TO KEEP HIM SAFE

TO KEEP HIM SAFE

A Debut Novel

GAYLE PARISH

Paperback: ISBN-13: 9781736188408
ISBN-10: 1736188402

Cover Design by and Layout by Theresa Marie Flaherty
(with special thanks to Michael Flaherty)

Turas Publishing
4833 Saratoga Blvd., No. 129
Corpus Christi, Texas 78413

www.turaspublishing.com

Dedicated to
mothers of children with special needs

For He will order his angels to protect you wherever you go.

— Psalm 91:11

Chapter 1

The day begins like too many others. I'm running late, gulping down a cup of coffee, grabbing a bran muffin, and then I'm out the door. My trusty 58 Caddy roars to life, and I'm off to work. After several rocky years, especially this last one, I often struggle finding the motivation to get out of bed.

When I'm late, every idiot seems to hit the road at the same time, but I make it to work and find a parking place. I take a deep breath and put on my game face. For just a moment I want to run away, to disappear, but I really do like my work. Adjusting to locked doors was troublesome at first, but that's how it is working in a Psychiatric/Addictions hospital. Although most patients come in voluntarily, the police sometimes bring in an individual who is deemed a risk to himself or others.

My first task is to check for new admissions. I'm relieved that there are only two new patients. As the only full time alcohol & drug counselor, I can be overwhelmed by too many new admissions on the same day. The amount of paperwork demanded by state and federal psychiatric oversight agencies for one person is amazing. I often spend more time doing paperwork than I do with patients. As I organize my day and give myself my morning pep talk, the buzzer blares, signaling a crisis, followed by the code green announcement calling all trained staff to assist.

The men discard their ties as the women remove their loose jewelry and scarves. We dash to the locked door into the unit. As we rush in, we're met with inhuman sounds emanating from a tall, thin, wild-eyed man in shackles fighting against three cops who are trying to restrain him. Long, matted hair and beard cover his features. The garbled, animalistic gibberish breaks my heart. Cases like this are the hardest for me. Our job will be to stabilize and evaluate him while he is on a police hold for evaluation.

As the attending nurse tries to sedate him with a shot, his flailing arms knock her away. He continues struggling, so some of our staff step in to restrain him. When he is under control, she gives him the shot.

Still he keeps on shouting and railing. I'm getting basic information for his admission from one of the officers, but he can't tell me much. He was found in Clear Creek Park, ranting, raving, tearing at his hair, and hitting his head against a tree. He became aggressive toward a man who tried to help, so that individual called the police. When the officers arrived, he ran. A foot chase ensued. They caught him. He fought them—giving one officer a black eye. Once in the police car, he continued his rant and tried to kick out the windows.

Something about his voice is familiar, but the sound is so contorted and tortured, it doesn't register. My heart skips a beat as I listen to that less-than-human wailing.

The medicine begins to take effect, and he is moved into the observation room, a small room behind the nurses' station. A security window allows the staff to keep an eye on him. He continues to fight as they get him into the room and in restraints. Finally his shouting becomes quieter and clearer. Then I hear, "NO, NO, NO; I WANT MOM, GET MOM GET MOM!! Moommmm."

My heart stops. Slowly I walk to the window and see deep blue eyes staring through. My breath catches as I look into the eyes of MY son. My son is lying there tattered, filthy, unkept, wild-eyed, fighting against his demons. His hair and beard are filthy, looking like a rat's nest. I haven't seen him for over two years. After a year in the state psychiatric hospital, he'd come home, and he seemed to do well for over a year. Then one night he left, taking most of his belongings. We searched everywhere. Although there were sightings of him, he slipped away every time. I lost hope that I'd ever see him again. Yet here he is!

My heart is breaking. I can't breathe. I choke back a sob, knowing I can do nothing to stop his pain. I can't even go into the room to comfort him. I have spent years helping others, but I can do nothing to help my own son.

With shaking hands, I fill out the admission form with his name and medical information, things I know by heart. I feel a gentle hand on my shoulder and turn to see Dr. Hendricks standing behind me.

"Lillian? Is it Dan?" he asks.

I can only nod.

"Okay, when you finish, why don't you take a few days off until we can stabilize him and arrange for his transfer. You'll be able to see him later, but for now you don't need to be here."

Before I can protest, he adds, "We'll have Alice come in to cover your groups for you."

I nod again, my throat too constricted to speak.

Chapter 2

After stopping by my office to retrieve my purse, I leave. Maggie tries to catch me but I just keep on walking. Driving in a daze, I turn the corner and realize I'm back to where it all began. I don't know how long I've been driving, but here I am on the block where we welcomed our Dan. The sight of our old home floods my mind with memories of those happy days. They warm my spirit.

It was such a happy day when Mitchell and I moved into our beautiful Craftsman house. We were so young when we got married—me at seventeen, Mitchell at twenty-two. I was such a young, innocent bride then—believing in happily ever after and all the trite things we told ourselves.

What a blessing that we received the unexpected inheritance from Mitchell's grandmother Hawke. Four years after our wedding, we used some of it for the down payment on our forever home. With a baby on the way, we were filled with hope and expectations and couldn't wait to get the nursery ready for our new baby.

• • •

"Hey, Sweet Pea! Throw me a beer, I'm parched."

Mitchell wipes his arm across his forehead and flicks his hand down to the floor like he's shaking off dripping sweat—but he's just exaggerating.

"How many boxes of these damned books did you pack anyway? Damn, girl. Don't you realize how heavy they are?"

I toss him a beer. "Sorry, but you knew when you married me how much I love my books." I can feel my cheeks crinkle with an easy smile, deepening my dimple. Mitchell loves the damned thing. He reaches across the books to tug me to him and kisses me.

I duck my head and pull away, laughing. "Think of it as carrying me across the threshold. Besides, this'll be the last time you have to move them. I'm staying here forever."

As I look at this beautiful old Craftsman four-bedroom home, my heart sings in amazement that we could buy it. I can see us sitting together on the wrap-around porch with a cup of coffee and picture our children running on the hardwood floors into the large living room where a huge, old-fashioned fireplace, complete with a pivoting arm for hanging pots, and a huge mantle where I'll hang all our Christmas stockings. The built-in bookcases on either side will be overflowing with my books—and lots of children's books. The oak pocket door separating it from the den will give Mitchell a quiet space.

I already know the kitchen will be my favorite room. It's been updated with the latest appliances, and the amount of storage in the walk-in pantry is incredible. The previous owners removed the wall between the kitchen and the formal dining room for an eat-in kitchen with an island seating four, yet there is still enough room for a large dining room suite. The bank of windows and sliding glass door to the backyard where our children will play provide a glorious view of the Big Horn Mountains beyond.

The four bedrooms upstairs may be more than we need now, but this new baby will start filling it. Our master bedroom with our very own private, huge bathroom already makes me feel delicious all over. Baby's room, one of the other three bedrooms, is across the hall from ours, with another bathroom nearby. A foot kicking me under the rib, *or was that a summersault*, reminds me this baby's about to make an appearance.

Having Mom to help us has been a Godsend. She's been working late into the night to clear things up so I can rest. Our room is ready first. The bed is all set up with our luxurious feather mattress—or our devil bed, as Mitchell calls it. "Once you lay down on it, you'll have a devil of a time wanting to get up."

It's nearly midnight when we fall into bed, exhausted. A light kiss and the smell of freshly brewed coffee wake me in the morning. If only I could just pull the covers over my head and not leave my devil bed for a week. Mitchell has other ideas.

"Come on, Sleepy Head, time's wasting. We've a lot to do before that little one makes an appearance." He runs his hand tenderly over my swollen belly, and the baby kicks his hand, startling him.

"That little thing packs a punch."

I sit up and stretch, reaching for the mug of steaming coffee. "What? No breakfast in bed?" I tease, giving him a lazy smile.

"You're lucky I figured out the coffee pot, but don't push your luck. Come on. We don't have much time before your mom gets here."

I grab some clothes on my way to take a quick shower and dress. When finished, I take a minute to stand and admire the fantastic view from our bedroom window. I'm feeling very blessed.

With Mom's help we manage to get somewhat organized in a couple of days. Now I'm on my own. Mitch's back to work. Mom should be resting. I should be, too, but I'm drawn to the nursery. I can visualize just how it should be. It won't take long, I think. *A coat of paint. Put the crib together. Arrange it all. I know I shouldn't. I really shouldn't.* But, I do. I grab a can of off-white paint, pour it in the pan, find a roller, and begin. Music is playing. Time slips away. Before I realize how quickly, I stand back, admiring my handiwork and rubbing my tired back.

The painting is done. The crib is in place, along with the changing table and the stacks of flannel diapers Mom taught me to fold. Even the diaper pins, with duck heads and puppy heads, are just too cute. I love how the light shines through the window, making the room light and airy. It's all ready. All we need is Baby.

I hear footsteps and turn to see Mitchell. I didn't realize it was that late. I have no idea what we're having for dinner, or if I have the energy to cook.

Mitchell tips his head to one side as he looks at me. "Hi, little Mama. Looks like you've been busy. Thought you were going to get some rest."

"I know, but after you left this morning I found myself in here. Then a paint roller fell into my hand, and before you could say 'Jack Sprat,' I was putting on the last touches. Between coats I put the crib together, and once the painting was done—well, you know the furniture insisted on being where it belonged. What can I say?"

"You know you're nuts, don't you?" He wraps me in his burly arms. As I relax against him, I realize just how tired I am. And so does he.

"Why don't you run a bath and have a long soak? I'll rustle up something for dinner."

"Sounds wonderful. You're too good to me. You know that, don't you?"

He smiles that lopsided grin I love. "I do, but what can I do? You're about to pop out that little one, so I've got to keep up my end of the bargain. Now scoot, get your bath. I'll see you downstairs when you're through." He turns me toward the door and gives me a little nudge.

After pouring some lilac bath salts into the big old-fashioned claw-footed bathtub, I run a bath and slide down in the water. It's heaven in a tub. *I may never get out.* I may not be able to get out. Baby kicks me twice as I begin to relax. The hot water soaks my aching body, my eyes feel heavy, and my head begins to nod.

• • •

I feel gentle hands lift me. "W-what's going on?"

"Shh, just rest."

Gently, I'm laid on the bed. I open my eyes slowly and see Mitch's face. He's got that look. And he's biting his lower lip. I know he's worried.

"What happened?" I ask.

"Just rest, honey. You fell asleep in the tub. When you didn't come down, I came to check on you, and you were asleep. You'd slipped down, and the water was almost to your nose. You scared the hell out of me. I got you out, wrapped you in a towel, and you know the rest of the story. It's a good thing you insisted on those gigantic towels after all."

"We haven't had dinner. Hand me my robe, and I'll be right down." I yawn and stretch.

"I've got a better idea. Stay here. I'll fix a couple plates, and we can eat by the window."

Glancing towards the window, I realize how much I love our room, especially the fireplace and double-hung dormer window where we've placed a small table and two overstuffed chairs.

Mitch returns with two plates and condiments on a tray, with a white towel draped regally over his arm.

"Your dinner, m'lady," he announces as he places a plate of fried chicken, plank fries, and a salad on the table.

I'm gaping, mouth wide open, like a carp. "You? Fried chicken? Where did you get chicken? It smells so good. I don't care. Just let me have it."

"What? You think I can't fry chicken?"

"Not when there isn't one in the fridge, I don't. So fess up. How is it we're having this yummy fried chicken?" I take a big bite. It's so damn good I lick my fingers.

Mitch raises his hands in surrender. "I give up. I'll confess so I can eat before it gets any colder. I saw a sign in Gatchell's Drugs window— Broasted chicken by the piece or the bucket. I thought it'd be a good time to try it. While you were bathing I ran down and picked us up some, then fixed a salad when I got home. Do you like it?"

"Mmm. It's delicious," I say, with my mouth full. This is something I will buy again. After eating my fill, I am scooted off to bed by my worried husband.

∞

Chapter 3

The first pain hits in the middle of the night. "Mitch, Mitchell! Wake up! Something's wrong." I lie in bed, panting.

His feet hit the floor before he's fully awake. "Is it time? We need to go to the hospital?" He reaches for my hand, "COME ON!"

As the pain subsides, I begin to laugh. Mitch freezes. "What's funny? Are you in labor? Do we need to get to the hospital?"

"Calm down, it's gone now. Maybe I overdid it today. RelAAAAX! OH, DAMN! Call the doctor. Tell him—whew—I might be in labor."

"It's 3 o'clock in the morning."

"I don't care—oh—whew. There, it's getting better. Maybe we should go." I sit up slowly. He pulls on his sweats as I reach for my robe, then change my mind—to hell with getting dressed. He guides me down the stairs to the pickup.

I watch the speedometer climb during our rush to the hospital. When another pain hits I bite my lip, stifling my groans so Mitch won't go any faster. Finally, he screeches to a halt in front of the Emergency entrance, jumps out of the pickup, and runs to look for help. Instead of waiting, I climb awkwardly out of the pickup. Before I can take a step, I feel something warm running down my legs. My water's broken. My knees begin to buckle as a nurse rushes to me with a wheelchair.

"Come on, little Mama. Let's get you into a room. Once the water breaks, the baby's usually close behind."

Mitchell fills out the paperwork while I'm wheeled to an exam room. As the nurse helps me into a hospital gown, she asks how often and how strong the pains are. Her line of chatter is somehow reassuring. Mitch catches up with us just as she helps me on to the exam table.

"I'm sorry, Mr. Hawke. I have to ask you to wait outside for just a minute while I examine your wife."

"B-but, can't he stay?" *I need him here.*

"No. I'm sorry, but he can't." She places my feet in stirrups at the end of the table. "Now slide down. Okay. Relax. Let your knees drop to the side. That's good, let's see what we've got."

Another contraction builds as she begins examining me. "You're doing great. Now pant like a puppy when the contractions hit." She demonstrates by blowing out short breaths. "That'll help."

I pant while she completes her examination. "You're dilated to about five, so we need to get you up to maternity, and I'll call the doctor."

Over the next couple of hours the contractions become more frequent and more severe. *If I hear "pant" one more time, I'll show them "pant."*

"We're getting close, Lillian. You're doing good." I hear the reassuring voice of Dr. Cranston as another pain rocks me.

"Mitch," I whimper.

"MITCHELL HAWKE, where the hell are you?!" This time I shriek.

"Lillian, we're going to give you something for the pain, remember—"

"To pant," I say through gritted teeth, thinking, *yeah, sure, pant. How'd you like it if you were the one splitting in half, and I was telling you to pant through it? How about I accidentally kick you in the nads and tell you to pant?*

What I do learn about having a baby is that all dignity is lost. They shave your most private parts—even when you're having contractions and in terrible pain. The person you need the most, your husband, is relegated to the waiting room. As the pain assaults your body, you rue the day you became pregnant and swear you'll NEVER do it again.

Finally, a shot takes the edge off the excruciating pain. Then, about the time I think I can't go on—it ends.

"It's a baby boy, Mrs. Hawke." I hear the cry of my precious baby and know it was worth it.

"A little boy? Can I see him? Where's Mitchell? Does he know? Thank you. I'm sorry." I know I'm babbling, but I can't seem to stop.

The nurse comes closer, holding him so I can see his little face. "We need to get him cleaned up, weighed, and measured. Then we'll bring him to your room, and you can hold him. Yes, someone has gone to tell your husband." She hurries away with my precious baby.

Dr. Cranston pats me on the arm. "Congratulations, Lillian. You have a healthy baby boy, and you did really well. Do you realize it's the 4th of July? Bet you won't forget his birthday," he says with a tired smile. "Get some rest now. I'll be back to see you later, but now I'm going to talk to Mitchell."

Though I desperately want to see my baby, suddenly I'm so exhausted. My eyes feel heavy and begin to close.

I wake in a different room, in a clean gown and a regular hospital bed. Mitch is asleep in a chair by the bed, holding my hand. I run my free hand over my tummy. For a minute I can't figure out what's wrong. Then I remember. We have a baby boy. Now, I'm wide awake.

"Mitch, Mitch, wake up. We have a boy, a baby boy. Have you seen him? What are we going to name him? Mitch, I want to see our baby."

He smiles with that lopsided grin I know so well and tenderly smoothes back my hair. "Yes, I saw him, but only through the nursery window. He's so little, Lil."

There's a tap on the door, and a nurse enters with our baby. "I have a little guy who wants to meet his mommy and daddy." She lays him in my outstretched arms. "I'll be back in a half hour. If you need anything, let me know." She hands me a small bottle of what looks like water. "Try getting him to drink this. If he fights against the nipple, keep trying. He really needs to drink it."

As soon as she's out of the room I lay him on the bed and unwrap him, while keeping an eye on the door so as not to get caught. I don't know what I think will happen if they catch me looking at my own son, but I'm still furtive in my examination. Mitch and I are in awe as we count ten little fingers and toes, two eyes, two darling ears, a little nose, and a sweet little mouth making suckling noises. He begins to fuss, so I wrap him up and see if he'll take the bottle. He latches on and sucks it dry. I look at Mitch. My heart swells with love when I see a tear slide down his cheek. I hold the baby out for him.

"Oh, Lil. I don't know. He's so little. What if I hurt him?"

"You'll be okay. Make sure you support his head." I lay our tiny son in Daddy's arms.

He holds him awkwardly, as though he's made of glass. "Hello, little man. I'm your daddy. How about we call you Daniel, after Mommy's Daddy? Would you like that, little guy?" Then he looks at me. "How about Mommy? Would she like that?"

"Mommy would love that," I manage to choke out.

∞

Chapter 4

"No, Danny, no. Get off there. NO! You can't climb the cupboard, Danny. Stop it."

To think he'd been the perfect baby. He slept all night by three months old, sat up, rolled over, started walking, talking, and feeding himself—all on schedule, according to the doctor. As soon as he learned how to walk, it turned into a run as he explored every nook and cranny of the house. Gates at the bottom and top of the stairs, safety locks on the cupboards and over the light plug-ins are now installed, so those busy hands can't find so many things to get into. Yet his antics make me laugh.

"Come on, big guy. You better settle down if you want a birthday party." He wiggles free, giggling.

"Mama, let me go."

"No, I won't let you go." I hug him tight again.

"But Mama, ou gotta lets me go. It my birfday. Daddy says I play on my birfday. I free." He holds up three fingers proudly for me to see.

"You're three?" I ask, and he nods. "Do you want Grandma to come to your birthday party? Do you want ice cream and cake?"

"Oh, oh, oh, Gamma come. Icream, I lub icream. Daddy get Gamma?"

"First you have to be good and let me get things ready. Yes, Daddy's getting Grandma and you, young man, take puppy outside. I'll be right out."

"Tum on buppy, we go outside." He runs out, his chubby legs churning, with Leo the puppy right behind.

Mitch tied balloons and streamers to the trees, chairs, and along the patio to decorate the yard and filled a #2 galvanized washtub with ice to keep drinks cold. Eight children, plus their parents, and a couple of our elderly neighbors who've taken a shine to Danny are expected. It's a beautiful day for a party. The guests begin arriving just as Mitch and my mom get back.

"Gamma, Gamma!" Danny hurls himself into her arms, wraps his little arms around her neck, and gives her a sloppy kiss.

Gently, she disengages from his stranglehold. "Hi, Grandma's precious boy."

I notice her wince and hurry to take the wiggling worm from her. "Come on, Danny. Let Grandma sit down."

Mom gives me a wan smile as she sits in the closest chair, trying to hide her pain. But I can tell she's hurting.

"Are you okay, Mom?" I've never seen her look so frail. This isn't my I-can-do-anything mom, and I'm concerned.

"Don't worry about me, honey. I wrenched my back, and it's a bit sore. It's Danny's birthday. We're here to have a good time. So, let's get this party started."

The kids are running and playing, with 'buppy' in the mix. As squeals and laughter fill the air, the adults raise their voices, talking over the hubbub. Mitch is our entertainment as he leads the kids at play. Everyone seems to be enjoying the party. When Danny spies the presents piled on a table, we gather everyone together so he can open them.

His grandma hands each one to him after rescuing the card so she can record who gave what. There's a set of cap pistols with a holster, a cowboy hat, a teddy bear, a baseball glove, a ball, a small black truck, coloring books with crayons, some story books, a stick horse, and a barnyard set with a tin barn with a silo to put together, and assorted animals, and corrals. We plan to save our special present for later.

I carry out the cake, shaped like a pickup, and place it on the table. Danny is so excited when he sees it.

"Truck, truck. I want truck," he yells and tries to grab it. As I slice it, his eyes get big and fill with tears. "Mama broke truck," he says as the tears begin to fall.

Mitchell scoops him up. "Hey buddy, it's okay. Mommy made the cake to look like a truck. See, it's cake. Mmm. Good cake." He slips a small piece in Danny's mouth.

The tears dry in an instant. "Danny want cake, Mama. Danny want cake." I serve him the first piece with ice cream on the side. Crisis averted.

After the last guest has gone, I look around our once beautiful back yard—it looks like a hurricane blew through. Then I realize Mitchell's folks haven't called today. They're usually the first to call on special days. The thought niggles at me as I begin cleaning.

Mom, too, begins gathering paper plates that were thrown on the grass, but she's moving slowly. To assure myself she's okay, I join her, and I'm surprised to see a tear trickle down her cheek.

"Mom? Are you okay?"

"I'm good." She reaches up and pats my cheek. "I was thinking how much your daddy would have loved this. It was a great party, and Danny's a lucky little boy. Now, let's get this mess cleaned up."

Danny comes barreling around the picnic table toward us with his holster and cap guns strapped on and Leo on his heels. "Tik em up," he shouts at his grandma. She raises her hands above her head, then quickly lowers them and wraps him in a hug.

"You little munchkin, you. You taste like cake and ice cream. I'm gonna eat you all up." With that she covers his little face with kisses while he wiggles and giggles—a wonderful snapshot of a wonderful day. As he runs off, I see a flash of pain cross her face.

I've been concerned for a few months now, but she refuses to admit anything's wrong. I've tried getting her to the doctor, but she always has an excuse. I've scheduled an appointment for her tomorrow, and I will not take no for an answer. We're getting to the bottom of this.

"Mom, you are staying with us tonight, aren't you? I can take you home tomorrow. Danny would love for you to read him a bedtime story."

"Not go bed."

"Not right now, but wouldn't you like Grandma to read you a story when you do?"

"Gamma tay. Gamma read me tory."

"That's not fighting fair, Lil, using a little boy to get me to stay. As long as you let me help you clean up—"

"Okay, but please don't overdo it."

Danny finally settles down after his bath, and he's dressed in new pj's ready for bed. He and his grandma find a book. Then she tucks him in so she can read it to him.

I'm in the living room, resting with a cup of coffee while Mitchell is on the phone, when I realize we still haven't given Danny his present from us. We'll give it to him tomorrow. I was already nodding off when Mitch walked in with a beer.

"You want one?"

"No, my coffee's fine. Who was on the phone so long?"

"It was Mom, apologizing for not calling earlier to talk to Danny."

"I was wondering what happened. What's going on?"

Mitchell sighs, takes a deep breath, then he tells me. "You remember my brother, Christopher, and all his problems, don't you? He's gotten himself arrested, again. He was involved in a liquor store robbery, and the clerk was killed, so he's facing some serious prison time. He's calling Mom to bail him out. She's torn, but Dad says absolutely not. They're not spending any more money to bail him out. From now on, he's on his own. Mom's upset—he's her baby, and she feels it's her job to take care of him—even if he doesn't appreciate it. The only time they hear from him is when he's in trouble. I didn't know what to say, so I just listened. I haven't seen or talked to him in nearly fifteen years. The sad thing is I could probably see him on the street and not even recognize him."

I see the pain in his eyes and reach for him, hugging him tight. I hold him close for a long moment. "I'm sorry you and your folks have to go through this. I wish there was something we could do. I might sound selfish, but I am so grateful for our little Danny. We're blessed, aren't we?"

Chapter 5

Danny is up early. I hear him slide down the stairs on his bottom—his favorite way of tackling the stairs. Mitch and I are in the kitchen as he comes hurtling through the door. The one package he didn't open at his party yesterday is waiting for him on his chair. I chuckle, watching his eyes grow large when he sees it. His little hands begin ripping paper, but he stops and stares when he sees the picture of the big yellow Tonka dump truck on the box. The surprise on his face is priceless.

"Daddy, is dis cake?" I try not to laugh, but he's so darn cute.

"No, baby. It's your birthday present. Do you want me to help you?"

"Yes, yes." He grabs at the box and with his daddy's help, manages to get the truck out—it's almost as big as he is.

Breakfast was a lost cause that morning. The sound of him and that truck echoed throughout the house, along with Leo yapping. For the first week he even slept with it.

• • •

It's almost a year later, and I never tire of watching him. He's grown so much in the past year, but there will be no big party this year. We gave him his birthday present a month early since we're not sure what will be going on by his birthday. He's been outside enjoying it since almost the first light.

He sees me at the window and waves. There'll be no sleeping with this present in his bed—I'm worried he'll want to sleep in the yard with it. He makes another pass around the yard on his new, big, green John Deere pedal tractor, towing the trailer behind. Last year's dump truck rides in the trailer filled with rocks—and God only knows what else. He's tried to coax Leo to ride in it, but Leo jumps out and runs alongside.

They are quite a pair, the best of buds.

The tinkling of a bell breaks my reverie. "I'm coming, Mom—glad to hear you're awake." I leave her morning medicines and a glass of water on her bedside table while I help her to the bathroom, then back to bed.

She's so frail. I'm almost afraid to touch her for fear she'll break. This year has been tough on her. Sometimes I regret insisting she go to that doctor's appointment. Of course it's not rational, but at times I think, *If only we hadn't gone!* Those tests could not have revealed *uterine cancer.* Those terrible words would remain unspoken, and she'd still be hail and hearty.

"How about I fix a slice of dry toast and some tea after you've taken your medicine?"

"No, Lil. I'm not hungry, and I don't want those pills. They make me gag, and then come right back up as fast as I swallow them."

"But, Mom. You need to get your strength back."

A weak smile plays on her lips. "Ever the optimist aren't you, honey?"

I choke back tears and force a smile. "Like my mama taught me."

She reaches for my hand. "I need you to do something for me."

My heart drops as I look into her eyes, "Anything, Mom."

Her words are measured and firm, "I need you to call Dr. Irwin. Tell him I'm ready to go back to the hospital. Then I need you to bring that precious little man in to visit me before we leave."

I can't answer. I'm frozen. I want to run away. I want to curl up on her lap and have her make it better. I want my mama to stay with me, to hold me, and keep me. I don't want to do this. Dr. Irwin's assured her when it's time, he will not let her suffer, and he'll see she's kept as comfortable as possible. Selfishly, I want to keep her home, but it's not an option. I don't want her to— I shudder.

"Are you sure, Mom? Maybe he'll come here to see you. Maybe we can hire a nurse if you need more care. Maybe—"

"No, Lil. You need to do what I ask," she says gently.

This short conversation has taken so much out of her. I can't put her through anymore. "Okay, but before I do that, let me make you a cup of tea. Just a few sips?" I don't mention the medications again. I know she'll refuse, as she has for the last couple of days. She doesn't answer—she's drifted off. I square my shoulders, take a deep breath, and walk out of the room.

No matter how hard I've steeled myself for this moment, I'm not ready when it comes. Deep down I knew there was no avoiding it. When I call Dr. Irwin, I'm put right through.

"Hi, Lillian, Dr. Irwin here. I understand she isn't doing too well?"

I choke back tears. "It's hard to tell. She's sleeping a lot, refusing medications as she throws them up shortly after she's taken them. She never complains—but this morning she asked me to call you. She wants to go to the hospital." My voice breaks, but I hold it together.

"Then that's what we'll do. We'll start an IV to keep her hydrated and administer her medications. I'll make the arrangements. I can meet you there at two this afternoon. We'll transport her by ambulance."

"God, I hadn't even thought of that. Yes, an ambulance would be good. She can hardly bear sitting up even with the bed raised." I can't hold back the tears any longer.

"You're doing the right thing, Lil. We'll keep her comfortable and ease her pain. I know it's hard, but we have to think of her now."

I gulp back my tears and wipe my nose. "I know. I know. But I hate this. You have no idea how much I hate it."

"I know, but we have to do it for her. I'll see you at two."

I stand staring at the phone. "Mama? Mama?" A little hand tugs at my blouse. "Why you cry? You got a boo boo? Danny kiss it better, Mama?"

I scoop him up and hold him tight.

"Mama, you squeeze too tight, I can't breaf."

I loosen my hold and swoop in for kisses on his dirty little face. "Grandma wants to see you, little man. You have to sit real still and not jump around."

"I know. I not a baby. Gamma tell me we have to be real quiet. I do be quiet. Wait, I got something for Gamma. Let me go. I go get it." He takes off on a dead run, but slows when he's close to Grandma's room. He tiptoes past the door then is off running again. In moments he's back with Blue Bunny clutched in his hand. "I want give bunny to Gamma. Bunny make Gamma feel better."

He's had Blue Bunny since birth. He sleeps with him every night, and he won't go to sleep without his bunny. Yet, here he is giving his gamma his prized possession. He doesn't wait for me but takes his bunny to Gamma's room.

"Gamma?" He whispers, tiptoeing to her bedside.

She stirs, her eyelids fluttering open. "Come here, sweet boy." She reaches out to him. "Lil, will you put him here beside me?" She pats the bed. "I need to hold him once more."

Gently, I put him on her bed. He lies down snuggling close to her. "Gamma, I bring you bunny. Blue Bunny help you."

Her frail hand strokes his face. "Thank you, baby. I know bunny will help me." They lie quietly—Danny and bunny wrapped in Gamma's embrace. Two thirds of my heart entwined. I don't know how I'm going to get through this.

"Danny? I have to go to the hospital. Then I'll be going away. I'll love you always, and I'll always be with you."

"I know, Gamma, I lub you, too." He kisses her gently on the cheek.

Her eyes fill with tears as she holds him. "You're my blessing. I hear you got a fancy tractor today—for your birthday."

"I did. It wonnerful. Me an' Leo play wid it. It got trailer, I put toys in it, and pull wif the tractor." His blue eyes, so much like hers, sparkle.

"You go have fun. Thank you for letting bunny stay with me for a while. I'll send him home when I no longer need him."

"I know." He pats Gamma's hand, slides off the bed, and tiptoes out of the room. He calls for Leo and we hear him running toward the back door.

"Lil? Did you call the doctor?"

"I did, Mom. He'll meet us at the hospital, and he's sending an ambulance for you, Mom. I don't want this, I'm not ready, and I feel selfish."

"I don't like it either, Lil, but it's time. I'm tired, the medicine isn't helping, and the pain is becoming unbearable. I don't think God will let me suffer much longer. I've had a good life." She pauses, then whispers, "If I could have one thing before I die, it would be for you and your sister to be close again—and I wanted to be here when the new baby comes. I guess I'll be watching from the other side."

I'm stunned. "How did you know? I haven't even told Mitch."

"Oh, honey. Don't you know—moms know things?"

For a moment I see the feisty mom who raised me. I take her hand, and we sit quietly. She pats my hand. "You've always been such a joy to me. Thank you for taking such good care of me this past year. I don't know what I'd have done without your strength. Now, you have things to do, and I need to rest." Tears swim in our eyes as we embrace.

I can barely see through the tears as I leave her side. She's right. I have things to do. First, I need to call Mitch.

"Mitch, honey. Mom's going to be admitted to the hospital this afternoon. Is there any way you can come home?"

"I'm sorry, Lil. I can't, I'm so sorry. I'm in Casper today, remember? I'll get there as soon as I can. I have a couple things to finish, but I'll be there as soon as I can. I love you."

I feel so alone. I should call my sister, but I can't right now. Instead, I call Trudy, my neighbor, to ask if she'll watch Danny until one of us gets home.

"I don't know how long we'll be, Trudy."

"Don't worry about it, Lil. I'd love having Danny for however long you need. I'll be over in an hour to get him. Will that work?"

"Thanks, Trudy. That'll be great." She's one person I can always count on. Her daughter is grown and moved to Denver, so she's not able to see much of her only grandson. She adores Danny and loves spending time with him.

I check on Mom. She's still sleeping. I make a peanut butter and jelly sandwich and take it out to Danny. "Danny, let's have something to eat." He clambers up on a chair and begins wolfing down his sandwich—Leo poised to snatch any crumbs that drop. As he eats, I explain to him Mrs. Andrews will be coming to pick him up while I go to the hospital with Grandma. Once he understands Leo can go with him, he's fine.

"I like Mrs. Andews. She make me cookies when I tay wid her."

"A big truck, called an ambulance, will come to take Grandma to the hospital. I'll go to be with her for a while."

"I know. Bunny told me. That's why I gib Bunny to Gamma. He take care her, then come home to me." Danny hops off his chair, he and Leo playing chase.

I'm left with my mouth gaping, staring after him.

Chapter 6

We lost Mom only three days after she went to the hospital. I was devastated. This new baby and Danny needing me are what got me through it. One day at a time became my reality. Mom's last wish that my sister and I become closer didn't happen. Reggie flew in for the funeral and left the day after. That time's all a blur. Maybe she tried. I'm not really sure.

Now we're preparing for the new baby, and I feel the excitement returning. Mitchell asked me just a few weeks ago, "what do you think Mom would say if she saw how you drag yourself through each day?" That realization hit me hard.

I could almost hear her voice, "Lillian, get your chin off the floor. Knock it off. Take care of your baby and your husband. Get off the pity pot before you get stuck and end up with a ring around your ass." Poor Mitch. The look on his face when I started laughing was priceless.

Danny now spends more time in the den, the room we fixed for Mom. Some mornings I find him sleeping in her bed. When we brought Blue Bunny home, he placed her carefully on Gamma's dresser. He doesn't talk about Gamma and, when I tried to explain about her dying, his response was "I know, Gamma told me."

Now another big change is in store for him; the new baby is due in a month. Today's Saturday, and we're moving Mom's furniture upstairs to one of the spare rooms and making the other into Danny's new bedroom. Mitchell and I move his bookshelves with books and toys, his bed, dresser, and clothes out of the nursery into his new room. Although dormer windows are in all the bedrooms, ours is the only one

without a built-in window seat for storage—the one in Danny's room
will make an excellent toy box.

Danny is on the verge of tears when we begin moving Mom's furniture, until he sees it taken upstairs. Then he calms down, but remains
unusually quiet as we move his things out of the nursery and again
when we tuck him into bed.

The next morning, he isn't in his room when I check.

"Danny, Danny?" I call. Mitch comes running.

"What's wrong?"

"Danny's not in his room, and some of his toys are missing."

"Did you check the guest room?"

There he is, curled up in the middle of Mom's old bed, sound
asleep. His favorite trucks are neatly placed on one of the bookcases,
and Blue Bunny's standing guard. I notice his big yellow Tonka truck
has been left behind.

"I think he's chosen his room, Lil. For now, let's use the other one
for a playroom. After all, he's got enough trucks to fill a warehouse.
There'll be plenty of room for them and, with his love of art, I can
make him an easel to use in there. Think of how much he'll enjoy that."

"Maybe we could get rid of the flowered bedspread?"

"I wouldn't bet on it. He seems pretty attached to it all," he says
with a laugh. "He'll probably outgrow it—for now let's just keep it
simple."

I worry how he's going to feel about the baby. I was afraid he'd
blame the baby for taking over his room when we moved him out
of the nursery. Claiming Mom's bed as his own made the move go
well. When I tried to explain to him the baby would be here soon, he
shocked me. "I know, Mama. Gamma told me." For him, it's like she's
still here.

• • •

Now baby Sarah has joined us. She's named for my mom, and I can
feel Mom smiling down on us. I'm excited to be coming home with
her. Danny is waiting on the front porch with Trudy. Clutched in his
hand is a Raggedy Ann doll. Mitch told me Danny picked it out for

his baby sister. When I get out of the car he stands, watching as I walk up the steps with the baby in my arms. Mitchell pulls up a wicker chair so I can sit down.

"Danny, want to see your baby sister Sarah?"

His eyes widen as he peers into her little face—she's looking back at him. He leans over for a closer look. Her little arm reaches for him, so he holds out his finger. As she curls her tiny fist around it, I hear his quick intake of breath.

In a hushed voice he says, "Mama, she likes me. See? She got my finger." His smile is dazzling. "Mama, she so little—and she got no hair? Why she got no hair? Does she want her dolly?" He pushes Raggedy Ann gently toward her as she clings to his finger.

"Honey, she's too little to play with dolly. We'll put her in her crib. Is that okay? Soon she'll have lots of hair, just like you. Will you help me take care of Sarah and make sure Leo doesn't get too feisty around her until she's a little bigger and can run and play with you both?"

"I can do that, Mama." He spies Leo sitting across the porch. He raises his hand and points his finger. "Leo, baby sister can't play wid us right now. You hab to be good and not hurt her." Leo lets out a little bark.

"Daddy, we got baby sister now, don't we?"

"Yes, sport, we sure do. You're a big boy now, and I know you'll help Mama when I'm at work, won't you?"

He nods solemnly. "I big boy. I help Mama wit baby Sawrah." We all stifle a laugh because he's so serious.

"Come on, little man. Let's get Mama and baby Sarah in the house. Would you carry Mom's purse? I'll get the rest of the things out of the car." Mitchell puts the handle of my purse around Danny's neck.

After a quick peek, Trudy says goodbye. "I'll be over in the morning to see if you need anything—if that's okay?"

"I'd like that." I know she's dying to hold Sarah. Through this pregnancy, she's been such a support. Tommy, her only grandchild, is four already, and she hasn't even seen him yet. It's breaking her heart. A widow on a fixed income can't afford bus or train tickets. She's been such a rock for me this past year—I should talk to Mitch about treating her with plane tickets to Denver for Christmas.

Sarah's not the easy baby her brother was. Those first months, her internal clock was upside down, sleeping days and crying nights. Since I'm nursing, it's me who answers the call. *Too bad boobs aren't detachable.* Once I purchase a breast pump, I share the joy of nighttime feedings with Mitch, who is a trooper. *Ahh! Sleep, perchance to dream.*

When I awake, the sun is shining in my eyes. It's a moment before I realize it's the middle of the day. I'd only meant to sit for a minute or two. It's too quiet. No Leo barking. No Danny laughing, and no baby crying. I leap from the chair and peek into the back yard for Danny, but he's not there. My heart is pounding. Where is he? Where's Leo? I call them—no answer. I race up the stairs to check his room, but he's not there either. I rush to Sarah's room and, there on the floor next to the crib, sits Danny and Leo. Danny is paging through one of his books, 'reading' to his baby sister who lies quietly as if listening to him.

"Dan—"

"Shhh, Mama. I read baby Sawrah a tory. She take a nap. I take care her, you sleep. Daddy say I help Mama."

I swoop this sweet child into my arms. I glance in the crib and realize Sarah is following us with her big brown eyes, her Raggedy Ann snuggled close to her.

"You're such a big help, Danny. I'll tell Daddy what a good helper you've been today. Would you like Mama to bring you some cookies and milk? We can have them in here."

"Oh, yes. I want free cookies and Leo want two. Sissy don't get cookies. She a baby."

"You wait here and finish your story to Sissy. I'll be right back." As I turn, I see Blue Bunny on Sarah's dresser.

"Danny, why is Bunny in Sissy's room?"

"A'cuz Bunny take care Sissy for Danny, Mama, and Daddy. Bunny take good care of her. Gamma say so." I feel the hair on my neck rise.

∞

Chapter 7

"Danny has a doctor's appointment today for a physical and to make sure his immunizations are up to date before he starts kindergarten. Did you remember? I'd like you to be there."

"I've got a busy day, Lil. I'm not sure what time I'll be home tonight. This project has to be completed today, or we'll have to pay a hell of a penalty."

He's working longer hours lately. Business is good, but I expected his workload to lessen when he took on a partner.

"Damn it, Mitch. I scheduled the last appointment of the day hoping you could at least meet me there. It'd be nice to have some help with the kids—but also for you to hear what the doctor has to say. I'm concerned that Danny is becoming more withdrawn and is still talking baby talk, unlike most children his age. The only person outside our family he'll have anything to do with is Trudy. Before long he'll be in a classroom full of kids he doesn't know, plus the teacher. I need to know he'll be okay. Why can't Larry step in and help? Isn't that why you took on a partner?"

"Lil, maybe it's because you hate the idea he'll be out of your sight for a few hours everyday. Face it. Your baby boy's growing up. He'll be fine once he's around other kids his age. He talks baby talk because you think it's cute when Sarah does it. He wants your attention. Besides, Larry's got his hands full, too. Business is good—it pays the bills and buys us groceries. Now, I've gotta run, or I'll be late."

He barely brushes my cheek with a kiss as he hurries away. "Wait," I call, "did you check the oil in the car?" But he's already in the pickup. I'll have to do it myself. *Like most everything around here lately.* I take a deep breath and try not to be mad. But, damn, the only thing he does around here anymore is eat, sleep, and sometimes grace us with his presence the whole day Sunday—unless he's playing golf with Larry or some of his business acquaintances. It hurts to see him and Danny drifting apart. I can't remember the last time he even took him for a short run to the store. Danny needs his daddy.

After breakfast the kids take Leo outside to play. With plenty to do, I get busy with housework and laundry. Danny's playing with his trucks. Sarah toddles after him on her little chubby legs. He sets up an area of her own so she won't disturb him and his road building. Of course, she doesn't always stay there. Yet, he's patient when he moves her out of his little 'town.' Lunch is peanut butter and jelly sammies at the picnic table and, before I know it, it's quick baths and off to the doctors.

Of late Danny insists on having one of his toy hot wheel trucks with him. He picks the choice of the day to carry, and Sarah drags her well-worn Raggedy Ann. She considers herself a big girl now that she's walking. She hates to be carried, so our progress to the doctor's office is slow. Another mom with three children is in the waiting room when we arrive. Sarah hurries to the toy box in the children's area to play with a little girl.

"Good afternoon, Mrs. Hawke. How are you?"

"Good, Bessie. Danny's here to see Dr. Wright." She checks my insurance and current information and tells us it'll be a few minutes.

"Danny, why don't you go play with the toys like Sissy?"

"NO! Don't want play wit kids. You make Sissy come here."

Two little boys are playing with toy trucks. I thought surely that would pique his interest, but he won't leave my side. Their mother notices and turns to me. "Looks like your guy is a little shy. My oldest was like that when he was little, but now he's in 6th grade with not a shy bone in his body."

"He's used to being with just my husband, me, and our daughter. Sadly, we have no other small boys his age in our neighborhood. We're hoping kindergarten will help."

"It helped my boy—he really blossomed when he started school."

"That's good to know."

Bessie calls the other woman to take one of her boys in to see the doctor. I offer to watch the other boy and the girl while she sees him. She cautions them to be good. They wave and go back to playing.

The little boy—about 3 or 4 approaches Danny, carrying a toy truck. He holds it out. "Do you want to play trucks wif me? You play mine. Can I play yours?"

"NO!" Danny jerks away and tries to climb on my lap.

"Danny, he wants to play with you. He doesn't want your truck."

"No play, make him go way."

The poor little guy looks crestfallen. His sister comes and takes him by the hand. "Come on, Tony. You can play with me and the little girl." As she leads him away he turns and waves at Danny, who ignores him and climbs up in the chair next to me.

It isn't long before we're called back to see the doctor as the other mom is coming out.

"Mrs. Hawke, how is everything? Any concerns or is this a routine physical for school?" Dr. Wright asks.

"I'm concerned that he isn't progressing. He still talks baby talk. He won't have anything to do with children other than his sister—it seems his 'spark' isn't there anymore." After taking a calming breath, I add softly, "Mitch says I baby him too much."

Danny's quiet throughout the exam. When Dr. Wright asks him some questions, he gets no response. He even offers to let Danny listen to his heart but he refuses.

"Mrs. Hawke, other than appearing to be quite shy, I don't see anything wrong with his health. He's in the normal range of height and weight for his age. His heart and lung sounds are good. Let's see how he does in Kindergarten before we get too worried, shall we? Expand his social circle so he becomes more comfortable away from you. You might try a half-day in a daycare program for a couple days a week until school begins. He and his sis could both go, giving you a few hours to pamper yourself, too. How is Sarah?"

"She's good, loves everybody and everything. She made herself at home in your waiting room with the other children there. Danny watched everyone and refused to play, even when one of the other little boys approached him. I'll take your advice though. How about the baby talk?"

"Encourage him to say the words correctly, but don't nag him. It may be that you and he have gotten into this pattern of communication. With Sarah learning, it's easy to fall into that pattern. If it doesn't improve, we could consider a hearing test and speech therapy." Clearly, he was finished. "Bessie will give you a copy of his immunization record. Let me know if his social skills don't improve."

I nod. I guess I expected more.

As we leave the doctor's office I decide to treat us. "How about we go to the Burger Barn for hamburgers, Danny?"

"No, want go home, Mama, want p butter n jelly."

"Danny, you and Sissy have been so good, I think we need to do something special, so we're going to the Burger Barn. We'll have hamburgers, French fries, and an ice cream milkshake. I know you like ice cream, Danny. Doesn't that sound good?"

"Bambburger, bambburger," Sarah chants.

It's early, and not many people are there. I order, and we find a place to sit. As other families begin to trickle in, a couple with five stair-step children sit in the booth across from us. They are all laughing, making funny faces at each other. I smile at their antics, antics that have Sarah laughing too, but Danny doesn't even smile. He sits stiffly, pushing his French fries around his plate, muttering all he wants is p butter n jelly.

I can't help but wonder what happened to my fun little boy who, like Sarah, didn't know a stranger.

• • •

The attempt at daycare is a disaster. Danny may be the first kid to get kicked out of daycare. He refuses to participate in anything and, if anyone gets close to Sarah, he pushes them down. I get the call within an hour of dropping them off.

Mitchell is working day and night to get all his jobs completed.

When he is home, all he seems to do is correct Danny and talk about 'making him grow up.' I miss him. I miss us, and for the first time, I'm afraid. I'm afraid for us—but mostly I'm afraid of what's happening to Danny.

Chapter 8

Danny didn't do well in Kindergarten. In fact, we held him back to repeat it, enrolled him in speech therapy, and made many attempts to interest him in some group activities. Art is the only class he seems to enjoy—he loves painting, drawing, and coloring. His only other interest is trucks and other types of vehicles.

• • •

Sarah, however, is in her element at school. She loves everything about it. Now that she is in first grade at the same school where Danny is in third, we hope he will look forward to going with her. He should be four years ahead of her instead of only two.

The house is quiet, and I'm having a quick cup of coffee and reading on the patio before starting the housework. *This is heaven!* Chirps and trills of robins and meadowlarks serenade me as a gentle breeze ruffles the pages of my book. I'm lost in the world of espionage in *The Hunt for Red October*. Although I listen for the sound of the phone, I pray it won't ring. I don't need a call with a problem from the school—I'm praying for things to be calmer this year. But, of course, the shrill ring of the phone summons me from my reverie.

"Hello?"

"Hey, Lil." What a relief it is that it's Mitch and not the school. "I thought I'd better let you know I won't be home tonight like we hoped. Something came up with this job in Gillette. It'll be tomorrow before I can get away."

"But, Mitchell. You promised." Damn, I hate the whine in my voice.

"I know, Lil. And you know how these jobs are—about the time we think it'll go smoothly, something throws a monkey wrench in the mix. How are the kids?"

"I know, Mitch. It's just that we miss you. It feels like you've been gone most of this past year. I don't understand why all your jobs lately take you so far from home." A heavy sigh escapes before I can stifle it. Mitch hates when I do that. "The kids are doing okay. So far, Danny is getting on the bus with Sarah without much of a problem. Sarah loves school and is full of stories when she gets home. Danny seems to be okay. He spends a lot of time outside in the evenings. In fact, he spends hours out there building roads and stick houses and playing with his trucks. I love watching Sarah play with him and hearing their laughter. You know Danny doesn't laugh much anymore." This time I'm able to stifle a sigh. "You're missing so much—I wish you were home more."

"I know. Maybe I'll take a couple of weeks off around Thanksgiving, and we could ask Mom and Dad to come for a visit. They aren't getting any younger, and it would be nice for them to spend time with the kids and us. What do you think?"

"That's a great idea. We need to see more of them. It's been almost two years since we made the trip to Texas to visit them. That's the last time you took any time off. Will you call them?"

"Yeah. I'll call them and make the arrangements. I'll check the price of plane tickets. We'll have to pay for the tickets since they're strapped for cash after all they've been through with Chris. Damn that brother of mine. I wish he'd get his shit together. He's going to be the death of them if he doesn't."

"It'll be good for the kids to get to know them better. Don't be too hard on Chris. The last time I talked to your mom she said he'd been doing better, taking some classes, saying he might as well take advantage of the programs the prison offers."

"I'll give them a call when I get home and make arrangements. Give the kids a hug and I'll see you tomorrow evening." The phone goes dead.

• • •

The next day after the kids are on the bus, I decide to go shopping for a special dinner for tonight, when Mitch gets home—hamburger for the kids and ribeye steaks for us. Mitch loves his charcoal grill, so he can do the cooking. I'll make potato salad, and we'll eat on the patio. This will be a special homecoming. Maybe it'll encourage him to find some way to be home more. My heart is light as I carry out my plans.

"Hey Lil. I'm home. Where is everybody? Isn't anyone going to meet the weary traveler?"

I'm startled awake by his booming voice and the slamming of the front door. When I check the clock, it's almost one in the morning. I must have fallen asleep on the couch—waiting for him.

"Shhh, you're going to wake the kids," I call as I stumble toward the door.

"Hey there, Lilly girl." He wraps his arms around me, lifting me off my feet. "Give your old husband a kiss, home from slaving to keep you in the comfort of this grand old house."

The stench of beer on his breath makes me gag when he covers my mouth with his. "Mitch! You're drunk." I push him away. "Please don't wake the kids. They have school tomorrow."

"Please don't wake the kids. They have school." He mimics. "What's the matter, don't want old Dad to see your babies? They're my kids too, you know. Maybe they want to see old Dad for a while. Danny! Sarah! Daddy's home. Come on, kids. Daddy's home," he shouts as he starts up the stairs.

When I try to move past him, he pushes me into the wall. I lose my footing and fall, landing two steps down with a thud.

"YOU HURT MAMA!" Danny yells, lunging from the landing onto his dad, flailing and pounding him with his fists.

I'm afraid Mitch will lose his footing and fall, so I hurry to pull Danny away. "It's okay, Danny. I'm okay—I slipped. Daddy didn't hurt me." His breathing slows, and he begins to quiet down. Mitch stares like he'd never seen this little boy before.

"I'm going to take Danny to bed. Why don't you get a cup of coffee—there's some in the pot. I'll be down in a minute." I cradle Danny in my arms and carry him to bed. He's getting too big for me to lift, but

I just want to get him settled—and not kill his father. I've never been this angry. *Who the hell does he think he is—coming in drunk?* I don't want him dead, I want him to feel as bad as I have tonight.

Danny crawls into bed when I set him down, immediately falling asleep with his arm draped over Leo—like nothing happened. I walk slowly down the stairs, struggling to calm myself before I confront Mitch.

He's already repentant. "Aw, Lil. I'm sorry. I was an ass. I didn't hurt you, did I? How's Danny? I've never seen him like that before. He can really throw a punch." He sounds almost proud.

"Danny's fine, no thanks to you. He thought you were hurting me. What the hell do you think you're doing—coming home drunk at this hour? We planned a nice dinner, the kids made your favorite lemonade, I made potato salad, and bought ribeyes for us and hamburger for the kids. We expected you to fire up the grill. But you'd rather hang out with your buddies and get drunk. I don't know what's going on with you, Mitchell Hawke, but I know I don't like it. You're pulling away from us more and more. We need you here with us, Mitch. Danny needs you."

Now he's sullen. "You don't need me, Lil. You've got your babies. You've made such a mommy's boy out of Danny that I can't get him to leave your side. You need to let him grow up. You can't keep him a baby forever. Look at what you're doing to him, for God's sake."

My head spins, my stomach clutches. I try to speak, but nothing comes out. I feel like I've been sucker punched. I hang on to the counter to keep from falling. *Who is this man? Where did my loving husband go, and when did he leave me?* Tears prick my eyes but I refuse to let them fall. I swallow down the bile surging in my throat.

"Mitch, you're drunk. I'm not going to fight with you. Either drink some coffee or go to bed. We'll talk when you're sober." I turn on my heel and stalk outside to the patio and collapse in a lounge chair. Then the tears fall.

Chapter 9

Life has settled into a guarded normal the last few weeks. Mitch works closer to home once more so he's here in the evenings. That means he and Danny are spending more time together. One trip to the construction site, where Mitch gave him a grand tour of the big dump trucks, excavators, backhoes, and bulldozers, was all it took. Now he is excited to go with his daddy. We hope this will break him out of the developmental stage he seems to be stuck in. Although he still dislikes going to school every day, he's not fighting it anymore.

As I sip my second cup of coffee at the dining room table, I look longingly at my favorite lounge on the patio outside. Leo lifts his head and follows my gaze. I'd love to be taking a break there, but not with the winds howling and dirt and leaves blowing. There's already a chill in the air.

The ringing phone startles me. "Hello?"

"Mrs. Hawke?"

"Yes."

"This is Mr. Meldrum, the school principal. We have a problem. Danny has been in a fight with a first-grade boy."

"Oh, my gosh." I'm on full alert. "What happened? That isn't like Danny."

"Can you come and pick him up from school? He's in the nurse's office."

"Is he hurt? What happened?"

"I'm not sure. Apparently he thought the little boy hurt his sister and claims he was defending her. The little boy isn't hurt either, other than a nosebleed, but he was scared. Danny is much bigger than he is."

"I'll be right there. Can I pick Sarah up at the same time? They usually ride the bus together."

"Yes. I'll have her brought to the nurse's office. I'd also like you and Mr. Hawke to join the school nurse, Danny's teacher, and me this evening to discuss his behavior and progress. Would 6 work for you?"

I'm stunned. I thought we were making progress. This forces me to face reality. "I-I'll try to reach my husband about the meeting, but I don't think there'll be a problem. I'll come get Danny right now." I grab my car keys, run my fingers through my hair, and rush out the door.

"Mama, Mama, I wanna go home! Mama, I go home." Danny charges at me as I enter the office. Sarah's crying, and for a moment I feel sorry for the poor nurse. She blows a loose tendril of hair from her face and sighs in frustration. One side of her blouse is no longer tucked in, and her skirt is twisted with the back zipper nearly in front.

"It's okay, Danny." I kneel and gather him in arms. "We're going home in a minute. I need you to be quiet while I speak with the nurse. Okay? Then we can go home."

Then I see Sarah. She's sobbing. "I don't want to go home, Mama. I want to stay here. I want to do my work. It's not time to go home. I want to stay." She throws herself down on the bench and continues to sob.

"Sarah Lorraine Hawke! You need to quit crying so I can talk to the nurse. When you get home you can practice your cursive letters. Tomorrow you can show your teacher. How's that?"

"I-I can do that?" she hiccups. "I can play school?"

"Yes, you can. But you need to quit crying. Okay?"

She smiles her angel smile and nods, wiping her tears.

I extend my hand to the nurse. "I'm Lillian Hawke, in case you haven't guessed."

"Jane Gothard, school nurse."

Danny broke in. "I taking care Sissy. Dat boy push Sissy, and I hit him. He not hurt my Sissy. I take care her."

Sarah sits up and tells him, "That boy didn't hurt me, Danny, I told you not to hit him. We were playing, and I fell down."

"But I take care Sissy."

"I think I understand, Danny. But you can't hit other children. If Sissy needs help, she'll ask a teacher."

"B-but I take care—" he insists.

"Enough, Danny. We'll talk about it at home. Now gather your things so we can go home. Miss Gothard, thanks for everything. I hope they weren't too much trouble. I believe I know what happened."

"It's all part of the job. It took some time to calm Danny down. He was convinced his sister needed him. Eventually I got him to tell me about his little car, and that seemed to calm him."

"Danny is very protective of his sister. Thanks for everything. I guess we'll see you later?"

We go by Mitch's office, only to find he's left early. I need to find him, fix something for the kids to eat, and shower before it's time to leave for the meeting. Thank goodness Betty, Mitch's new office manager, said she'd babysit. According to Mitch, she took Danny outside to see some of the equipment while he dealt with a customer, and he seemed to enjoy being with her other times when he'd been to the yard. She'll be at the house in 5:30.

Thank God Mitch is home when we get there. "Hey, I came home early to surprise you. All I found was Leo. He said he didn't know where you'd gone. What are the kids doing home already?" He leers at me, "I had some plans." Then he notices how distracted I am. "What's going on?"

I fling myself into his arms. "Oh, Mitch. Danny hit a first-grade boy. He says he was protecting Sarah, but she said the little boy hadn't done anything. They were playing when she slipped and fell, then Danny came running over and hit him."

"Hey, hey, take a breath. It's okay. We'll figure it out. He's only sticking up for his sis. We can't blame him for that." I can practically see his chest puff out.

"The principal wants us to meet with him, Danny's teacher, and the school nurse at 6. I already talked to Betty, and she'll babysit. She'll be here in an hour."

"Let's hope they aren't going to make a big deal out of this. He's only standing up for his sister."

"I know, but there may be more going on though. Why else would we be meeting with all three?" That worries me, but before I can think too much about it, I realize the kids have to be fed. "Mitch, could you make Danny and Sarah a sandwich while I get a quick shower?"

"Sure. Hey, kids. How'd you like some of dad's famous peanut butter and jelly sammies?"

I want to stand under the hot water forever, to wash all the anxiety and fear away. Our beautiful baby boy seems to be slowly disappearing as I watch helplessly. Glimpses of that energetic little boy appear once in a while, then in a flash he's gone, a mask drops, hiding him. Sarah is already ahead of him with what she's learned. A few nights ago I found her reading to him as he stared vacantly at Blue Bunny on her dresser.

Mitch's voice startles me. "You better hurry, Lil, or we'll be late. We should go to dinner after the meeting, just the two of us."

"Yes, we haven't done that in a long time." I slip into a simple shirtdress, and slide my feet into a pair of flats. With a few quick strokes, I pull my strawberry blond hair into a ponytail and remind myself I need a trim. A flick of mascara, a swipe of lipstick, and I'm ready to go.

The ride to the school is quiet—we're both lost in our own thoughts. I wish we could just skip over the next hour or so.

"Glad you could make it." Principal Meldrum welcomes us. "You've met Danny's teacher, Mrs. Miller, and our school nurse, Ms. Gothard."

I feel like I'm back in school, summoned to the principal's office.

Mitch finds his voice first. "Please, Mr. Meldrum, can we cut to the chase. You've asked us to come here tonight, so I'm assuming it's about more than the trouble Danny got into this afternoon."

"You're right. We're concerned about his progress, or I should say lack of progress. We want to give him the best education we can, but what we're doing doesn't seem to be working. Mrs. Miller, would you share with the Hawkes your concerns?"

Mrs. Miller, who is usually poised and always in control, wrings her hands as she clears her voice. "First, let me say, Danny is a sweet boy, but he won't participate in any class activities. Today is the first I've seen him display any emotion. When he comes to class, he takes his seat at his desk in the back of the classroom. I've encouraged him to move closer to the front, thinking he might have a hearing or vision problem. I've tried everything I can to engage him in class." At this point, she's looking directly at me. I squirm just a bit. "In fact, I've sent three notes home asking you to call or come in, but I've gotten no response. After today's incident, I felt it was imperative we meet to discuss a plan to help him. I'd also like Ms. Gothard to share her assessment of Danny—she's been monitoring and documenting his behaviors over the past two weeks at my request."

I remain outwardly calm despite the urge to be indignant. *This is no time to blame anyone.* "I never got any notes. I would have called."

Ms. Gothard may still be troubled about this afternoon, but she remains calm. Her voice is slow and measured. "I've been observing Danny in the classroom and on the playground. My concern is the way he isolates himself. The only other child I see him talk to is his sister. If she's busy playing with friends, he sits where he can watch her. I've had to chastise the children who taunt him. Danny doesn't seem to notice unless they try to touch him or the little toy pickup he carries. Then he starts rolling the toy in his palms, faster and faster. After his outburst today, I have to admit I'm concerned how he will react when or if he's pushed too far. His lack of social skills is bothersome—but his lack of class participation even more so." Almost as an afterthought, she adds, "he can barely write his name."

Mitch and I sit in stunned silence.

Mr. Meldrum gives us a moment before he says, "As principal I don't usually get involved unless the teacher requests it. We've discussed Danny on more than one occasion. That you haven't received the notes is upsetting to me. I wonder if he did that deliberately? Of course, we should have followed through with a phone call to your home." He looks towards Mrs. Miller for support. "We recommend that you have him evaluated by professionals at the Child Development Center. They are trained to administer the appropriate testing instruments to determine what, if any, psychological or learning disabilities we may be dealing with. Then an individualized plan could be developed that would be best for Danny. If necessary, we have a resource room for children with disabilities." I'm not sure either of us absorbs the full impact of what he is saying. "We are asking you to help us help you," he concludes.

Mitch is on his feet. Now he is the one who is indignant. "Are you saying our son is retarded?"

"No, Mr. Hawke," Mr. Meldrum responds quietly. At 6 foot 2, Mitch can be intimidating when he's angry, but the principal is unfazed. "We're saying that what we're doing is not helping Danny, and we feel it unfair to him to not find something that will. He's behind in all his classes. We don't know if it's because he can't, or because he simply refuses to do the work asked of him. That is why we recommend trained professionals to evaluate him." Then he adds, "I'm afraid that he can't return to school until he's completed an evaluation."

"B-but—" I don't even know what I want to say. I want to run from their words and yell, scream, call them liars, make them see the sweet little boy who makes up his own games, watches over his sister, loves his family. I want to say it's my fault for keeping him close to me, away from other children. If only I could curl up in a little ball and let someone else deal with this. I want my little boy to be like any other little boy—that's what I want more than anything.

Mitch must think I'm about to lose it, so he takes charge. "Lil and I need to talk about this. Give us the information on the center. How do we tell him he can't go to school because he defended his sister?"

My fear is that Danny will like this outcome. "I'll make the arrangements." I say. "All we want is what's best for our boy. I don't know what else to say. Maybe I've been in denial, telling myself one of these days he'll wake up and want to learn like Sarah; one of these days the little boy who used to run, play, laugh, and give big hugs will magically reappear." I stand and extend my hand to the principal. "Thank you so much for your concern." Then I turn to Mitch. "Do you want to ask anything else, Mitch?"

"No, not right now. Probably as soon as I leave, but right now I can't think of anything."

In the car I let the tears fall. Mitch reaches for me, and we hold each other. We are a couple united in our pain. Our hearts are breaking. I know, even if Mitch hasn't said anything, he's thinking of his brother Chris. That has to make it even more frightening for him. Tonight we're two wounded souls trying to digest all we've heard. Not a night for a 'date' when we only want to be safe in our home with our children.

Chapter 10

Until three weeks ago we had not heard of the Child Development Center, yet here we are, baring our souls for the last few hours. Our turn is finished. Now, we wait for Danny to complete yet another evaluation.

At home he's been a little angel since he no longer has to go to school. He was upset at first because Sarah wasn't staying home with him, but once she explained to him how much she likes school, he just accepted it. The first day was the worst—he waited at the window all day watching for the bus. That night I heard her speaking to him quietly. Whatever she said seemed to soothe him. Since their talk, he waves goodbye when she leaves. Weather permitting, he plays outside with his trucks and his ever-expanding town and roads. Otherwise, I'll find him in the playroom, either coloring, painting, or playing with his trucks—seemingly lost in a world of his own.

I've answered questions about his birth, my family history, medical, and emotional problems on either side of the family. They need to know the age he first rolled over, sat up, said his first words, crawled, walked—and on and on. How do they expect a person to remember every tiny detail? Mitch is going through the same questions with his family history, but he doesn't have to answer his questions in such detail. The problem for him is that he doesn't really know his family history. His parents are reluctant to talk about it. We know Chris has 'problems' but not really what that means. If they won't discuss Chris on the phone, I will sit down with them when they come for Thanksgiving.

We meet with Linda Parkin MSW, the Program Coordinator, when Danny is finished with his evaluation. "Mr. and Mrs. Hawke, we're done for the day. We need you to bring Danny back tomorrow. We have a few more steps to do a complete evaluation." She leans down to Danny. "Will you come and see me again tomorrow? We'll play some more games. How would you like that?"

"I bring my truck?"

"Yes, Danny. I'd like you to bring your truck to show me." Straightening, she looks at us. "Will you be able to do that?"

"I won't be able to—but you can, can't you, Lil? Surely you don't need both of us?"

"Actually, all we need is Danny. He'll be spending the day with us. Can you drop him off at nine and pick him up at three?"

I have so many questions, but now is not the time. "I can bring him tomorrow. We'll contact Mitch's parents tonight. Hopefully, I can fill in some of that information in the morning."

"That would be helpful—the more family history, the better. Sadly, some families are not very forthcoming, especially when it comes to mental health."

Danny waves at her as we leave. "I want go home. I want see Sissy."

"Should we stop by Burger Barn and get Sissy a hamburger and fries?"

"Yep, Sissy like bambugger. I like p butter n jelly."

"We know you love peanut butter and jelly."

He laughs, and my heart lifts. He doesn't laugh much anymore, but when he does, it gives me hope.

Our timing was perfect. The school bus pulls up just as we get home.

"Sissy, Sissy. We got you bamburger and fies. Mama and Daddy, too. I have p butter n jelly."

Leo is running in circles, trying to greet us all at once. Mitch and I eat in silence while Sarah chatters, telling us all about her day at school. Although I try to pay attention, she doesn't seem to notice whether we're listening or not. She exudes joy from her pert little nose to her toes.

After Danny and Sarah are bathed and tucked into bed, I shower while Mitch cleans up the kitchen. While he's showering I open a bottle of wine and take it up to the bedroom and light the fireplace. Normally, I don't drink much, but tonight I feel like a glass. Mitch hasn't had a drink since the night he came home drunk and we had that nasty fight.

I want to call his parents and get some answers. And we need to talk about what's going on. "Come on, Lil. Let's call it a day. We can call them in the morning. We need to get some rest." He leans down and kisses me tenderly and thoroughly.

He hasn't kissed me like that for a long time. At first I'm a bit surprised, then I feel my body responding. As I rise to meet him, he slips the robe off my shoulders, tugs my nightgown over my head, and wraps me in his embrace. His hands slide down my back as his kisses deepen. Heat sparks between us. *God how I've missed this.* A low moan escapes my lips as I pull away for a breath before I meet his lips with a hunger that threatens to consume me. My hands reach inside his robe to find him naked—and obviously up to the task. As we explore each other's bodies, he guides us to the bed and gently lowers me. His hand lightly brushes a nipple, sending a wave of need rippling through me. My body begins to pulse. I wrap my legs around him as he enters me, my breath is raspy with desire as he slowly begins to move. I'm overcome with a passion like nothing I've felt before—his arms tremble. "Oh, Mitch! Please, please, now, NOW!" I feel him shudder and his arm twitches. My body pulses as I ride the wave, not once but twice. He collapses on me and rolls to my side, still holding me in his arms. We're spent. I trace a finger down his cheek, wanting to stay in this moment forever.

The fire burns down, but we're loath to move from our embrace. He pulls the covers over us, still holding me close. A teardrop falls where our cheeks touch, but it's not mine. I cling to him and hold him tighter. His words are muffled when he speaks. "I've always been so afraid this would happen. I thought if we took care of him, gave him love and structure, everything would be okay. I feel so guilty, thinking I was wrong to marry and bring a son into the world. What if I passed the crazy gene down to him?" I want to comfort him, but he won't let me speak.

"I saw so much of Chris in Danny when he was little." Mitch was five when Chris was born. I want to take away his pain, but he needs to talk about this.

"Danny was fine when he was little. So, Chris was, too?"

"Everything seemed fine until he was about six. He was a loner like Danny, too, and fell behind in school, isolated himself, and acted out. The first time he was arrested, it was for shoplifting—he was only twelve. I remember his angry outbursts and him being in and out of jail. Then he ended up in the state hospital, yet he's still a mess."

He pulled away to look at me. "We can't let that happen to Danny. We can't. I don't think I could live with that." He's holding me so tight I can hardly breathe.

"Honey, it's not your fault. Why didn't you tell me before? We can get through anything together. We'll get him the help he needs."

I feel him nod, then we are both silent.

∞

Chapter 11

When we arrive, the receptionist escorts us to a conference room where Linda Parkin, our case manager, welcomes us. She greets us pleasantly, indicating that we take a seat at the table where several others have already gathered. "Good Morning, Mr. and Mrs. Hawke. Thank you for coming in. We've run Danny through a battery of diagnostic tests. He's been examined by Thomas Harden, our audiologist." As she mentions each professional by name, they stand and smile warmly at us. "Mary Smith is one of our speech therapists, Dr. Lawrence Moore is a child psychologist, and Becky Schrader, who has a Masters in Education, administered educational testing. Becky is our liaison with the school district, also." She nods, and they take their seats.

"I'm the case manager assigned to your son's case. We're here today to go over the reports prepared by each of the therapists. After we discuss the results, we'll give you our recommendations."

Before we begin, she asks if we'd like coffee or something else to drink and directs us to a pot of coffee, pitchers of juice, and ice water on the credenza. "Please help yourself."

Both Mitch and I are pleased that Linda, who has a master's degree in Social Work, is our case manager. We've had the most contact with her since this all started. It's reassuring to see a familiar face.

"I'll get it, Lil. Coffee?"

"Thanks, Mitch. Yes, please. Black."

I take a deep breath and relax as everyone gets their drinks and settles back at the conference table. While I wait for Mitch to bring my coffee, I notice the pale green walls that I suppose are meant to soothe. The lone painting of a relaxing mountain scene softens the starkness of an otherwise sterile room. At least the heavily padded chairs are comfortable. Mitch fidgets with a pen, disturbing my sense of calm. I gently take it from him. I know he's anxious, but I don't know how to reassure him. Part of me wants to run away. I want a do-over—to go back to when Danny was born. I wonder for a moment if having the flu when I was pregnant might have caused it. Could I have done something differently? *I've got to stop this.*

When everyone is settled, Linda begins. "Let's get started. We'll go over the results and recommendations. There's no need to take notes as we'll be giving you a written report." I quickly put Mitch's pen in my purse. I have nothing to write on anyway.

"We'll start with Dr. Hayden, the audiologist."

He indicates Danny hears a ringing or sounds in his ears at times, but his hearing is normal. "I recommend annual exams in case the ringing gets worse. It could be tinnitus."

The speech therapist recommends speech therapy to help him over-come a tongue thrust—and to develop age-appropriate speech patterns.

Dr. Moore, the psychologist, tells us he could get a better overall picture of Danny's behavior and mental health if he spends more time at the center. "Danny is socially inadequate and immature for his age. That means he is physically and emotionally unable to cope with the normal stress of living."

Mitch shuffles in his chair. He doesn't like what we are hearing. Neither do I.

"The plan is to involve Danny in speech therapy—as recommend-ed by the speech therapist. He'll also be in a socialization group where he can develop more mature social skills. To move forward with his education, he'll participate in some math, English, science, and other classes here. Our goal is to ease him back into the public school system when he's ready."

Mitch is the first to find his voice. "How many hours a day will he be here?"

"We're recommending 9 to 3, much like a regular school day. We have a small bus to pick him up and bring him home. We have no kitchen, so we ask that you send a sack lunch with his favorite foods. You will be apprised of all of his progress and activities. We hold weekly staffing meetings to continue developing the best plan of treatment for him."

"Could I stay with him the first day? He doesn't do well with change."

"If you ride the bus with him and spend the day observing, then ride home together on the bus in the afternoon, that should help with his transition—and reassure you about the program. After that you'll have to allow him to do it on his own. Will that work for you, Mrs. Hawke?"

"Yes. I guess I'll have to look at it like I'm sending him to school?"

"Exactly."

We finalize the plan. By the end of the meeting my head is spinning with so many emotions—hope, sadness, relief—relief that he's finally getting help so he'll be able to have a normal life. Yet fear, too, that this is only the beginning of a long road.

We're both quiet on the ride home. Mitch's jaw is clenched, and his knuckles are white from clutching the wheel so tightly. I want to reassure him it'll be okay, but I'm afraid the jumble of emotions will come tumbling out if I begin. When we finally reach our home, I'm anxious to get inside, thank Betty, and let her leave. I need to spend time with Danny and tell him about our plan. I need the rest of the day to go well. Since Sarah won't be home for a couple of hours, I'm going to relax, then fix a nice family dinner. Of course, that will be fried chicken, mashed potatoes, and gravy.

The house is quiet when we walk in. Betty's reading, but I don't see any sign of Danny. My heart leaps. "Where's Danny?" I ask, looking around.

"Oh, I didn't hear you drive up or I'd have called him down. He's upstairs in the playroom. He's been really good all day. When I check on him every once in a while, he's playing with his toys. He came down long enough to have his lunch—p butter n jelly sammie with a glass of milk. Does he ever eat anything else?"

Mitch went over some of what we'd learned and the plan for him to be at the center through the day. "Looks like you're stuck in the office and on the job now." He tries to laugh but it comes out strangled.

"Oh, you poor man." She places her hand on his.

"Betty, I really appreciate all you've done. I think we've taken you away from your job long enough. Danny's starting at the center on Monday. I'll get Sarah on the bus before Danny's bus comes, and I'll be spending the day with him."

She looks at Mitch, not at me. "But you'll want me here for Sarah when she gets home, won't you, Mitch?"

Before Mitch can respond, I answer, "That's okay, Betty. I'll be talking to Martha next door. Her daughter rides the bus with Sarah, so I'll ask if she'll watch her until I get home. You've been a blessing to us. I hope you know how much I appreciate it." Betty's disappointment is painfully obvious. I wonder why it took me so long to realize young Betty has a crush on my husband. It's about time I pinch her happy family fantasy in the bud. Mitch will have to deal with it at the office, but I won't in our home. Poor girl, to him she is a good kid—a young, good kid.

"Mama, Daddy, you home!"

Leo is at Danny's side. He greets us by spinning in circles.

"We sure are, sport. What would you like to do the rest of the day?"

"We go see big trucks, Daddy?"

"Is that what you want?"

"Yes, big truck. Wanna see big trucks." His face lights up in anticipation.

"Betty, why don't you take the rest of the day off? Then come into the office in the morning."

"Oh, but Mitch, I could come and help with Danny."

"No. Dan and I are fine. I don't want to see you in the office until 9 in the morning."

Is that a tear in her eye?

"If you're sure, Mitch." She pulls her coat on, watching him with Danny.

I walk her to the door. "Take care and drive safely. Again, thanks for all you've done." I give her a little hug.

She hesitates, looking back towards Mitch. "Bye, Mitch." He doesn't respond, and she leaves.

Should I say anything? I smile and think, *absolutely not!*

"Lil, do you mind? Danny and I are going to the yard? I need some time with him right now. I hope you understand. Why don't you put your feet up and relax. I don't know about you, but I feel better now that we have a plan. I don't feel so lost."

"Of course I don't mind. Will you talk to him about going to the center?"

"I thought I might, but I'll play it by ear."

I hug them both and send them on their way. With a couple of hours to myself, I know just what I'll do.

I pour myself a cup of coffee, then head upstairs for a long, hot bath. As I slide down into the water, my tears blend with the water in the tub.

Chapter 12

Eight inches of newly fallen snow blankets the neighborhood; trees are draped in veils of white, and shadows of Christmas reds and greens shine faintly through the limbs. I rest my head against the cold windowpane, thinking about Christmas. Our best-laid plans are once again out of our control. We should have picked up Mitchell's parents by now. They were due to fly out of Amarillo this morning, but all flights from north Texas were canceled. Early yesterday morning, the storm rampaged from Canada to Texas. We'd bought their plane tickets to come and spend the holidays with us.

With a wistful smile, I remember their Thanksgiving visit here last year. Sarah, though shy at first, spent every waking moment with them—we hoped they'd come more often. Now we're shooting for late spring, maybe combine Christmas and Easter—with all the trimmings. Sarah would love that. She had been so excited all week. I dread seeing her disappointment in the morning when we tell her they couldn't come. With all the time and attention we give to Danny, God knows she could use a little of that, especially from Nana and Papa.

This year clear lights decorate our Christmas tree, much to Sarah's disappointment—she wanted twinkling colored lights, like those her friends have. Because we've discovered Danny has a problem with certain colors, especially yellow, with red and green close behind, I learned the hard way that twinkling lights are a definite no-no. The first time, he saw them in the middle of a store. At first he just stopped and stared, mesmerized, when suddenly he rushed to the tree, trying to tear the lights off. Somehow, I got him under control and to the car before anyone called the cops.

In many ways he's done better over the past year and a few months. His reading and writing are better—at least he can write more than just his name. His printing is about second-grade level, and we believe that might be as good as it gets. Most kids look forward to a break once in a while, but not Danny. He's been broody since the center closed for Christmas.

Even planning Christmas dinner presents problems. At least now he won't get upset if there's food on the table he doesn't like. His preferences in food are strictly limited to peanut butter, grape jelly, milk, pancakes, oatmeal, fried chicken, mashed potatoes with cream gravy, and plain sugar cookies. I worry about his nutrition— he won't take vitamins. It's almost impossible to get any medications in him. Sometimes I can mix a pill into his food, but if he gets the slightest hint of a strange taste, that's it for the meal. He won't eat another bite.

As I sip a lukewarm cup of tea, I realize how much I've learned since Danny started at the center. They still don't have a conclusive diagnosis. They've mentioned many possible diagnoses, but they're still guesses—possibly Autism, obsessive-compulsive disorder, oppositional disorder, hyperactive, or others I can't even remember. Right now the focus is on behavioral modification—treating the symptoms more than having an actual diagnosis. We've tried so many medications—and always it's a struggle for Danny to get them down. None of them seemed to make any difference. With each new possible diagnosis, I research extensively and learn about disorders I didn't even know existed. That's why I applied for the therapy technician position at the Child Development Center and started taking college courses to learn as much as I can to help our boy.

Mitchell, too, is learning, but with each failed attempt I can sense his frustration and discouragement grow. More and more he's reminded of his brother Chris—and his fear Danny will follow down the same path as his uncle. He's losing hope and patience with the whole situation, and he seems to be withdrawing again from Danny and Sarah, and from me.

My heart breaks watching this man as his hopes and dreams slip away. He was so proud the day our little guy came into the world. He shared the same hopes and dreams other daddies have of things they'll do with their sons; fishing, watching sports together—football, baseball, racing. Racing is the only one that holds Danny's attention. He could watch trucks race all day and wander around the pits looking them over. If there are no trucks racing, a car race will do.

Danny is happiest in the playroom or in the backyard surrounded by his trucks of various sizes. His town and roads are ever changing. I am thrilled that his love of painting has really blossomed this past year. He's created some really nice pictures. The adjustable easel Mitchell built for him is something can use into adulthood. It's also portable, one he can carry along with a matching oak box for his supplies.

The pictures he creates reveal his moods—the darker the picture, the darker the mood. Sometimes I feel the weight of the world on my shoulders. Mitchell works hard to pay the bills and put food on the table, but he's spending more and more time at work. At first I thought he might be seeing someone—that would have been the case if Betty had her way. He let her go with the excuse he didn't need extra help during the winter months, but he told me her attention made him uncomfortable.

The house remains quiet as I gaze at the falling snow. The muffled sound of church bells marks midnight. This is my favorite time of day—when everyone else is sound asleep—time all to myself, no one wanting a piece of me. I can sip a cuppa, read a good book, even shed a tear and let go. Homework for my abnormal psych class isn't due for a couple weeks, so I just need to relax and enjoy, hoping sleep will come soon. In this moment, I'm enjoying the blinking lights on our neighbor's house—it's all decked out for Christmas. I sip my tea again, but it's cold now. I marvel that a storm so severe has turned our neighborhood into a winter wonderland.

A scream shatters the stillness of the night. In the midst of the crashing noises above me, the cup slips from my fingers and smashes to the floor. I take the stairs two at a time, in a rush to get to the playroom.

Danny's walking in circles. His hands are fluttering. His mouth is wide open, and his screams are ear-splitting screams. In the middle of the floor, surrounded by destruction, is his big yellow Tonka truck. Blue Bunny's insides are ripped out. Trucks of all sizes are smashed and lie broken on the floor. Mitchell staggers in, wrapping his robe around him.

He reaches out and grabs Danny by the arm. "What the hell! Danny! Stop screaming right now." Danny breaks free, and the crescendo intensifies. Mitchell reaches for him again, but Danny sidesteps, his agitation increasing. As I step between them, Sarah appears in the door, clutching her favorite blanket. She's wide-eyed and shaking, staring at her brother and the two of us.

"Mitchell, take Sarah out of here. I'll take care of Danny."

He hesitates before turning away, shaking his head, and cursing under his breath. Just as he reaches her, Sarah sees the tattered Blue Bunny, who's sat on her dresser her entire life—put there when she was a baby, a gift from her big brother. Tears trickle down her cheeks as she reaches toward him.

"Danny? Why?" She whispers so softly I barely hear her.

All sound stops as his eyes meet hers.

"NO. NO. NNOOOO. Not ME. Yellow did it. Yellow—" he cries, then begins pacing and flailing again.

Mitchell starts for him once more, once more I position myself between them. "Mitchell, take Sarah out. NOW!" Slowly he turns, reaches down, and picks her up gently. With one last glance at Danny, he takes her out of the room, his shoulders slumped and looking like he's aged twenty years in the last few minutes.

"Danny." I say his name quietly, but he doesn't seem to hear. Slowly I move toward him. He doesn't even know I'm here. When his back is to me, I wrap my arms around him, pinning his arms to his sides. He struggles to break my hold, but I don't let go, all the while whispering reassurances in his ear.

"It's okay Danny. Mom's got you. It's okay. We love you. We love you, Danny." Around and around the room we move as I keep repeating the same reassurances. My arms ache and my back is hurting, but that's nothing compared to the aching in my heart seeing him like this. It's never been this bad before.

Finally, he begins to quiet, allowing me to settle with him on his beanbag chair. I lose track of time while we sit. Then I feel his body begin to relax. As if a switch is thrown, he's asleep and gently snoring.

I loosen my hold and let him rest against me. I'm exhausted in body and spirit. I feel broken, like the toys strewn around the room.

∞

Chapter 13

I must have fallen asleep with Danny snuggled up against me. When I look up sleepily, Mitch is standing in the doorway. Danny is still sound asleep.

"We're going to have to do something. You know that, don't you?"

"But what, Mitchell? What do you suggest?" My voice cracks and I hear the desperation creeping in.

His eyes are damp with unshed tears and red from lack of sleep as he looks first at the destruction in the room and then at our son, who looks so innocent and vulnerable. A sob shudders through his body as he slowly slides to the floor. "I don't know. I don't know, but we can't subject Sarah or even Danny to this again. We might need to s-s-send—" His shoulders quake with sobs.

I want to go to him, to hold him the way I'm holding Danny, to tell him everything will be okay. As I pull away, Danny mumbles in his sleep and curls up in the warm spot I've left. I try to stand but my cramped legs won't move, so I crawl to Mitch and wrap him in my arms. He clutches me to him.

I can't find the words to convince him it won't happen again, that it's an anomaly, just a one-time thing—that when Danny wakes he'll be the sweet little boy we first brought home when he was born. God, that's what I want to say, but I'm frozen in a nightmare—afraid to move or I'll wake the sleeping tiger. What if I set him off again, and I can't control him.

I didn't know a person could feel so much pain, and yet—when I see his sleeping face, the face of an angel—I can't connect this little boy to the one in the midst of the chaos of a few hours ago.

I'm the first to pull away. We have to clean up this mess before Danny and Sarah wake up. I pray Danny will be okay when he wakes up and can tell us what happened. If only it wasn't him that caused this. What if someone got in somehow and did all the damage? Maybe Danny walked in and found it like this. Is that what set him off? That's the answer I want. If we don't find out what happened in this room, how can we prevent a repeat in the future? The most heartbreaking is the destruction of Blue Bunny, my mom's guardian as she lay dying, the protector of Sarah all these years. Suddenly, as though cold, icy fingers were sliding up my spine, a sense of panic rises and I think—*Sarah! Danny wouldn't hurt Sarah—Would he?* I drive those thoughts away and pull myself up.

Mitchell remains quiet. I reach my hand out to him. "We have to clean this up. We can't leave this mess for Danny to see when he wakes up, and Sarah shouldn't see any more than she already has. Speaking of Sarah, where is she?"

Mitchell stands, runs one hand through his hair, and with the other, wipes the tears from his weary face. "She's asleep in our bed. She didn't want to go back to hers, so I let her crawl into ours. She cried herself to sleep. She kept asking me, 'Why?' But how could I answer—I keep asking the same question."

When he begins to pick up bunny and his stuffing, I reach out and touch his arm. "Honey, why don't you fix us some coffee? You can bring some trash bags when you bring the coffee. I'll get started here, if you'll check on Sarah. I need to know she's okay, but I don't want to leave Danny in case he wakes up. Someone needs to be here when he does—at least until we clean up the room." For the first time I notice the only area of the room unscathed is where his easel stands with his paints.

Mitchell looks helplessly down at the empty shell of fur and the stuffing strewn about that was once our faithful friend and asks me, "Do you think you could fix him?"

I choke back a sob. "No, I'm afraid he's torn too badly. Why don't you put him in a bag so they won't see him." I can't fall apart now—there's too much to do. Taking a deep breath, I pick up the twisted, broken cars and trucks. All but the big Yellow Tonka have some damage. The destroyed ones go in one pile, the ones to repair and keep in another. Danny sleeps on as I work, unaware of our anguish. I straighten and sort through his things like a robot—I feel frozen, numb.

Mitch pauses at the door when he comes back with my coffee. "This looks much better. You got a lot done. Almost back to normal, but kind of empty. What are we going to do with all of this?" He points to the pile of crumpled toys.

"Throw them away, unless you want some parts off them first—they can't be fixed. Let's get them out of sight. You might salvage those in that pile."

I stare at the big Tonka truck for just a moment. "Put that up in the rafters of the garage or someplace out of sight in the basement." I'd put it in the back of his closet, behind a suitcase, thinking one day he'd want to play with it again. Now I never want to see it again, but I can't bring myself to throw it away. "Remember not so long ago when it was his favorite? I don't think I told you what he said. 'Big yellow bad—big yellow tell me do bad things.' I didn't think much of it at the time. I thought it was his imagination working over time, now I wonder—"

We work together putting everything back the best we can. Other than fewer cars and trucks, it looks much the same—although his favorites are missing. I worry about how he'll react. We're not sure whether we can leave him alone, sleeping in the beanbag chair, or if one of us should stay with him. Mitchell is at the end of his rope, and I'm exhausted. I just want to take a hot shower, hold Sarah close, and figure out what to do.

It's all I can do to keep from screaming like Danny did last night. I don't want to be a grown up. I don't want to deal with this. I'm sure Mitch feels the same. Just for today, I want to disappear and let the world go by, and not be responsible for anything. Just once I'd like to fall apart and let someone else clean up the mess. I'm so flippin' sick of being strong.

"Mitch, I'm going to check on Sarah, then take a long, hot shower.

Will you keep an ear out for Danny in case he wakes up?"

"Are you sure it's okay to leave him?"

"I have no idea, but we can't sit here waiting for him to wake up, and I sure as hell don't want to wake him. He has to be worn out. I know I am. You need some rest, too, and we need to talk. Let me get a shower. Okay?"

The hot water cascades over me. I want to stay here forever, feeling safe, like I'm behind a waterfall where the troubles of the world can't penetrate. I feel anger bubbling up inside. Pretending I know how to deal with a child as confounding as Danny is exhausting. Hell, the professionals are only guessing. It's like a science experiment. They poke and prod him. They 'observe' behaviors, suggest treatments, and prescribe medications. Then out of the blue, a new set of problems appears. Our family histories have been explored with a fine-toothed comb. They dug into my pregnancy as though I did something to cause it. Our marriage, our communication styles were questioned. Even sexual abuse was implied and explored; and yet, at the end of the day, Danny's still a tortured young boy, as confused and lost as when we began. Just a few short hours ago I thought we'd made progress. But two days of a broken routine and with company expected, things are far worse than they've ever been.

"Lil? Are you okay in there?"

The water has gone cold. Quickly, I turn it off and reach out for a towel.

"Here, let me help." Mitch wraps me in the towel and holds me tight. "I was worried. You've been in there quite a while."

I let myself relax against him. "Are the kids still sleeping?"

"Yes. I just looked in on them before I got you a fresh cup of coffee. All is quiet." He holds me for a few more minutes, then briskly rubs my arms, turns me to dry my back and hands me the towel. "I thought we could have a few minutes to ourselves."

"I'd like that. How about starting a fire downstairs, and I'll be right down?"

"Sounds good."

I towel dry my hair and pull on my comfy sweats—my go to when-I'm-feeling-down clothes. Sarah's snuggled on her daddy's pillow, her arm around Malcolm, her teddy bear. I have no clue where she came up with his name. Bless this 'normal' little girl, with her loving heart and happy smile—the opposite of her brother. Where he's a puzzle, she's an open book. He's standoffish, and she's a hugger and a snuggler. Her smile lights up the room, but the pain I saw in her eyes when she spied Bunny will haunt me for a very long time. I check Danny. He's still sleeping in the beanbag chair—looking as innocent as his sister.

The brightness of the sun surprises me as I descend the stairs. I'm shocked by the glare off the newly fallen snow—I'd forgotten about the storm outside. A fire crackles in the fireplace, and I breathe in the fragrance of the pine log. I don't see Mitch, so I step in the kitchen to refill my cup. I hear a sound and turn toward the picture windows where he's slumped in his Grandma's old rocker, sound asleep. There's a movement just outside the window where a bird sits on a drift of snow. Neighbors, snow shovels in hand, venture outside. In the distance a snowplow is already at work on the streets.

"Mitchell? Come on, honey. Come on over to the couch. You'll be more comfortable there." He mumbles but lets me help him up. Not quite awake, he lets me guide him to the couch and help him lie down. I cover him with the afghan Mom made that last year before she died. It's his favorite. We need to talk, but he needs his rest. As I turn, I see the Christmas tree is still lit. *Good Heavens, only one more day till Christmas Eve.* But right now I have more important things to do.

"You've reached the office of Dr. Landry. I'm sorry we aren't in right now. Please leave a message, and we'll get back to you."

Doctor Landry is a child Psychiatrist. We need the kind of help she can give us. I leave a short message about what's happened and pray she'll call me back. If Danny wakes up and is still agitated, I'll give him anti-anxiety medication to calm him until we can get him to the doctor. I can only pray he won't need it. Somehow, we need to make this a good Christmas for Sarah.

Chapter 14

The house is quiet, too quiet. My family's sleeping, and hopefully resting. I'm beyond tired, yet wound tight as a top, on the verge of spinning out of control on this rollercoaster ride we call our lives. Just when things level out, when I think I can relax, wham. Out of the blue, another problem slaps me in the face.

Resting my face against the cool window, I watch the neighborhood come to life. Neighbors clearing their sidewalks wave to each other. A few children, bundled against the cold, emerge to build snowmen and start snowball fights. As their joyous laughter reaches my ears, I drink it in. That laughter is what's missing in our home. Once in a while something will set Sarah off in peals of laughter, but I can't remember the last time I heard Danny really laugh.

The patter of bare feet on the hardwood floor tells me Sarah's coming. She's dragging Malcolm behind her, rubbing sleep from her eyes.

"Mama? Where's Daddy?"

"Daddy's asleep on the couch. He's really tired, so we'll let him rest. Okay?"

"Okay." She looks so forlorn. Her hair is in tangles, and her pj's are skewed from sleep.

"You doin' okay, cookie?"

"I'm okay, Mama. Mama? Danny didn't mean to hurt Blue Bunny and break his toys, did he?"

"No, honey." I pull her into my arms and breathe in the sweet smell of lilac that envelops her. "He didn't mean to do it."

"Danny says yellow truck is mean. It tells him to do bad things. But his yellow truck can't do that, can it?"

"No, it can't. Sometimes Danny gets confused."

"That's why he goes to that center place, isn't it, Mama? So they can make him better. And he won't be conpused any more?"

"Yes, that's why he goes to the center to learn and get better." I hold her tight.

"Mama, Mama. Look at the snow. Oh, Mama, look at the snow. That's Margaret and Tony building a snowman. Mama, can I go play with them and help build their snowman? Can I, Mama? Please?"

How I envy the innocence of her youth as I watch her let go of the pain and slide into pure joy. "First you need to have some breakfast, then we'll bundle you up, and you can go play."

"Will you come, too, Mama? Will you come play, too? Please?"

"We'll see. Mama has to be right here when Daddy and Danny wake up. But maybe later I'll come out and play in the snow with you."

She wriggles out of my arms and skips into the kitchen for breakfast. "It's almost Christmas, isn't it, Mama? When will Nana and Papa be here? I can't wait to see them."

"Oh, honey. Nana and Papa won't be coming. There's too much snow for their airplane to fly them here. We have to wait till spring for them to visit."

"But, Mama, I want Papa and Nana for Christmas. Couldn't Santa bring them on his sleigh?" For a moment she brightens, then she's crestfallen. "He can't, can he? Toys for all the girls and boys will fill the sleigh."

"I'm sorry, baby. It'll be a good Christmas anyway. If they come at Easter, we'll put up a tree and have Chriseaster. What do you think of that?"

She giggles. "That's funny, Mama. Can we do that, have Chrieaster when they come?"

"Yes, we can. And this will be a good Christmas, or I'll eat my new shoe." Her burst of laughter warms my heart.

After hurrying through breakfast, she rushes upstairs to get dressed. I follow to help her with her hair and to make sure she chooses her warmest clothes. Then I check on Danny.

I tread softly as I approach the playroom door, hoping he's still asleep. When I push the door open, he's already hunched over his drafting table, and papers are strewn all around him. He's frantically drawing a big, yellow truck with angry, red eyes for headlights. The grill is shaped into an open mouth drawn into a grimace, with sharp, jagged teeth. Little cars and trucks are crushed under its oversized wheels.

I stifle the gasp that nearly escapes—so I don't startle him. Touching his shoulder gently, I whisper, "Danny?" But he keeps on drawing. The other papers strewn about him are more pictures of the same angry truck.

When I hear the phone ring, I'm torn between answering it or trying to pull Danny from the trancelike state he's in. It might be the doctor, so I run downstairs for the phone.

Mitch, who's not quite awake, answers just as I reach it.

"'Low. No, this isn't Dr. Landry—you must have the wrong number."

I grab the phone before he can put it down. "Hello, Dr. Landry?"

"Yes, Mrs. Hawke. Your message sounded urgent. I'm snowed in, and I imagine you are, too, or I'd say bring your son right in. How is he?"

"He's quiet now. When I checked on him, he didn't know I was there, even when I touched him. It's like he's in a trance. He's drawing all sorts of pictures—a big, ugly, yellow truck with angry human features, crushing smaller ones." I swallow a sob. "I don't know what to do for him."

"Did something happen recently to precipitate the incident last night?"

"It shouldn't be the Christmas tree we just put up, because it's decorated with only clear bulbs—lately he's been bothered by colored lights. He doesn't handle changes in his routine very well, or company either. The Child Development Center is closed for the holidays—otherwise he'd be there every day. Plus, we've been preparing for Mitchell's parents' visit over the holidays, but bad weather cancelled their trip."

"Have any of his medications changed recently?"

"Not really. We've tried different medications this past year, but to no avail. Getting him to take anything is a challenge. He has a prescription for anti-anxiety medication I was going to give him if he got agitated, until we can get him in to see you. The center's been helpful, but he needs to see someone like you for a more in-depth evaluation."

"If he has another violent outburst you need to call 911 and get him to a safe environment. He may have to be hospitalized for an evaluation." She hesitates just a heartbeat, then asks, "Are there any other children in the home?"

"Yes, his little sister. I've convinced myself he'd never hurt Sarah. He sees himself as her protector. But last night he must have taken the stuffed rabbit he gave her when she was a baby. It was destroyed, along with most of his favorite toy trucks in the playroom."

"See if you can give him the anti-anxiety medication now. As soon as weather permits, bring him to my office." She hesitates once more, then continues, "It is extremely important you call 911 if he loses control again or becomes a danger to himself or others. Please do not hesitate to call 911—you'll be doing what's best for him, and you must keep him and your daughter safe." Before ending the call, she gives me her contact information, and I assure her we'll follow her instructions.

Mitch is right behind me, his tired eyes shimmering with emotion. "I'm sorry. I almost hung up on her. I didn't know you'd called anyone."

"You were already asleep when I called her. I know we should have talked it over, but I didn't want to waste another minute. We can't stand by while he spins out of control."

He nods his head, letting me know he's not upset. "What did she say?"

"She said to give him the anxiety medicine to keep him calm until we can see her. When I checked on him, he was drawing—he's zoned out, but drawing. Sarah's ready to play in the snow with the neighbor kids."

As if on cue, Sarah trundles down the stairs in jeans and bundled in her favorite sweater. She throws herself into her daddy's arms. "Daddy, did you see the snow? Did you? I'm going to go play with my friends.

I'm going to make a snowman. Can you and Mama come, too? Can you?"

"Whoa, Nellie. Slow down the horse." He chuckles, using one of her favorite phrases. "I did see all the snow—fun for you, but work for me. You go have fun with your friends. Mama and I have to take care of some things."

I help button her into her winter coat and slip on her snow boots while she pulls on gloves and stocking hat. Her beaming face puts a smile on my face. With a quick hug, she bolts out the door.

"Later, gators."

"'While, crocodile," we say in unison. *Ah, to be a child again.*

While I tell Mitch about my call with Dr. Landry, he sits with his head in his hands, shoulders slumped, and staring at the floor. He doesn't say anything. I wait for a response—I don't know what more to say. At least we have a game plan, just in case.

The sizzle of the fire inside, burning low, and peals of laughter from outside ring in my ears. I'm living in a divided world with hopelessness about Danny crushing my spirit, yet the sound of pure joy and abandonment from our precious daughter fills my heart. Feeling torn in two, I reach for a log and put it on the fire.

A slight sound on the stairs grabs my attention. Danny's coming down. still in his pajamas, with his arms at his sides, his hands flailing in slow motion. With eyes downcast watching his feet, he descends the stairs. As he reaches the bottom step Mitchell spins towards him, his face twisted with rage. He strides towards him with such fury. I reach out, desperate to grasp his arm and stop him.

"Please, no," I whisper, not even sure he could hear my words. Mitch stops, looks at me and back at Danny. Then he draws in a deep breath.

With gritted teeth, hands clenched tightly, he spits out, "For two cents I'd whip his ass, just like my dad did Chris'. I WILL NOT have him tearing up our home and scaring the holy hell out of his little sister. I will NOT tolerate it! Do you hear me, Lil? I will not!" He turns on his heel before I can answer, rips his coat off the hook, and slams out into the cold air and snow.

Sarah must have heard the door slam. She comes running as fast as her legs can manage in the deep snow. "Daddy. Daddy. You came to play with me!" She throws herself at him, expecting he'll catch her—but with such force he's knocked down as he steps off the porch. She slaps the snow off his coat, and her giggles fill the air—his anger dissipates and laughter softens his features.

Danny makes his way to the kitchen, totally unaware of what just happened. He walks with a stiff-legged stride that's developed lately. His lips move but no words escape, and his hands move to some internal rhythm. He pulls a spoon out from the silverware drawer and climbs up on his favorite bar stool, waiting.

"Would you like some oatmeal?" I ask, but he just sits there staring. "Danny, I need you to answer me. Would you like some oatmeal?"

"Yes, oatmeal." He doesn't look at me.

As I make his oatmeal, I think about the pills in my pocket. How do I hide a bright orange pill in an off-white meal? I pour a glass of milk and set it in front of him. Then I have an idea that might work. "Would you like a slice of bread?" I ask, knowing he doesn't eat toast but likes bread. He likes to pull it apart, roll the pieces into little balls, pop them in his mouth and swallow them whole.

When he says, "Yes," I place a slice on a napkin for him. He tears it apart and starts rolling the pieces.

"Can I help?"

He nods, indicating it's okay, so I take a few pieces and roll them like he does—one I roll around the pill. Silently I pray he won't pick today to start chewing them. I add some sugar and milk to his oatmeal and set it in front of him.

"It's hot, so be careful."

He takes a bite of oatmeal and a sip of milk, then pops a rolled up piece of bread in his mouth and swallows. With each bite I watch closely until he swallows that last piece. He wipes his mouth and slides off the stool.

"Danny? Do you remember what happened last night?" When

there's no response, I lift his chin so he's looking into my eyes. He doesn't try to turn away. He just stands there. "Danny, can you tell me what happened to your toys?" His eyelids flutter, and he shuffles a bit in place.

"What toys? I got trucks and cars. Big Yellow doesn't like my little cars and trucks." Now his hands begin to flutter. The last thing I want to do is agitate him, but I need to know what he remembers.

"Danny? Did you break your cars and trucks? Did you tear up Blue Bunny and make a the mess in the playroom?"

He stares into my eyes, with little change in expression. "Playroom not a mess. I draw, not hurt Blue Bunny. Sissy has Bunny." He looks away. "I want go outside. Can I go outside?"

I let go of his chin, and his eyes look down at the floor. This is an exercise in futility. He doesn't understand what I'm talking about, and the medication is already making him sleepy. That's why we don't like using it.

"Danny, how about a bath first, then maybe we'll go outside?"

"Okay, Mama. Take bath." He repeats, "I take bath," as he makes his way up the stairs.

"I'll start your bathwater while you get your clothes."

"Okay, Mama. I get my clothes."

How can this be the same little boy who was so frantic a few hours ago? By the time he's through with his bath, his eyelids are drooping. It's probably the meds, the fact he's had so little sleep, or a combination of both.

"Danny, why don't you put on clean pajamas and crawl into bed for a while. Would you like that?"

Without a word he pulls on his pj's, crawls into bed, and pulls up his covers. He's almost asleep before his head hits the pillow. I lean down and kiss his forehead, then go to my room and crawl into bed. Mitch can be in charge. For now, I'm not going to worry.

∞

Chapter 15

Christmas is especially quiet this year, but the day turns out okay. Sarah's thrilled with her Raggedy Ann and Andy dolls and the wooden wagon for pulling them. Danny's shown little interest in his new paints and trucks, instead sleeping on the floor most of the day near the tree. No huge feast for dinner this year, yet plenty of leftovers remain. A twenty-five-inch television, our family present, now occupies the den—our new TV room, and Mitch and Sarah are enthralled by it.

The next day is our emergency appointment with Dr. Landry. Glancing outside on my way to get Danny out of bed, I'm thankful the streets are plowed.

"Come on, Danny. Let's go. We've got to get ready."

"No, don't wanna." He squeezes his eyes closed.

"Daddy's bringing his new, big truck home just for you."

"I get ride in big truck?" Eyes wide open now, he pulls himself out of bed.

When Mitch brought home the new 1964 four-door crew pickup, Danny's reaction was amazing—the first we'd seen like this in a long time. He couldn't wait to go for a drive. Today it's an enticement to take him to see Dr. Landry.

"Ride in truck." Danny repeats as he heads for the door.

We're ready when Mitch pulls up out front and revs the engine—to Danny's delight. He grabs two of his new toy pickups, and he's out the door. Sarah is staying with the Thompsons while we're gone.

Danny's engrossed in watching his Dad. His excitement tickles Mitch, who explains each dial on the dash. The sun's shining off the banks of snow, and the streets are sanded. Although I'm really nervous about our appointment, I need answers—yet, I'm afraid of what they will be. Moms are supposed to take care of their children no matter what. The thought of trying more medicines that make him dull and lethargic makes me cringe, yet his illness is doing just that anyway. Today I'm hoping for answers—even if I don't like them.

I'm so deep in thought I don't realize we've arrived at Dr. Landry's office until Mitch shakes my arm. "Lil, earth to Lil. We're here." That's my guy, with his dry sense of humor, trying to 'jolly' me into thinking everything's going to be okay. It's his way of hiding his own fear and reassuring me.

"Come on, Danny. Let's show Dr. Landry your new pickups." He's dozed off again, and I gently jiggle him awake. Thank God, he takes my hand and crawls out of the pickup, docilely following us into the office.

The reception area's a welcoming place, with a gas fireplace emitting a warm, hospitable glow. Overstuffed easy chairs invite us to sit down and enjoy the warmth. Table and chairs are tucked in the corner with a big wicker basket of crayons. Stacks of paper on one bookshelf are ready for taking, along with an assortment of children and young people's books that fill the built-in bookcases along the wall. Danny's drawn to the paper—he takes some and sits at the table. He places his trucks on the table and begins to sketch.

A young lady in her early twenties stands to greet us. "You must be the Hawkes. Dr. Landry will be with you in a few minutes. These are the papers I need you to fill out." She slides a clipboard to us and asks for our insurance card to copy.

Since we began this search for answers, I've filled out countless forms. Mitch is reading over my shoulders. When filling out the family history section, I hesitate at the question asking for history of mental illness, depression, etc., and an explanation. When I mark "yes," I feel Mitch stiffen beside me. "What do you mean by that? Who's the loony in your family?"

This is where I have to tread carefully. "Mitch, what about your uncle and your brother Chris? Think of all the problems they've had.

Your uncle died drunk and homeless, never able to hold a job. You and your parents told me how he withdrew from the family. Chris was in and out of jail from the time he got into your parents' liquor and tore up the neighborhood on his bicycle when he was twelve." I'm whispering now. "He ended up in juvie then, and it got worse. You haven't seen him in years, since he killed the clerk in that liquor store robbery. He hasn't accepted any visitors since he's been in prison. All the letters you and your mom send come back unopened."

"Okay, so my uncle was a little strange. So was the other one. He covered it up better and made all kinds of money. Then he left the money to some guy he had as a roommate for years. There might have been something hinky, but crazy? I'd say unique."

"But Mitchell, don't you think we need to let the Doctor know in case there's a connection—"

"So, now it's my fault?" His face is turning red.

Before I can respond to him, the receptionist tells us the Doctor is ready to see us. "I haven't finished filling out our personal information."

"That's okay. Dr. Landry likes to go over that information with the patient and the family."

"Danny, it's time to see Dr. Landry." I tap his shoulder, but he shrugs my hand away. His eyes are locked on what he's drawing—trucks, over and over—the same theme we've seen all week, a big, mean-looking truck with little broken ones beneath its over-sized tires.

Another young woman in brightly colored scrubs kneels beside Danny. Her voice is soft, nearly a whisper. "Hi, Danny. I'm Marcia. Can I see your picture? You draw really well." She slips into a small chair next to him. "Is it okay if I sit with you while your mom and dad speak to Dr. Landry?" Danny ignores her.

She turns to us. "Dr. Landry would prefer talking to you both first—if Danny will stay here with me?"

"Are you sure? I thought she was going to evaluate him."

"Yes, she is, but she needs time with you to discuss what's been happening. She also needs a more detailed family history without Danny present. She'll explain it all to you, if you don't mind me staying here with Danny."

I'm torn, and I can tell Mitch is, too. We never know how he'll react to strangers, but right now he's engrossed in drawing. He probably won't miss us, so I slip my hand in Mitch's—Dr. Landry is waiting for us in the doorway of her office with an easy smile that calms my nerves just a bit. "Please come in." She motions for us to enter into her office. "I hope you didn't have any problems with the streets."

Her office, like her, is soothing. The seating area feels more like a living room. Simple, decorative lamps on end tables next to softly cushioned chairs light the room with a gentle glow. Floor-to-ceiling bookcases line the walls—the lower shelves contain children's books, papers, and art supplies. On one side, her desk sits unobtrusively. It feels as though I'm visiting a friend's home rather than a doctor's office. Glancing around appreciatively, I see a Norman Rockwell painting titled "Mysterious Malady" over her desk. Moving closer for a better look, I have to smile. A barefoot little boy, wearing a fedora, plaid shirt, suspenders, and Levis is concentrating on pouring medicine into a spoon while a sad-looking dog in a box, covered with a blanket, looks on.

She glances at the painting and smiles, too. With a sweep of her arm, she signals us to take a seat. We choose two overstuffed chairs that are close together. Mine is very comfortable, reminding me of my favorite chair at home.

"Mitchell, I'm glad to meet you. I met Lillian and Danny at the Child Development Center when I was asked to do a consultation. I was hoping we made some headway."

"We hoped so, too, until this last week—now he's worse than ever. I hope you can tell us what we need to do for him. We've got to do something before he's completely out of control and hurts someone or himself." He chokes back a sob as he winds down.

"I'm sure this must be frightening for you and Lillian. My goal today is to develop a game plan beneficial for all. First, I need a clearer picture of the whole family—not just you, Lillian, Danny, and Sarah, but a more complete family history from both of you. That's why I asked Marcia to distract Danny while we talk. She's trained to work with troubled children and will communicate with him verbally or through his drawings. She'll ask him to draw specific things, then see how he responds."

When she asked Mitch point blank about his family history, including siblings, and extended family, I was surprised when he shared with no hesitation. "What do you need to know? I have one younger brother—I'm five years older. I had a little sister, but she died in an accident when she was three or four. I was nine or so when it happened, so I don't remember much at all. My parents have been married for forty years or so. Mom's an only child. My father's two brothers are both deceased. There's really not much to tell about my family. My brother's been away from the family for years, and my parents live in Texas. We don't see them much. They were supposed to come for Christmas, but the weather ruined that."

I find myself reaching out to touch him. He doesn't want to talk about this—he guards the family secret fiercely. "Mitch, maybe we should tell Dr. Landry about your brother." I prod gently. Immediately, he tenses even more.

"I knew it, Lillian. There you go. We're not even in here two minutes, and already you're pointing the blame at my family. Just because he's in prison and a bit messed up doesn't mean Danny will end up the same way. We're better parents than my folks. We can figure this out, and Danny will be okay. Isn't that why we're here— so Dr. Landry can help him? Damn it, Lil. It isn't my fault he's like he is. It isn't." He stops, embarrassed by his outburst, and looks down at his hands. I realize he's blamed himself all along. I grab his hand and hold it tight.

"I know, Mitch. I know. It isn't your fault, but if telling Dr. Landry about our families will help her, we have to tell her everything—the bad with the good. We have to help her help Danny."

"That's easy for you, Lil. Your family isn't the one that's all messed up in the head—it's mine."

Dr. Landry gives us both a few minutes while Mitch regains his composure before she speaks again. "If we can talk about it, maybe we'll learn something that may help Danny. It isn't about blaming anyone. We're looking for the pieces of a puzzle to get a better picture. We can do that if you're open and honest about your family history. This will take time. We won't get to it all today, but let's at least begin. I'd like both of you to write out your family histories in greater detail and bring them to me the next time we meet. This outline will assist you. With this added information we'll develop a better course of treatment in the long run."

We agree. Then, with Dr. Landry's gentle encouragement, Mitchell opens up about his brother. He tells her about his angry outbursts, legal problems, and that he is serving a life sentence for murder and refuses to see any of his family.

"I appreciate your willingness to open up and share this painful information with me. I truly believe it will be helpful both for Danny and for you. You've opened a very heavy door. Please don't let it shut again. When you leave, please continue looking openly at your family dynamics as you write your family history for me. Will you do that?"

Mitch nods his head in agreement.

"Lillian, though I do know some of your history I expect you to be just as honest when you put together your family history. Genetics play a huge role in our physical and mental makeup."

She stands, indicating we're finished. "I think we've kept Danny waiting long enough. It's time for me to see him."

∞

Chapter 16

"No, no, no. Mama, mama, noooo." Those words reverberating from the waiting room tear at my heart. Something crashes to the floor. I'm paralyzed at first, and when I start for the door, Mitchell holds me back.

"I'll go." He scrambles toward the sound with me close behind. Dr. Landry is there before either of us. Danny has crawled into a corner—his arms full of papers. Dr. Landry approaches him, but he pulls away, gripping his drawings tightly. Marcia gently touches her cheek where evidence of a bruise begins to appear. Her hair is in disarray. Her blouse is torn, yet she speaks calmly to Danny while slowly working her way around him. As she draws closer, he becomes more and more agitated. The sounds he's making are deep and guttural, almost a growl, and the naked fear in his eyes is more than I can bear.

Mitchell and I both realize what Marcia's trying to do. He motions for her to stop. Danny is so focused on her and Dr. Landry that he's not even aware we're in the room. Mitch moves cautiously toward him, but Danny suddenly bolts for the outer door. In one step Mitchell is behind him. He wraps his arms around him, all the while murmuring reassurances. Danny struggles to break Mitchell's hold on him, but his arms are held tight. His hands flail and flutter, and he kicks with his feet. Mitchell pulls him close against his chest, slowly drops to the floor, and wraps his legs around Danny's to keep him from hurting anyone.

Torn papers, upset chairs, colored pencils, and crayons are strewn across the floor. Marcia's cheek is swelling and turning dark. She's obviously been struck by something to raise such a bruise. I'm appalled.

Danny's never hurt anyone before. And I'm shocked because he was doing so well with her when we left the room.

Although his screams are subsiding, he still struggles. Mitchell is more patient with Danny than I've ever seen him. This tells me he was listening when I explained how to deal with Danny's outbursts. He holds Danny, whispering calmly to him until Danny finally settles down. Mitchell loosens his hold, but his total focus is on Danny.

Dr. Landry and Marcia slowly move away from them, but Danny never takes his eyes off them. Dr. Landry gestures for me to join them on the other side of the room.

"What happened? Do you have any idea what set him off?"

"I'm afraid I did." Marcia replies. "Dr. Landry wanted to see his drawings, but when I started to gather them to bring them in with him, he became upset. He started throwing things, knocked over some chairs and then, when I tried to get behind him like Mr. Hawke, he threw his head back, catching me on the cheek before I could restrain him."

"I'm so sorry. He's never hurt anyone like that before." Tears slide down my cheek—impatiently, I wipe them away. I look toward Dr. Landry for answers. She's watching Danny begin to struggle once more. The strain on Mitch is obvious as he tries to calm Danny again.

"Mrs. Hawke, I'm afraid we're going to have to sedate him, then admit him for a complete workup. Are you okay with that?"

"I-I don't know. Isn't there something more we can try at home?"

"Lillian, please give me permission to sedate him—we'll talk about the next step when that's done. Mitchell can't continue restraining him this way."

Once I've given my consent, Dr. Landry leaves to get the shot while Marcia has me sign a permission slip so it can be administered. Danny's voice becomes shrill with a keening wail that sends cold chills up my spine. It's taking all of Mitch's strength to hold him. I didn't realize how much he'd grown until I watched their struggle.

"Mrs. Hawke, Lillian. We need to do this for Danny. This shot of Thorazine will calm him. I've asked Marcia to call for an ambulance to transfer him to the hospital. This is difficult, but it's for the best. Will you help us hold him while I give him the shot? I need you to remain calm. Can you do that?"

I nod, struggling to hold back tears, but I follow her lead. She means to come up on his blind side. Mitchell is talking to him, trying to distract him.

"Lillian, can you expose his hip for me? You and Mitchell will have to keep him still."

I must keep calm. I must keep calm. When I loosen his belt, he jerks his head toward me. His nostrils are flaring, and his eyes are wild. He doesn't even recognize me. He's acting like a cornered animal. I quickly undo his belt and pants, pulling them down enough to expose an area for the shot. While I lean into his shoulder and hold his leg to help Mitchell, she swiftly administers the shot. I back away, and a little wet spot appears on his shirt—I didn't realize I was crying. Mitch, too, can't keep his tears from falling. It seems like forever, but in a few minutes Danny's quiet. Mitch still holds him in his arms, gently now—as though afraid to let him go.

"Why don't you lay him there on the rug so you can get up, Mitchell. The ambulance will be here soon." Dr. Landry calmly encourages him. "That's good. Here, let me help you up."

When he stands, a shudder wracks his body. I gather him into my arms, and we cling together as our tears mingle.

Dr. Landy gives us a few minutes to comfort one another before she says, "I know this is so hard for you both, but we must discuss what will happen when the ambulance arrives."

Once again Dr. Landry's calming influence steadies us—this is not the time to fall apart. Danny needs us.

"Let's go back to my office. Marcia will let us know when the ambulance arrives."

We return to the same chairs we'd just left while Dr. Landry goes through Danny's drawings.

"He's really talented. How long has he been drawing?"

"He started when he was two or three—mostly trucks. He's obsessed with all kinds of vehicles, but mostly trucks. That's how we usually calm him down, by getting him to talk about trucks."

"I'd like to keep these to look at more closely. But for now, let's focus on what happens next. I'd like you to meet us at the hospital. Trained personnel will be with him on the ambulance should the medication begin wearing off. We don't know how he'll react. While he's in the hospital, he'll be under observation. We hope to create a safe environment where he can help us understand what he's going through. Our goal is to keep him just long enough to stabilize him and develop a regimen that includes appropriate medications to prevent these types of outbursts. Do you have any questions?"

"Can we stay with him?" Mitchell asks. "He's never been away from us overnight."

"No, I'm afraid you can't. Sarah needs you, too. He'll be in good hands, and you can visit him."

When Dr. Landry's phone chimes, she answers, "We'll be right out." Then to us, she says, "Before we go, you'll need to sign these papers giving permission to transport and admit him to the hospital."

We both sign, knowing it's best for Danny.

∞

Chapter 17

I don't remember the drive to the hospital. As soon as we get there, we rush to Admissions. "Our son, Danny Hawke, was just brought in by ambulance to be admitted. Can we see him?"

"If this is his first admission I'll need you to fill in some paperwork."

More paperwork—of course. The clerk hands me a clipboard with the standard forms—asking for family history. I look for a place to sit in the somber waiting room. We choose two uncomfortable chairs by a small window with a view of a little garden.

After glancing at the questions on the top form, Mitchell erupts, "For Christ's sake, Lil. How many times do we have to do this?" He strides to the receptionist, "Excuse me. We just came from Dr. Landry's office. She has all this information. Why do we have to do it again?"

Patiently, she explains they have no access to the doctor's records. These are for the hospital's records to allow them to give our son the best treatment possible. "Is there anything else I can help you with, Mr. Hawke?"

"You haven't really helped with anything," he mutters as he begins pacing.

I finish the questionnaire on autopilot—pregnancy, birth, weight, trauma, and so on. Again they ask for mental health history, and I jot a short summary. I'm sure they'll ask the same damn questions when we meet them.

I hand it to the receptionist. "Someone will be with you shortly." She returns to her typing, discouraging any further discourse.

Has it been minutes or hours? Mitchell finally drops in the chair next to me. While we wait, I feel nothing at all. A door opens nearby, drawing my attention, and my heart begins to race. I don't want to do this. I don't want to be the mom who sends her child away. Mitch squares his shoulders. With a visible shiver, he holds his hand out to me.

"Mr. and Mrs. Hawke? Please come with me. My name is Judith Monroe. I'm the intake worker. We need to go over a few things before you can see your son. He's getting settled in his room, and it's my understanding that's going smoothly."

With a death grip on Mitchell's hand, I stumble along, trying to keep up. He gently pulls his hand from mine so he can put his arm around my shoulders. He leans down to whisper in my ear, "If she asks one damn thing about our flippen' family history, I'm going to tell her we're all nutty as hell. Are they admitting one little boy or writing a book?" He hugs me tight and barely smiles.

Her voice drones on, and I respond appropriately as she repeats each question I've already answered in writing on the form. But the responses screaming in my head are very different from the monotone answers she hears from me. *Can't anybody read, for God's sake? Are you all so stupid? Why do I have to repeat and repeat and repeat it. Just read the damn paper and take me to my child.*

Mitchell is now answering the questions as these thoughts whirl in my head. I feel myself slowly shrinking away.

"Mrs. Hawke, Mrs. Hawke? Are you okay?"

"Goddamn it. Can't you get me some water? Lil. Lillian." Mitch's voice seems so far away. Did he just slap me? He never slaps me. "Lillian, honey, are you okay? Don't scare me like that."

"W-what happened? Why am I on the floor?"

"You passed out. Here, take a sip of water. Are you okay?"

I struggle to sit up, but his strong arms pick me up and set me in the chair. "Ms. Monroe, I don't mean to be rude, but can we hurry this along? We need to see what's going on with Danny. My wife has just about had it for one day. Our little girl at home must be wondering what the hell's happened to us. Frankly, I'm out of patience with all this bullshit. Now, either get me to where I can see my son or get me Dr. Landry."

She hesitates briefly, "I'll see what I can do, Mr. Hawke. We don't want to burden you more than you already are." She leaves quickly.

"Damn, I should have gotten pissed an hour ago. Are you sure you're all right, Lil? You scared the holy hell out of me when you slid off that chair. Don't ever do that again, okay?" He holds me tightly and doesn't let go until we hear someone approaching.

"I've been to the nurses' station, and they say we can go back now. You'll be able to see your son for a few minutes."

Danny is settled in a small room with just a bed with rails on both sides. He's sleeping, though not peacefully, so I don't even try to touch him. It breaks my heart to leave him there.

• • •

We're both exhausted when we get home. Sarah's full of questions. We try to explain why her brother won't be coming home for a while. Mitch calls his parents and goes over the same information with his mom that we shared with Sarah. I slip away for a long soak in the tub and let Mitch handle it.

A few days later we receive a letter from Mitch's mom.

Dear Mitchell and Lillian,

This is the hardest letter I've ever had to write. When you told us Danny had been admitted to a Psychiatric hospital I knew I had to do something. This is so hard because your dad won't like it, but it's time you knew more about your uncles and your brother.

I thought I hit the jackpot when I married Gordon. I pictured family dinners with his brothers—their families and ours doing things together, but that didn't happen. Samuel married and moved to New York. We rarely heard from them. He and Maureen divorced when Marsha and Tommy were small—he never remarried. He died at fifty-two and left everything he had to his closest friend. I realized then he was probably gay—but your father denies it.

Roy was a hell raiser. He could be all smiles and laughs, then turn like a thundercloud. Dad always said he had a split personality. The last time we heard from him, about a year or so before he was killed in that accident, he was living in Las Vegas. He called to tell us he'd quit drinking and was trying to change his life. Then he asked to borrow money again. Dad hung up on him.

Dad can be a bit moody at times, but he's not like either of his brothers. Neither of us talks about things that bother us, so we never even talked about the breakdown I had after we lost Millie—you were only 9 when that happened. I spent three months in a sanatorium—they said it was depression. I was never the same again. People didn't talk about mental health back then. When Christopher started having problems we just dealt with them the best we could. Dad whipped him more than once for lying. He blamed stuff on his invisible friends. But now, I wonder if he was really lying or if he heard them in his head. Maybe he did have a split personality.

Please don't be like Dad and me, thinking it will go away if you ignore it. Danny's not a bad boy. Get him all the help you can. Do it for him and for you.

We hope to come up this summer and spend some time. Give that precious Sarah a hug and a kiss for me. I see my Millie in her— sweet, good natured and funny. I love how she talks to me on the phone.

Enclosed is a letter for her and one for Danny, too.

I love you, Mitchell. I know I haven't said it much, but I do. And Lillian, I love you, too. You are a blessing to our family and a good mate for our boy.

Mom

Mitch finishes reading the letter and places it on the counter, gently smoothing it. To my surprise, he brushes his fingertips with a small kiss and touches it to the letter, a letter that expresses the most emotion I've seen or heard from his mom in all the time I've known her. For Mitch, it's just what he needed.

Chapter 18

When I awake in a tangle of bedding, arms and legs spooning with Mitch, he's holding me snugly against him—his breath warm on my ear. A smile plays on my lips as I recall our night of passion. I owe Mother Hawke a very inappropriate thank you card. Her letter and their call after was a Godsend for him and for me, too.

As I stretch, Mitch stirs, pulling me even tighter. I savor the feel of him against me, wondering if round three is about to begin. What a night. *What a night indeed.*

• • •

After seeing Danny and meeting briefly with Dr. Landry, I felt so numb—there had been little change. Dr. Landry's parting words rang in our ears as we headed home. "Why don't you take a few days off and not torture yourselves. Danny's in good hands. Have some fun, rest—just stay away this weekend. Danny's going to need you when he comes home. If you're completely exhausted, you won't be any good to him. Plus, Sarah needs you, too."

Fun? What? It's been so long, we've probably forgotten how. But we call the Thompsons and ask if Sarah can stay a bit longer. When Martha suggests she spend the night, we agree.

Mitch has a plan as we head out, just the two of us—he's turning down North Borah Street to our favorite little jazz club where he proposed to me. We haven't been there in a long time. At first it's as if nothing much has changed. Charlie greets us with a dazzling smile and welcomes us back, calling us by our first names. I shouldn't be surprised that he remembers us. He remembers everyone who steps into his place. It's still early, so we choose our favorite table in a cozy corner close to the dance floor.

Steve introduces himself as our waiter. "Our special tonight is prime rib with au jus, house salad, and choice of curly fries, potato planks, or onion rings." He offers us each a menu, "Or, you can make a selection from the menu. What can I get you to drink while you decide?"

"I'll have a Vod—no, I'll have a cup of coffee and a glass of ice water," Mitchell says.

"Same for me." When the waiter leaves, I tell Mitch, "You could have ordered the vodka if you wanted."

He reaches across the table and takes my hand in his. "I think it's best if I don't. That trap would be too easy to fall into again. If I don't keep my head clear, I could fall into the bottle and not come out. Some days that feels like the easy way out."

We sit in comfortable silence while our drinks are served. Mitch orders the prime rib for both of us—mine with curly fries, his with the planks. Steve repeats our order. Mitch nods and asks him, "Who's playing tonight?"

"A new band will be starting in fifteen minutes. Buddy Ray and the Boogie Boys are really good—and dancing's encouraged." He flashes a warm smile. Dim lights mask worn spots in the carpet in high-traffic areas, and some of the upholstered booths are beginning to look a bit shabby. Although our little club has not escaped the effects of time, the feeling of warmth and intimacy we always loved remains. It's good to see that has stood the test of time.

By the time our food comes, the place is filling and the band is tuning up, almost ready to begin their first set. The first bite of prime rib melts in my mouth. The food here has always been delicious. *Why don't we do this more often?* I can tell by the murmurs escaping from his lips that Mitch loves every bite as well.

The band starts with "When the Saints Come Marching In," their usual opening song—according to the bandleader, and it gets a lot of toes tapping. As we finish our meal the sweet sounds of "Georgia" fill the air.

"May I have this dance?" Mitch offers his hand with a slight bow.

"I would be delighted."

We sway slowly on the dance floor, lost in the music, enjoying the moment—no problems, only the two of us, the magic of music and movement.

After listening to a few more tunes and dancing a few more times, we make our way to the pickup for the drive home. Snuggled close against him, I trail my hand up his thigh higher and higher, enjoying the rush as lust flares deep inside. He pulls me closer and plants a quick kiss on my lips, eyes on the road. My hand is dangerously close to totally distracting him.

"Hey, lady. You sure make it hard for a guy to concentrate on driving, don't you?" I love his throaty chuckle.

When he pulls up to the house, he wraps me in an embrace that takes my breath away. Sweet memories of making out like this as teenagers almost make me giggle. The house is empty—no one to interrupt needing a drink, a story, or to ask just one more question. *How sweet this is!*

Mitch starts a fire and lights candles in our bedroom. With a sly smile, he tells me he's going to take a shower. I peel off my clothes and scamper to join him. We meet in a frenzy, like animals in heat. Our lust is almost frightening, burning white hot and spent in a short time. We are left panting, in a sweaty heap on the bathroom floor.

The second time around was so much sweeter, love making, not sex—taking it slow, enjoying the languid way hands trail across warm skin, murmuring sweet nothings, then falling asleep in the afterglow, the musky scent of sex surrounding us.

"Mama, Daddy!" The bedroom door explodes, and Sarah lands between us, clutching her dolls. "Wake up. WAKE UP!" She's so excited, she runs her words together. "The sun's shining, and it snowed more, and I want you to come play in the snow with me. Can we? Please, can we make a snowman?"

I snatch the blanket, pulling it up around us, trying to keep our naked bodies covered. Mitchell's trying to fend off this little person in snow clothes, who's attacking us with complete abandon. "Whoa there, tiger. Let Mama and Daddy get up first. Okay?"

Then it dawned on me. Why she was already dressed to play in the snow. "What are you doing here? Didn't you spend the night at the Thompsons?"

"I did, I did. But when I saw the snow I had to come get you. You said next time it snowed we'd make a snowman and it snowed again. Hurry up."

In our excitement last night we didn't lock the front door—hence the whirling dervish in our bed.

"Let us get up, and we'll be out in a few minutes. Go check on Leo, okay?"

"Okay, hurry up." The whirlwind we call our daughter is gone.

With one last embrace before we begin the day, I'm almost shy as I grin at him, remembering our wonderful night—and knowing he is, too.

She waits for us at the foot of the stairs, bundled in her snowsuit. With hat, scarf, and mittens firmly in place, all I can see are her bright eyes peering at me. She looks like the Michelin man, standing there with her dollies abandoned in their wagon.

When the doorbell rings, she runs to answer—it's her friend, Megan. She runs out to play with her, shouting as she leaves, "You promised me a snowman."

Chapter 19

"How about closing that door before you let out all the heat." Mitchell chuckles.

Lost in my thoughts, standing in the doorway watching Sarah with her friends, I'm thinking: *This is the way childhood should be.* Even as guilt tugs at me, I push it away. *Not today.* Today I'm going to play—I'm tired of reality, and for one day I'm just going to play.

"Bet I can build a bigger snowman." I challenge him.

"Ya think? I don't think you can. I take that bet and raise it with a snowball fight."

"You're on! Let me get dressed, and we'll see who's gonna win this bet." I race him up the stairs.

The neighborhood is alive with activity. All up and down the street families are out playing in the snow. I love our neighborhood. We've made good friends over the years, especially the Thompsons who bought Trudy's house when she moved to Denver to be with her daughter.

Martha waves. For a moment I hesitate, afraid she'll ask about Danny, and for today I don't want it to be about Danny. I want it to be about Sarah, and I want to feel young—if only for a few hours.

Cold snow smacks the side of my face, and there's Mitch beaming. The snowball fight begins—girls against the boys. Peals of laughter fill the air. Gobs of snow stick to everyone's coats and hats where they've been pelted with wet snow. We declare them all winners. Larger clumps of snow take shape as groups join together to build snowmen. Before long a family of snow people, a dad with cardboard hat, a mom with a scarf, and children of different sizes, emerge to stand guard along the sidewalk. Mitch joins a group of fathers and sons building a snow fort. When I see him step back, eyes on Mr. Andrew and his son working together, sadness threatens. But he steps back into the game, and I shake it off.

"Sorry I didn't catch Sarah this morning. Hope she didn't interrupt anything." Martha throws back her head laughing. "Did you and the big guy have a good night?"

I'm blushing like a schoolgirl. "We stopped for dinner at the Jazz club, danced a little, and went home to bed." I blush even deeper.

"Good for you. You have a bit of a glow this morning. Now I'm really sorry I let little Sarah crash your party." Once more she roars with laughter.

"Don't be silly, we're old married people. We don't have time for that foolishness." I can't help but join in the laughter.

• • •

The day flies by. Except for bathroom breaks, we spend most of it outside refilling coffee and hot chocolate mugs and heating a batch of chili that we eat from paper bowls with plastic spoons. The party breaks up mid-afternoon. We wrangle our happy, tired, little girl into the house with promises of more days like this to come. She's exhausted but not ready to stop.

"Wasn't this the best day ever? It's the best day I've ever had in my whole life." A twinge of sadness darkens her eyes for just a moment when she whispers, "If Danny were here and would play with us, it would be the perfect day." Then she brightens again. "Did you see my snowman? I gave him my scarf, Mama. And I gave him Daddy's old hat. Did you see them? Did you like them? Are you mad I gave my scarf away?"

"We saw, and he was wonderful. Now let's get you out of those wet clothes and into the bathtub to warm you up. You can put on your warm jammies, and you'll be all ready for bed when it's time."

She throws her arms around her daddy and gives him a big hug. "I love you, Daddy."

He chokes out, "Love you too, bug," before she races up the stairs with me following.

I pour in bubble bath and run a tub of water. She climbs in with a big sigh, and I start to leave.

"Mama? Can I tell you something?" her little face is serious. "Brenda says that Santa isn't real." Her eyes fill with tears.

I'm surprised this is on her mind at the end of such a glorious day. "What do you think? Didn't Santa just bring you Raggedy Ann and Andy?"

"I want Santa to be real—b-b but I saw you sewing my dollies, and I saw Daddy in the garage making my wagon. I didn't know it then, but on Christmas morning I remembered seeing the material in her dress and some of the parts for my wagon. So I think Brenda is right. I don't think there's a Santa. I think it's you and Daddy."

What do I say to her to keep the hope alive that comes with believing in Santa? "What do you think of when you think of Santa?"

"I dunno? Presents. Am I good? He makes us happy. I like it when we're happy. You and Daddy are happy except when you worry about Danny. I guess Santa isn't real, because I asked him to fix Danny. That's all I really wanted for Christmas—my brother to be happy and not get conpused anymore. So Santa can't be real."

"Oh, honey, I wish it were that simple. I wish all we had to do was ask Santa or God and Danny would be okay, but sometimes we don't get everything we want."

"Why, Mama?"

"I don't know, Sarah. Maybe we wouldn't appreciate it."

"What's pricate?"

Oh my lord, what have I gotten myself into? "It's when somebody does something for us, and we like it. You appreciated getting Ann and Andy for Christmas because it was something you like and wanted. It doesn't matter if Santa brought them or Mama made them, someone wanted you to be happy."

"Mama? If I don't believe in Santa, will we still have Christmas?"

"Yes, we'll have Christmas. Do you remember the story Daddy reads on Christmas Eve?"

"About the baby Jesus? The baby who was born with the sheep and the cows?"

"Yes, that's why we have Christmas, to celebrate His birthday. We give each other presents like the wise men gave presents to the baby Jesus on the night he was born."

She was quiet, deep in thought, "So if Santa isn't real, I could talk to Jesus, like I do at night in my prayers and not just at Christmas time, but all the time?"

"Yes, baby, you can."

She picks up some bubbles and blows them. "I don't think Santa's real. I think he's pretend, like when I have a tea party, and my dollies pretend to drink pretend tea and cookies. I love you, Mama, and I'm glad you're my Santa." She wraps her wet arms around my neck. I lift her from the bath and bundle her with a towel.

I'm dumbfounded. What a treat this little girl is. She never ceases to amaze me. If only all of life's problems were as easily solved as this. When Mitch comes to see what was taking so long, she tells him all about our discussion as she climbs into bed. Before she can finish, she's fast asleep between Raggedy Ann and Andy. Together, we pull a cover over her and tiptoe out, closing the door behind us.

It's the perfect end to a perfect day.

Chapter 20

Sunshine streams through the window, warm on my face, while I rinse the breakfast dishes. As the snow people outside begin drooping from the heat of the past two days, my heart is filled with the sounds of laughter from a really good weekend. Mitch is so much more relaxed since the letter from his mom. I'd heard about his uncles and Chris, but the death of Millie and the aftermath paints a new picture of my mother-in-law. I can't imagine surviving the loss of a child. She almost didn't. What helped Mitch the most was the reassurance of her love. We both know how difficult it is for her to talk about personal things and to demonstrate affection.

The weekend was good for us—for all those moments we could believe all was right in our world. Still I felt guilty on one hand, yet so happy on the other. Laughter had filled our home unchecked, not only by Sarah and her friends, but by Mitch and occasionally even me. Those are memories I hold dear. But now the weekend is over, and it's time to get back on life's treadmill.

"Sarah, you better hurry up. I see the school bus coming. You don't want to be late the first day back."

Sounding like a herd of horses, Sarah races down the stairway and across the floor.

"Mama, help me get my coat on. I can't get my coat on!" Frantically, she tries pushing her arm through a turned-in sleeve.

"Slow down, let me straighten this out. There you go."

She shoves her arm in, grabs her book bag, and dives towards the door. Halfway down the walk, she turns and races back. "Love you, Mama. Love Danny, too." She rushes back just as the school bus stops to pick up the group of children at the end of our driveway.

Love Danny, too. Those three little words jerk me back to reality. Our interlude of normalcy is over now. The time has come to return to reality.

• • •

It's been a month since Danny's meltdown and hospitalization. He was there almost three weeks before he showed any sign of improvement, but he was kept off all medications for the first two weeks to get a baseline of his behaviors in a safe environment. It broke my heart to see him thrashing, pacing, and speaking gibberish. Our visits just made him worse, so all we could do was watch him through the observation window. After an extensive workup, he was started on Haldol. Dr. Landry explained it wasn't a quick fix. She expected it to take a couple of weeks before we'd see any improvement—if it worked. Then, if it did help, periodic adjustments in the dosage would be required.

Last Friday when we saw him, we were able to go in his room. He became real quiet when we said anything, and he even looked at us once—but still didn't speak. At least the flailing and terrified sounds stopped. Some days I wonder if he'll ever be able to come home—if he'll ever be our Danny. I wonder if I can stand to lose him to this madness. I wonder what I did that was so bad to cause it—

I shake my head. *I can't do this!* Self-pity won't help Danny, and it certainly won't help me. I slam down the bowl I'm holding on the counter, and it shatters. All the hope I felt when I woke up shatters with it. *I don't want to do this anymore.* I don't want to meet with the doctor or be a grownup or make decisions or ask questions that have no answers. I want to grab my son and squeeze the illness out of him and *MAKE* him okay. I'm afraid if he doesn't get better, none of us will survive. *How do people do this? HOW?*

With a gentle touch on my shoulder, an arm draws me close, and I feel Mitch's choked cry against my hair. "Don't, Lil, don't. I can't tell you it's going to be okay. But don't let it take you, too. I can't do it alone. I need your strength." He holds me untill my sobs subside. I don't know what I'd do without him. Between the two of us we can shore up this crumbling foundation—not only to give Danny what he needs, but also to make as normal a home for Sarah as we can. Other people have. I know we can.

The shrill ring of the phone startles us. We both reach for it and knock it to the floor. We're like two Keystone cops trying to answer it.

"Hello?" I answer, laughing. "Sorry about that, we knocked the phone over in our hurry to answer it."

I hear Dr. Landry's laugh in return. "It's good to hear you laugh, Lillian. I hope that means you had a good weekend with Sarah."

"Yes, yes, we did. I'm glad we took your advice. But that's not why you called, is it?" My hand begins to shake holding the receiver. Mitch is as still as a statue, watching and trying to hear. I pull the phone away from my ear so he can hear what Dr. Landry's saying.

"You're right, Lillian. That isn't why I called. As we discussed, Danny's on Haldol. We considered the possibilities at that time. When we met on Friday you were both very discouraged, weren't you?"

"Yes, we were."

"We're beginning to see results, although there's still a ways to go. This morning when I saw Danny he was quieter and more attuned to his surroundings. He wants to see his mama and daddy."

"He wants to see us?" My voice squeaks with uncertainty.

"Yes, Lillian, he wants to see you." I can hear the smile in her voice.

"Mitchell, Danny wants to see us. Did you hear? He wants to see us!" I'm hitting him on the chest with my free hand, while tears stream down my face.

Mitchell engulfs me in a bear hug, crushing the phone against my ear, but I don't care. Our Danny's coming back—he wants to see us. Maybe, after all, God did hear my prayers.

"Oh, Dr. Landry, I'm sorry. In my excitement I forgot I was talking to you. Please forgive me."

"It's okay, Lillian. You're both entitled to be excited, but I must caution you, these are baby steps we're seeing. Can you come in at 11:30 to see Danny? If all goes well, you can have lunch with him, then we can meet at one. Will that work for the two of you? I know it's short notice."

I look at Mitch—he nods. "We'll be there."

"Good, see you at one. When you see Danny, let him come to you. Try to follow his lead." Before hanging up, she adds, "I feel confident this will be a better visit."

My heart leaps with joy. Danny's coming home soon. Mitch is quiet, looking out at the front yard, but a ragged breath escapes his lips as he turns to me.

"Lil, I don't know if I'm happy or sad? What kind of father am I? I love him. I do, but I don't know if I can go through all this again. I'm scared. I'm scared for us, for Sarah—but most of all for Danny."

I want to hang onto the excitement, but realize I, too, am afraid—afraid we won't know what to do or how to help him.

"Mitch, honey? I know what you mean. I'm scared, too. All we can do is love him and pray. Then listen to what the doctor has to say and do the best we can. Isn't that all we can do? Our best?"

∞

Chapter 21

Since the phone call, all I've been able to think of is Danny. The hours till we could get here crawled by so slowly. He's asked to see us. And we can't wait to see him.

Although we've been here many times over the past weeks, still I find the locked doors disconcerting. Once in reception we wait again until we can be buzzed through. Joanna assures us it'll only be a few minutes, but those minutes drag by as well. *Don't they realize how anxious we are?* Of course, they do—we're not their only concern. They have things to do besides rushing to take care of us. Finally, the lock releases with a 'shush,' and Joanna tells us to go on through.

When we stop at the nurses' station to sign in, I see a familiar face. "Hi, Ellen. Dr. Landry said we can see Danny and maybe have lunch with him." I'm talking too fast, so I take a deep breath and glance at Mitch. He looks as nervous as I feel. Somehow, that helps me calm down. I take his hand and squeeze it.

"Mr. and Mrs. Hawke, it's good to see you. Danny's had a good morning. He was up, showered, and dressed when the aide checked on him first thing this morning. He ate a good breakfast, too. Give me a sec, and I'll take you to him. His room's changed since you were last here." She finishes some paperwork, turns to another staff member to let her know where she's going, then takes us to him.

My heart's racing in eagerness. I picture him running to greet us with arms open wide. *Maybe our Danny will be back.*

Ellen taps lightly before opening the door. I notice this one doesn't have an observation window. "Danny, look who came to see you." She steps aside as we enter the room.

He's sitting on the edge of his bed, dressed in his new Christmas clothes, a white tee shirt and blue jeans—his favorite kind of clothes. His curly, blond hair is still damp and uncombed. He's looking straight ahead and doesn't move or acknowledge us. He looks so young it's hard to believe he'll be 13 in July.

My heart drops. "I thought they said he wanted to see us," I whisper through tight lips.

"He does—give him a few minutes. This has been a big morning for him. Have a seat and talk to him. He'll come around—give him some time. Let him come to you. Don't make any sudden movements towards him." She leaves us.

I've never felt so awkward. I'm his mom, and I don't know how to approach him. I perch on the corner of his bed. Mitch chooses a chair and sits down. "Hey, tiger, how ya doin'?" Mitch asks.

Danny doesn't respond. Looking around the room, I notice crayons and paper on the table, so I slowly move to one of the chairs there and sit down. Then I pick up a crayon and begin to draw. Mitch joins me at the table. We begin talking about home, Sarah, and the fun we had making snowmen and a snow fort this past weekend. Mitch talks about the crew truck. "Say Dan, I'm thinking about painting it. Should we—maybe purple?

"No, I like grey." He says quietly.

We both look at him. He's still not looking at us, but he did respond. Hope flares again.

"Guess that settles it. We'll give it a fresh coat of grey paint to spruce it up. Okay?"

"Okay."

Now my heart is racing. Everyone's quiet for a few minutes. Mitch and I continue drawing with the crayons. As I watch out of the corner of my eye, Danny slides off the bed and joins us at the table. He picks up a crayon and starts drawing a truck, but not an angry, destructive truck. He's drawing the crew truck. For a few moments, we all work silently on our drawings.

"I like to ride in the new truck."

It's all I can do to keep from reaching out and hugging him. I can't even talk.

"I like to ride in the new truck, too, Danny. It's a tough drivin' machine. I had to put it in four-wheel drive last week to get out of our driveway. You should have seen her break right through, didn't even spin a tire." Mitch continues to work on his drawing as he talks.

"Dan! Not Danny."

"Okay, tiger. Dan it is."

A soft touch tingles my little finger as Danny places his hand next to mine, fingers barely touching. He's done the same with his dad. Still as stone we sit, not talking, afraid to breathe.

"Mama? Where Sarah?"

Trying to keep my voice even, not to show how excited I'm feeling, I say, "Sarah had to go to school today. She said to tell you she loves you."

"Yep."

With a light tap on the door, one of the aides comes in. "Hi, my name's Arnold, I've been helping Danny today—"

"It Dan."

"Well, okay then, I've been helping Dan today. I came to check if you'd like to stay and have lunch with him?"

In unison, we reply, "Yes, if Dann—ah, Dan would like that." I look directly at him for the first time. "Dan, would you like us to have lunch with you?" His eyelids flicker, and for a brief moment he raises his eyes to mine.

"Yep."

"Then I guess it's settled. We're staying. What do we need to do?"

"Nothing. We'll bring your plates when we bring Dan's. He isn't too keen on going to the cafeteria yet—we'll be working on that. Today you have a choice of meatloaf with mashed potatoes and green beans or a grilled cheese sandwich with tomato soup."

"Want smashed taters." This rings loud and clear.

Mitch adds, "Guess it's settled then. Make that three meatloaf with smashed taters. We have a smashed-tater-eating champ right here."

Lunch goes well, with Dan scarfing down his mashed potatoes and part of mine. I keep reminding myself he no longer wants to be called Danny, and I'm concerned how he'll react when it's time for us to leave.

When I explain that we have to go, he lies down on his bed. "I tired. You go now."

Obviously, he's not upset. It seems we've been dismissed.

"Dan, would you mind if we give you a kiss before we go?"

"K," he says, and his eyelids flutter.

I fight the urge to take him in my arms and hold him and smother him with kisses. Instead, I lean down hesitantly and kiss his forehead. His hand brushes my cheek.

Mitch does the same. "Take care, tiger. Dad loves you."

"Yep."

As we turn to leave, he sits up.

"Dad?"

"Yes, Dan?"

"Take care my truck. Okay?"

"You betcha, tiger, I'll take care of your truck." Mitch's voice is thick with emotion as we both fight back tears. Our not-so-little-any-more boy lies back down and closes his eyes.

Baby steps. That's what we're taking—baby steps—steps we hope will bring our boy back home to us.

Chapter 22

"How did the visit go with Danny?" Dr. Landry asks when we meet in her office after our visit with Dan.

Both of us hesitate a minute. Mitch speaks first. "I think it went very well. One thing we learned is that he's growing up. He doesn't want to be called Danny anymore. And I'm no longer Daddy. With just a few words he made that very clear."

"Yes, he can be very concise with his words."

"Ellen suggested we let him come to us, so that's what we did. We just sat down at his table and started drawing pictures with his crayons. Lillian and I talked to each other about Sarah and stuff at home, but pretty soon he came and sat between us."

The memory of his tentative touch to both of us almost overwhelms me, "He touched us—just barely, but he reached out to both of us. I can't tell you how much that meant."

"That's wonderful, Lillian." Her smile tells me she understands.

"Oh," Mitch adds, "and he ate with us. No wonder he's grown so much."

"The best part for me was that he let us kiss him on the forehead."

"I'm so glad to hear that. I believe we've turned a corner. What do you think, Lillian?"

Trying to find the words to express what I'm feeling makes it difficult for me to speak. "I-I feel good about it, but it's so hard not to reach out and touch him, to let him know how much we love him." A lump forms in my throat. "Especially when he let us give him a kiss goodbye. I want a miracle, but I'm happy with how things went—even when he dismissed us." I manage a little laugh.

"He what?"

Mitchell explained how he told us he was tired and we could go. She bursts into laughter, and then becomes serious again.

"Lillian, I wish there was a magic cure, but you both know there isn't one. We are beginning to break the code in how best to treat him so he can have the best life for himself and for you."

"I know. I just want him to have a normal life again."

Dr. Landry leans forward and touches my hand. "Lillian, are you aware this is his normal? The agitation, the auditory and visual hallucinations are normal to him. He may not understand them or know how to control them, but he's familiar with them. We're trying to interfere with his normal so he can fit into our world."

"So where do we go from here? Do you know what causes it?" Mitch asks.

"We've been observing his behaviors. We've run him through a battery of tests. We've ruled out ADHD and oppositional/defiant disorder. With the hallucinations, we believe we're dealing with schizoaffective disorder with mania and possibly high functioning autism."

What? I don't want to hear this, so I interrupt her. "What? He's just a child. What the hell is that anyway?"

She hands us some literature. "This will explain it better than I can with the time we have."

The first lines jump out at me. I read the words out loud: "Schizophrenia is a mental disorder characterized mainly by hallucination, delusion, and disorganized speech while schizoaffective disorder has manifestations similar to schizophrenia, bipolar disorder, and autism." Now I'm speechless. I see the same shock on Mitch's face.

"B-But. How?"

"It's rare in children, but there have been other cases. There are treatments to help. I know it's frightening, but now we can develop a plan to help Dan—and you. The more you understand, the better you'll be able to help him and yourselves. We started him on a medication that appears to be working, as you saw this morning." I nod in agreement.

"We are putting together a team of helpers who will assist you in his transition home. Our goal while he's here is to get him out of his room, encourage him to become more social and attend the classes offered through the school. The teacher who comes here will be the same one teaching the class he'll be attending when he returns to school."

"School? You're going to make him go back to school?" My voice rises with what can only be hysteria.

"Yes, Lillian," she says gently and pats my hand again to calm me. "But this time an aide will be assisting him, not only with his lessons, but navigating the halls and cafeteria at the school. The aide will meet him every morning at your house and ride the bus with him. Arnold, whom you met today, will be his aide. He's someone Dan's already familiar with and likes."

"How long before all this happens?" Mitch asks.

"We're hoping on the weekend after next you'll be able to take him out on both afternoons. If all goes well, we'll then try for a whole weekend at home. Then, hopefully, the next step will be his release home. A liaison will be assigned to help you, answer any of your questions, and assist you in meeting Dan's needs."

So much information! My mind's racing. *Danny in school? Danny home?* "Are you sure it's a good idea to put him back in school? What if he gets picked on, what if kids laugh at him because he needs a helper? How do we protect him?"

"I understand your concern, but you and Mitch won't be able to protect him forever. We want him to live the best life he can. There will always be other people in his world, he'll be faced with meeting new ones, and he'll be in uncomfortable situations the rest of his life. With the medications keeping him on an even keel, we can work on the broader aspects of his life. I understand as parents you want to isolate him from the world and prevent any hurts that might be inflicted on him, but that would be doing him a disservice. He's physically growing up. He's going through puberty. Our job is to help him navigate the life he's been dealt. By working together, for his sake, we can help him. It won't be the life you expected for him when he was born, but at least it will be more than just existing."

I hear Mitch's ragged sigh. "I guess it gets down to trust. We have to trust the process, don't we? I say we do that, don't you, Lil?"

I nod in agreement. *I can do that! I think I can do that!*

Before we leave, we receive a copy of the treatment plan, sign and date the original and other papers. *So many papers.*

On the ride home we're both lost in our own thoughts, with so much to digest. I'm bombarded by such conflicting emotions. We have some answers—but God, what answers. I do want Danny home. I just don't know how we're going to make it all work. How will we take care of him and all of his needs and not neglect Sarah? I should be happy, instead I'm torn apart again. What kind of mother wouldn't be happy her boy is coming home. *Why do I feel such heaviness in my heart? Why am I so afraid?*

∞

Chapter 23

The crocuses next to the foundation are peeking through and bursting into colorful splendor. Here, on my hands and knees, cleaning out the flowerbeds as the world begins to awaken from winter, is my favorite place to be. I may be rushing it, but it's such a beautiful day. The flowerbeds have been neglected for too long—I want to get a head start while I have a chance. God only knows, time has been a premium over the past few years. At least now our life has settled into an uneasy routine, and I'm planning to take advantage of it.

For the last couple of years, our lives revolved around Dan, his appointments, his illness, and his support team. Everything else is scheduled around these things and what may or may not upset him. The transition from the hospital was a bit rocky, but with medication adjustments, behavior modifications, his aide Arnold, and tenacity, we've made it. Dan's in school—without Arnold accompanying him. Although he still struggles academically, at least he goes to school. He's been mainstreamed into the regular art class and, when left to his own vision, he excels. His view of the world is reflected in his artwork, and he branches out more all the time. Although he still loves his trucks, his paintings are more varied. The amazing thing is he can look at something once and reproduce it.

When he's not in school, he's going to the construction yard with Mitch—where Carl, one of our older employees, has taken him under his wing. Carl, the shop foreman in charge of vehicle maintenance, is a loner. Not one for long conversations either, they hit it off from the first. Carl saw Dan's fascination with the engine he was working on and asked if he'd like to help. Dan handed him the tools he needed as Carl explained what he was doing.

One day, he cleared a corner of the shop for Dan and gave him old engine parts to fiddle with. Dan loved it. He took them apart, cleaned them, and put them back together. Before long, Carl was bringing in small engines, like lawn mower engines, for him to repair. Dan knew exactly how to make them run. Dan would rather be at the shop or with his easel painting than at school.

Because we've been so intent on making the best of Dan's world, I fear we've sacrificed Sarah's world—and maybe even our own. Like Dr. Landry cautioned us, we've been walking on eggshells far too long, and it's time to quit making him the center of our universe. At the last appointment she reminded us again that he must learn to adjust.

We could start with small steps—like letting Sarah have her friends over once in a while—instead of her always going to their place.

The slamming of the door breaks my reverie, "Hey, Mom."

"Hey, Ladybug, want to help?" She picks up a trowel and joins me. We work in companionable silence for a while before I broach what I've been thinking about. "We have a birthday coming up, don't we? Any plans?"

"Mrs. Thompson said she would give me a party at her house. That's what I came to talk to you about. Would you mind?"

Of course, I mind. How sad is that—the neighbor lady throwing her a party when she should have one at home. "Tell you what." I say nonchalantly. "If it's not too big, how about we have it here? Maybe five or six of your closest friends?"

"But what about Dan?" She is such a sweet girl—her first thought is about her brother and how he might react. "Do you think he'll get upset?"

"Honestly I don't know, but we won't know if we don't try. Why don't we ask him?"

While we finish the flowerbed Sarah makes a plan to talk to him and Mitch this evening, and she is excited at the prospect.

I fix Dan's favorite meal and, while we're all sitting at the table, Sarah brings up the subject. "Hey Dan. I'm going to have a birthday next week."

"Yep. You will be twelve, almost teenie bopper."

"You know my friends—Mary, Betty, Gillian, Heather, and Francis? What would you think if I invited them for my Birthday party?"

"They silly girls. You like them. You should have Birthday party with them. I not come."

Obviously pleased, she flings her arms around her startled brother. He doesn't jerk away. Instead, he pats her awkwardly on the shoulder.

"Thank you, Dan. You're the best."

• • •

And so, it's happening—a houseful of giggling girls, a standing teddy bear cake made and decorated by our friend Martha, who's also helped to pull it off. And there are no explosions, just a 'normal' little family gathering. Dan eased part way downstairs at one point and watched for a few minutes. When everyone became very quiet, he shook his head as he turned to go back upstairs and said, "Silly girls," causing them all to giggle again.

As I step out of the shower, I'm humming—it has been such a good day. I pull on my old flannel nightgown, my grannie gown, as Mitch calls it. I'm going to do it. I'm going to tell Mitch the rest of my plans, since the day has gone so well.

After starting a fire, he brings hot chocolate he's made for us with whipped cream and a chocolate drizzle. He seems to be deep in thought.

Before sitting down, I kiss him on his forehead. "Penny for your thoughts."

"I'm not that cheap—my thoughts are worth more than a penny." He pauses, looking at me with that grin of his. "It's been a good day, hasn't it? I'll admit I was a bit hesitant when you broached the idea. She was one happy little girl, and it was so great to hear the laughter today. Dan handled it much better than I expected and, when she hugged him the other night, he didn't fight it. Maybe we're doing something right after all."

"Look at us, an almost 'normal' family. And while we're on a roll, I'd like to talk about something I really want to do."

"Oh, oh."

He ducks when I throw a pillow at him. "I'm serious. You know how much I love my part-time job as an aide at the Child Development Center?"

"Yes. Isn't that why you're taking classes at the college, to get a degree in child development?"

"When I started, that's what I thought. But truth be told, as much as I love my job, the clients, and the people I work with—I feel like I want more. I'm thinking of making a change."

"To what, a ballerina?"

"No, silly. The college is offering a course in Chemical Dependency Counseling. That's what I'd like to do—become a counselor."

"Wow! Where'd that come from? Isn't it dealing with even more troubled people?"

"In some ways, yes. At the center we have some clients with addiction in their family. Right now we have two little girls with alcohol syndrome because their moms were heavy drinkers during their pregnancies. I also work with a woman who's married to an alcoholic, and I see what it's doing to her and her family. It's tearing them apart."

"Honey, you know I support whatever you choose. I worry about you spreading yourself too thin—but if it's what you want. I say, go for it."

"Are you sure? If you are, I'll sign up for the fall classes. I'm not taking any this summer. I want to be home as much as possible."

When a slight sound catches my attention, I stop and listen. Mitch starts to say something, but I hold up my hand to stop him, ear cocked, listening. There it is again—the squeak of a floorboard.

Mitch leaps out of his chair. We rush into the hallway, in time to see a shadow cross from Sarah's room before Dan's door closes with a slight click.

Oh, no. Has this been too much for him after all? We bump shoulders trying to get through her door at the same time. Her nightlight shines a faint light. She's curled up with a smile on her lips, sleeping soundly. We know Dan's been in here, but why? We look around quietly so we don't wake her. On her little table, we see it. I cover my mouth to quiet the gasp. It's a picture of a wooden wagon, carrying a strawberry-blond-haired girl with a big grin, holding Raggedy Ann and Andy, with Blue Bunny sitting in front of her. A sandy, blond-haired boy is pulling the wagon, accompanied by a shaggy dog—Leo, our Leo who's been gone for over three years. A note lies beside it. In a childish scrawl, he's written, "happy birthday, sissy."

Mitch pulls me into his arms, and we hold each other, our tears merging together. *What is this feeling?* HOPE, I'm feeling hope.

Chapter 24

"Mrs. Hawke, Mrs. Hawke?" I jerk awake, befuddled, wondering who's calling my name. When I realize just who it is, I could crawl into a hole—and pull it in after me.

"Yes?" I answer.

"It's nice of you to join us. Did you have a nice nap? Maybe you aren't ready to be a student." I'm definitely awake now, but he continues his tirade. "You might want to rethink your choices. If you can't stay awake, you can't learn, and how do you think you'll ever pass my class?"

What an ass! Maybe if you weren't so damn boring, I could stay awake. And if I could get some rest, maybe I wouldn't be so tired. What the hell was I thinking? I thought I could work, take care of our home and family, and take classes three times a week. Now I'm not so sure.

"I'm sorry, Mr. Pierson. I do want to be here." I drink from my bottle of water and wipe my eyes as he returns to his lecture. What he's teaching is important for me to learn, but his monotone voice drones in my ear. Classification of drugs, family of drugs, their effect on the body, blah, blah, blah. This is the most boring lecture I've heard. I casually glance at the other students and see I'm not the only one struggling to stay awake. Although that makes me feel a little better, I'm no less humiliated for being singled out. Still struggling to stay awake, I doodle on a scrap of paper. His lecture is almost verbatim to the handout he's given us, or I'd take notes.

I'm so relieved this evening class is over, and I'm anxious to get home. By the time I turn down our street the skies are dark with rain clouds, and lightning dances across the sky, followed by the crash of thunder. As I step out of the car, another large bolt startles me, and a thundering roar almost deafens me. I scurry into the house as the sky opens and sheets of rain pour from the sky.

"Mitch? I'm home."

"In here."

I follow the sound of his voice to the TV room. Sarah sits huddled in his lap, eyes wide, watching the windows as lightning continues its light show. Each strike seems brighter, lighting the whole room as she clings to her daddy.

"Where's Danny?"

"Still in his room. This little munchkin must have taken the stairs in two leaps after the first lightning strike. I haven't had a chance to check on him. You take Sarah, and I'll make sure he's okay." All of us jump as another blaze of brilliant lightning flashes, lighting up the room for a second or two before thunder rumbles like a freight train. "Whew, that was really close."

"I'll go. Why don't you and Sarah light some candles and find a flashlight, just in case."

The house is lit up like daylight as I hurry toward the stairs. With a flash of light and a loud pop, all goes black, and our power is out. Glancing out the window, all I see is the neighborhood in darkness. Knowing I have to get to Danny, I feel my way up the stairs. There's a flashlight in our room, so I feel my way along as my eyes become accustomed to the darkness. I find the flashlight as another flash of lighting lights the skies. I listen for Danny, but all I hear is thunder rattling the rafters.

"Dan? Danny?" I call as I hurry toward his room. Throwing open the door, I shine the flashlight around. No Dan. Trying not to panic, I look under the bed, in the closets, even in the toy box. No Dan. *Where can he be?* I check the playroom, and that's when I see the trucks on the floor, all facing the window. I don't have time to wonder why. I only know I can't find Danny, even after another quick look at all the upstairs rooms, calling out his name over and over. No answer. No Danny.

"Mitchell! Mitchell! I can't find Danny!" I yell as I rush down the stairs. Mitch is at the foot of the stairs with his arm around Sarah's shoulders holding her tight. I take a deep breath to calm down so I don't scare Sarah anymore than she already is. She has a death grip around his waist, and with each flash of lightning she shudders. Our girl, who's never seemed afraid of anything, is beside herself.

With flashlights, we search the house, all the nooks and crannies, the garage, even the pickup and the car, but still no Danny.

"He doesn't seem to be anywhere." I hear the edge of panic in Mitch's voice. "Sarah? Did you see Danny when you came downstairs?"

"No Daddy, I was scared and I ran downstairs. I'm sorry, Daddy." A sob swallows the last word.

"It's okay, baby, it's okay. " He holds her tight, and we look helplessly at each other.

What do we do? Where can he be? "I'll check the backyard. If he's not there—" I shrug helplessly—then spin on my heel toward the French doors leading to the back deck.

"Lil, you take Sarah, let me go—" I'm already out the door.

I look in and under everything on the deck, shouting his name, trying to make my voice heard over the pounding rain. I rush headlong into the yard despite the continuing lightning flashes, immediately followed by the crash of thunder. *Where can he be? Is he afraid? Soaking wet?* The wind and rain pull at me as I rush to the garden shed and pull out everything to make sure he's not there. I look frantically under the rose bushes, while brambles tear at me. When lightning lights up the sky again, I see something out of the corner of my eye before the skies go dark again. I head in that direction, trying to make sense of what I thought I saw. The skies are alight again, and I can't believe my eyes.

"DANNY! What are you doing?" I sprint over to him. He's sitting on his old pedal tractor, soaking wet, naked, with arms outstretched to the heavens as rain pours down on him. I want to hug him and scold him at the same time. I call him again, but he doesn't answer. He seems transfixed, staring heavenward. I reach out to pull him off the tractor. He won't budge. When I take a firmer grip, he slaps my hand away, continuing to sit with outstretched arms as if in worship, a smile on his lips, as rain beats down on us.

I look toward the house to get Mitch's attention, but he's nowhere to be seen. I can't get Danny to go with me. I try once more to pull him off, but he's too strong and jerks his arm away. Hoping he'll stay on the tractor, I rush to the house to get his dad, dash across the deck, jerk the door open, and step inside. When my wet shoes hit the hardwood floor, my feet fly out from under me, and I go sliding across the floor, crashing into the corner of the island. Pain sears through my shoulder.

"Lillian, Lillian!"

Why is he yelling? I need to tell him something, but what? Danny! "Mitch, Danny's in the backyard on his old tractor. I couldn't get him to move. You've got to help him. Call an ambulance. We need help." I try to move, to point—but my arm doesn't move. A searing pain hits, and all goes black.

∞

Chapter 25

"Danny! Danny!" I yell as awareness returns. Throbbing pain in my shoulder jolts me fully awake when I try sitting up.

"Shhh, Lil. It's okay. Danny's fine, but you need to stay still. You've broken your shoulder. They had to operate, and you still need to rest." Mitch presses the call button for the nurse.

The nurse comes in quickly with a needle. "Here you go. This should take the edge off." I feel the needle prick in my hip—I'm grateful for the relief I know is coming. Within minutes I feel as though I'm wrapped in a warm cocoon.

"What happened? I remember lightning and the thunder. Danny was out in the rain and cold—" I begin to thrash around. "Danny, we've got to get Danny."

"Lil, it's okay. Dan's okay. Sarah got him out of the rain. The medics checked him over and he's doing fine."

I want to ask more questions but find myself drifting off. *Suddenly the wind and rain are pelting me. I can see Danny, but the harder I try to reach to him, the farther he seems to be from me. When the wind lifts him, he tumbles about as I try to catch him. Instead of fear, he has a look of glee on his face and waves as the wind takes him away. The skies darken, and I can't see him. I've lost him. I've lost Danny!! I fall to the ground sobbing, NO!!! Danny, NO! Come back.*

"Lil, wake up. You're having a nightmare." Mitch's voice is muffled as if he's far away. I struggle to reach him. Slowly, as though the fog has cleared, I awake, my cheeks wet with tears.

"Oh, my God, Mitch! I was dreaming the winds had taken him away, and he was smiling. He seemed happy to be tumbling about in the storm. I remember now. He was sitting on that little tractor, mesmerized by the storm—almost worshiping it. Tell me again that he's okay."

"He's okay, Lil. But he's back in the psych ward. He was suffering from hypothermia by the time we got him off that tractor. Physically, he recovered quickly. The problem is he hasn't uttered a word since. He's unresponsive and shut down." A sob escapes from deep within him. I reach with my good arm to sooth him.

"What's the doctor telling you?"

"The standard BS. He's under observation, trying different meds, no straight answers. They won't or can't say if he'll ever come back to us. I didn't know whether to stay with him or be here with you. They say he doesn't seem to know if I'm there or not, so I've been trying to check on him and be here for when you woke up. Plus, call Sarah at the Thompsons to make sure she's doing okay. I've been so worried. It's been three days now. You've been in and out. You were in shock and hypothermic, besides your broken shoulder."

We're both in tears. I try to wrap my arm around him, but the bulk of the cast and the pain keep me from doing it. All I can do is pat his head.

"Mitch, I think I'm back among the living. I need you to go home, get some sleep, then go pick up our girl and hug her tight. She had to be, and probably still is, so scared without any of us there for her. I know she was terrified by the storm. I can only imagine how frightened she was to see Danny like that. I remember how she took care of me when I was on the floor in so much pain, how she let go of you, in spite of how scared she was, to be there for me. Yet you tell me it was Sarah who managed to get Danny off the tractor?"

"Yes, it was. When the paramedics got there, one helped you while the other one went out in the yard with me to get Danny off the tractor. Lil, he fought us like a wild man. Sarah must have seen it. She came out, walked up to the tractor, held out her hand, and said, 'Danny, come with me.' Lil, he took her hand and crawled off the tractor as the paramedic wrapped a blanket around him. He held her hand until they gave him a shot and loaded him onto the ambulance. By that time

Martha was there, and she took Sarah home with her."

"Bless that girl. Please, Mitch, go take care of our baby. She needs you now more than anybody. She needs to know her world hasn't all been torn apart. And if the doctors will let you, bring her to see me tomorrow. But, Mitch, I don't want to see you again until tomorrow afternoon."

"Are you sure?"

"I'm positive. Now go." As he stands to leave, he seems to have aged years. His face is lined, shoulders are slumped, and a look of defeat seems to engulf him. "It's all going to be okay, Mitch. We'll make it through this. We're a tough bunch." I try to smile to reassure him.

"I know, Lil. It's just—sometimes I wonder. Do you need anything before I leave?" He leans down and tenderly brushes my lips with a kiss.

"Would you ask the nurse to come in on your way out?"

"Why? What's the matter? Maybe I should stay."

"No, Mitchell, you don't need to stay. I only want to ask her some questions about my shoulder. And if you must know, I need to use the bathroom. And maybe get something for pain. Now go! Shew, give a girl a little privacy." I wave my hand at him as he slowly leaves the room.

The tears begin as soon as he's out of sight. I talk a good story, but I, too, wonder how much more we can take. What does the future hold? How will we care for Dan if he stays shut away in a world of his own? Did I cause this by going back to school, changing the status quo, by not being there as much as I should have been?

And as a mom, there's always the question—*could I have done more?*

Chapter 26

When a sound awakens me, I see Mitch slumped in a chair by my bed—I didn't hear him come in. His eyes are closed, so at first I think he's sleeping—until a tear slips down his cheek, his shoulders begin shaking, and he covers his face. He's unaware that I'm awake, watching him—the pain in my heart is almost palpable for the man I love. If only I could reach out to comfort him, but as I move the physical pain in my shoulder reminds me why I'm here.

"Oh, Mitch." The words slip out before I realize I've said them out loud. He drops his hands, wipes his eyes, and looks at me with a wan smile.

"Hi, babe. Sorry, you caught me at a bad time." He stands, stretches, and turns toward the window. He's trying to put on a brave face to spare me.

"Has something happened to Dan?" Fear prickles my skin.

"No. Dan's fine. In fact, he's responding to the medications and drawing already. I checked on him before I came here this evening."

"How's Sarah? She's not with you?"

"She's doing okay. I asked her if she wanted to come. Honey, I'm sorry. She said she'd rather wait until you come home. On a good note—it sounds like we can take you home tomorrow. I told her that."

"I can't wait to go home. But how am I going to function? Of all the times to be left-handed—with a broken left shoulder. I'll be helpless using a knife and fork, writing, even brushing my hair will take some practice. At least Sarah's been helping me in the kitchen and, if Dan were home, under some circumstances he could help, but—" I *can't let myself go there.* "Is that what's got you down?"

His eyes are brimming with unshed tears. "No, we'll manage. I talked to Regina, and she's on her way—should be here in the morning for a couple of weeks."

"My sister's coming?" I interrupt him.

"Yes, your sister's coming. I called her about your accident, and she graciously said she would come help out. And, Lil, we need the help, so I said we'd appreciate it." His voice is strained. I can tell he's at his wit's end. As conflicted as I am about her visit, I hold my thoughts. Maybe it'll be good for the two of us to spend some time together. We haven't seen each other since Mom died. Cheyenne isn't that far, but for some reason neither of us makes the effort. A phone call every few months and a letter once in a while are about it.

"Lil, there's something more I need to tell you. On the night of the storm Carl died."

"Why would you say something like that, Mitch." I try to push it away. "It can't be true, can it?"

"That's what I thought, too, when I got the call from his neighbor. During the storm, lightning hit that big cottonwood in his yard, and one of the branches broke through his front windows. Apparently, when he'd tried moving it out of the way, he had a heart attack. His neighbor found him. There wasn't anything he could do. He called the ambulance, but Carl was already dead. They said it was quick, and he didn't suffer. I can't believe he's gone. He's been with me since I started my business. He was much more than an employee—I was closer to him than I am to my own dad. He was like a kind grandpa to Danny. I don't know what I'll do. It's as though my foundation's been ripped away. Besides you, he was the only person I could talk to about what's going on. He was a good listener—never said much, but when he did I knew it was true and important."

After a struggle getting out of bed, I go to him—I still have one arm to hold him. "I'm so sorry, Mitch. Sometimes life is so unfair. It kicks you when you're already down. He was a special man—we've been lucky to have him in our lives."

We hold each other, not wanting to let go. There's nothing else I can do to comfort him. To think, with everything he's been through, now he has to deal with the loss of his good friend, his father figure. Carl was a comfort to Mitch and a good friend to Dan. *Oh, my God. What are we—how are we going to tell Dan?*

"Mitch? How do we tell Danny? How will he react?" I begin to panic at that prospect.

"I don't know, Lil," Mitch says as he runs his hand through his hair. "Right now I don't know much of anything. I'm on autopilot. Putting one foot in front of the other." His shoulders shudder as he pulls in a deep breath. My heart aches watching him. "We need to get you back to bed. I want you coming home tomorrow."

"It's what I want, too, but I need to see Danny first. I need to see that he's safe."

"I know. That's why I talked to the doctor and made arrangements for us to see him once you're discharged. She feels he's improving. He's back to drawing and painting—that's a good sign. I've stopped by, but he doesn't respond to me. It breaks my heart. According to Dr. Landry he's compliant and does the tasks they ask of him, but he hasn't said a word since he was brought in. They've been worried about pneumonia because of the hypothermia, but no sign of even a cold. We can be grateful for that. Sometimes it's hard to see the light when his dark voices take him from us."

"I agree, but it's important that we keep looking. We have to keep fighting against his darkness to bring him back to us. I worry how he's going to take the news about Carl. Did he have any children? Do you know if any arrangements have been made?"

"I don't know if any arrangements have been made, but I don't think there are any relatives—at least none that he's spoken of to me. His wife died a few years ago, but he did have a son who passed away at about Dan's age in a skiing accident. His son had a learning disability—that's what drew him to Dan. Carl was the one who suggested I bring Dan to the shop when he learned about his love of trucks. His attorney called this morning requesting I come in and see him on Wednesday."

"What does he want with you?"

"That's what I asked, but he said he'd rather not discuss it over the phone, so we'll have to wait. Now, my girl, I need to get home to Sarah, and you need some rest. Tomorrow's going to be a big day. She can't wait for her mama to get home." He leans down and brushes my lips with a kiss. "I love you, Lil. I don't think I tell you that enough."

With my good arm wrapped around his waist, I don't want to let him go. "I love you, too, Mitch. We get caught up with so much going on, we forget to say it enough. One thing I've never doubted is our love for each other. Give Sarah a hug and my love. I can't wait to see my precious girl."

"We lucked out there, didn't we? Now unhand me—I've got another girl waiting at home for me to fix her my special dinner of hot dogs with pork n beans. We're even going to break out the good paper china."

Hearing him laugh feels so good. As I unwrap my arm from his waist, I say, "Give her a big hug from me—and don't burn the water." As he turns to walk away I slap his backside playfully.

"Don't be cheeky with me, woman, when you're not in any condition to follow through." He winks suggestively and saunters out the door.

God, how I love that man!

Chapter 27

It's amazing what we take for granted—like getting dressed. I'm going home, but I can't figure out how to put my clothes on with one shoulder, my chest, and my left arm covered by a lovely Spica cast with a bar immobilizing my arm out like a wounded wing. The nurse walks in as I'm helplessly staring at my clothes.

"Doctor's signed your release papers so let's spring you from this joint." She's smiles, trying to cheer me up. "Would you like some help dressing?"

"My question is how? Do you have a bag I can wear for a top?" I hold up the tee shirt Mitch brought for me to wear home. "Somehow I don't think this is going to work."

"That does appear to be a slight problem, now doesn't it? Let's get you in these slacks, then we'll figure out something for the top."

I can hear the laugh in her voice, but none of this is funny at the moment. "Since the important parts are all covered, I could go topless." The sarcasm rings hollow even to my ears. *She's only doing her job.*

"Yep, you could do that and start a new fad. I understand your son's quite the artist. We could have him paint a blouse on your cast when I take you up to see him, but it would be an off-the-shoulder blouse. I can see all the young girls coming in for shoulder Spica casts." She giggles. "Let's see what I can do with this old hospital gown." Sliding it over my good arm, she snaps it to close the shoulders and the sides. Before I know it, with some draping, a bit of tying and ingenuity, I'm covered. I survey her work in the mirror and admit it's not too bad— except for the faded color, which makes my pale complexion even paler.

With my left elbow out and my left hand raised in a queen's wave stance, I see some humor in the situation. "Does this make me look fat?" When that too-often-asked question falls from my mouth, laughter bubbles. "We can start a new clothing line with a wounded wing as our trademark." One more look, and I lose it. Laughter erupts into a full-blown belly laugh—a laugh I can't control. The poor nurse is drawn in until tears are running down our cheeks. It feels so good. It's been too long since I laughed like this.

"What's this, having a party without me?"

"Oh, h-hi, Mitch. Do you like my ragbag blouse? We're going to start a new business. What do you think?" His stunned expression elicits more laughter. I wipe away the tears. "Regina and I'll have to go through my closet to see what I've got that's ready for the rag box and make me some new blouses. Or, as the nurse suggested, I can have Dan paint one on the cast. And I won't need a blouse." The mention of Dan brings me back to earth. I begin to pack the overnight bag Mitch brought in.

"Hazel, thank you for your kindness and this lovely blouse. I was feeling sorry for myself this morning, and you definitely brightened my day."

"That's okay, Mrs. Hawke. It's what they pay me the big bucks for. Don't worry. You'll be a two-armed woman again before you know it. In the meantime, you've got one heck of an excuse to get out of chores you don't like. Let others wait on you for a while. Now, have a seat in your chariot here." She motions to a wheelchair.

"But I can walk. I still have two good legs. We're not going to the car—we're going to see Danny first."

"I know, and I'm your trusty tour guide. Now have a seat so we can see that talented boy of yours."

The pensive look on Mitch's face on the elevator ride to the sixth floor reminds me he's struggling with the same questions I am. The biggest is how do we tell him about Carl. How will we make him understand that his good friend will no longer be there when he goes to the shop? I choke back a sob, remembering how he looked the last time I saw him. I'm afraid of what I'll see today and how he'll handle my new look.

Mitch approaches the nurses' station. "We're here to see Dan Hawke."

"Yes, Mr. Hawke. Dan's in the activity room where he spends most of his time. Nelda Pitsch is his aide today. Let me call her." She calls for her over the intercom. "Nelda's been his aide since he was admitted."

The first thing I notice about Nelda is that her smile lights up the room. People who work with troubled individuals have the most open and caring personalities and a positive outlook on life. "Nice cast." she says drolly.

I find myself relaxing and begin asking her about Dan, his mood, progress, and if he's said anything. I feel Mitch's hand on my shoulder as if to reassure me.

"He's making progress, but has a way to go before he'll be ready to go home. He spends most of his days drawing or painting. In the beginning they were dark and angry but this morning I notice more detail and more color. He's slowed down and is working on a very nice painting. He's really quite talented."

We enter a large, open room with a seating area much like a home living room—with couches, a couple of easy chairs, and a television. Bookcases line the walls with books and games filling the shelves. A few people mill around, some looking out the windows, two appear to be reading, and one young girl with vacant eyes is rocking back and forth clutching a doll. A young man with a loping gait hurries towards us, his voice booming as he calls, "Hi, Ms. Pitsch!"

"Inside voice, Joe, inside voice." Cautions Ms. Pitsch.

"Oh, sorry. Inside voice," he says a little quieter. "Who are you? I'm Joe. Do you know my mom? Would you tell her to come see me? I want to see my mom."

I don't know what to say or do as I look at this young man with his ebullient greeting and such sad eyes.

Ms. Pitsch gently takes Joe's arm. "Joe, these nice people have come to see their son. You need to let them do that. Remember what we talked about this morning, about interrupting?"

"I'm sorry, I keep hoping—" His voice trails off.

"I know you do, Joe, I know. How about you helping me?"

Like an eager puppy wanting to please, he answers. "YES. I mean, yes, I would like to help. Can I? Do you want me to help the broken lady?" He reaches toward the wheelchair.

"No, Joe, not that. Hazel is doing that. I need you to pick up the Lincoln logs where someone dumped them. Could you do that, pick them up and put them where they belong or maybe build me something with them? Could you do that for me?"

"Yes, I can do that. I will build you a cabin then put all the rest away." He turns, eager to do what she's asked. "Sorry, broken lady, I can't help you. I have my own job to do now." He hurries off with his unsteady gait. I can't help but wonder what his story is.

"He seems eager," Mitch says.

"Yes, he is. He'll do anything for anyone who's nice to him." She points toward the far corner of the room. "There's Dan."

He's sitting with his back to the corner, by a large plant that almost hides him from view. He's tucked himself between it and the window near a small table covered with art supplies. Seated behind an easel, he's concentrating on his work.

"Look who's here, Dan."

His eyelids flutter, but his eyes remain on his work. We both say hi, but he keeps on working. "Is it alright if I look at your pictures, Dan?" His head barely moves in a nod. I look through the sketches in his sketchpad and see trucks, but not angry ones. These have lots of jagged lines and angry looking clouds. "Is this the lightning?" Again, a slight nod. This is going better than I feared.

"Hey," Mitch starts, then hesitates. "Mom's going home today."

"Home?" I can't believe it. He's talking to Mitch.

"Yeah, Dan, home, to see Sarah. Sarah misses you, Dan. So do Mom and I."

"Sarah?" He raises his head to glance first at his dad, then me. His eyes get big when he sees my cast. Tentatively, he reaches toward it. In a hushed voice he says, "You have a wing? Like an angel? Carl have wings, too."

We're both dumbstruck. Why would he think that? How would he know? "Dan, why did you say Carl has wings?"

There's no answer. He's turned back to work on his painting. Mitch moves closer to look at his work. I hear an intake of breath as his eyes widen. His face pales, and tears fill his eyes. He looks from the picture to me, then to Dan. "Can we show Mama your picture?" Dan nods slightly. Mitch turns it towards me.

In an old pickup, angled toward the heavens, is a figure in the driver's seat wearing a smile of joy, his hand raised as if waving goodbye. Wings jut from his back. Lightning bolts slash the skies, dark clouds graduate to light, and in the distance are two figures in the light—his gamma, and a shaggy dog, Leo. The man in the truck is the spitting image of Carl. With a gasp, I realize we don't have to tell him Carl's gone. *He already knows.*

Chapter 28

Home, my haven, is where I find my strength. Walking through the house, I find myself by the French doors in the kitchen, looking out into the back yard. Flashes, like a disjointed movie, ripple through my mind, nudging memories of the fear I felt as I struggled to get Dan in the house. My heart clutches, and I drag in a long breath, reminding myself that he's safe, and I'm home where I belong. I sense Mitch's presence behind me. When I turn, he's watching me from across the room.

"We're gonna be okay, Lil."

As I cross the room toward him, the memory of that night returns like a slap—I'm crumpled in a heap at the end of the island. I reach out to touch it with my one good hand. "You know, it doesn't look so dangerous in the light of day. Does it?" The lightness I try to interject into my voice as I look at the corner where I broke my shoulder comes out in a whisper instead. "I'm glad it's no worse for the wear."

Mitch approaches and tries to hug me. Although his intention is great, the question is how to accomplish it. Reaching towards him with my good arm ends with me knocking him with the arm in the cast. He retreats with a hand raised. "Hey, watch the weapon." A smile plays on his lips. "Let's say for now that I'm giving you a big hug? Can you feel it?"

We burst out laughing. God, it feels good to laugh together. Laughter is the best medicine, and I need good medicine. Healing laughter lends to healing minds.

Sarah comes barreling through the door like a Tasmanian devil and throws herself at me. Thank God Mitch is close enough to scoop her up before she can hit me, and we both end up in a pile on the floor.

"Whoa, slow down, Nellie. Pull those reins in before you knock your mama for a loop."

She notices the cast for the first time. "Oh, Mama!" Her eyes fill with tears. "Does it hurt?"

"It's not too bad, baby." I brace myself against the counter. "Come on, Sarah. Give Mama a hug. I've missed you, lady bug."

Slowly, she moves towards me, but stops short of touching me. "Mama, I don't want to hurt you." She sniffles and tries to stop crying.

I reach for her. "Oh, baby. You aren't going to hurt me. Come on, give me a big hug." When she wraps her arms around me, all my fear drains away. I'm home with my family. We'll meet the world head on.

"How about we fix some lunch, then Mama can rest. What do you think?" Before she can answer I hear a familar voice.

"What if you let me fix lunch while you and Sarah take care of my little sis?"

Regina? In the excitement of coming home, I'd forgotten about her being here. I'm not sure I'm up to this. We've never been really close—at least not since we were children, before Daddy died.

It's hard for me to let someone else help me, especially in my own home. Regina and I are almost strangers, even though we're sisters. Barely seventeen when she left home, she only came home sporadically, with a few phone calls here and there, and a rare letter once in a blue moon. I have no idea what she's up to these days, but from the look of her, she must be up to something. She looks so much like Mom that it throws me. Looking like Mom isn't the biggest shock. What throws me for a loop is that she's going to become a mom herself. Evidently there must be a boyfriend somewhere. My hand is shaking when I reach for her.

"Regina, I didn't see you come in." When she clasps my hand, I realize she's as nervous as me.

"I wanted Sarah to see you before I interrupted. I'm really sorry to hear what happened." She pulls me into a gentle hug.

"I can't tell you how happy I am you've come." I'm surprised, but the words are true. I am glad she's here.

The rest of the day goes by in a fog. Finally I'm tucked into bed, to rest, to sleep, and hopefully not to dream. Then it's a repeat for a few more days—they go by in a haze. At least yesterday I got through without the aid of pain pills. Hopefully I'll be more aware and involved now.

When I wake up and try getting out of bed by myself, I feel like a beached whale. *Forget about that, not today at least.* I lie there listening to Sarah and Reggie chatting easily. A twinge of jealousy nips at me. Sarah's taken to her Aunt Reggie as though she's always been a part of her life, but I'm still having trouble adjusting to her willingness to be here. Over the years it seemed she didn't really care. Yet, it's soothing to me to have another adult helping while Mitch is at work. I'm basically helpless, at least until this Spica cast comes off. I'm hoping soon she and I will find time to really talk. There has just been so much going on since I came home from the hospital.

Mitch met with Carl's attorney the next day about the contents of Carl's will. What a shock to learn that Carl left his house and savings to us. The savings will be held in trust for Dan and Sarah's education. We'll have to decide what to do with the house—to rent, sell or—?? His insurance policy paid for his cremation, covered his outstanding bills, and divided what was left between The Senior Center and the Alcohol Rehab Center. We had no idea that he was a recovering alcoholic with thirteen years of sobriety. He didn't want a service, but many of his friends are asking to hold a celebration of his life at his favorite fishing spot, down the path from his home on Clear Creek. They're making all the arrangements. Hopefully, I'll be out of this cast by then.

With a soft knock on the door, Reggie calls out, "Lillian, are you awake?"

"Yes, come on in." She shoulders her way through the door carrying a tray. Once more I'm taken aback by her appearance—the resemblance to Mom still shocks me. At 5' 8", she's four inches taller than me, her hair is auburn like Mom's, and she has the same deep blue eyes as Mom. With my curly, light red hair and light blue eyes, I take more after dad—just like my Sarah. The rounded belly on my single sister still surprises me. Who would have thought that at almost 36 she'd be having her first baby? We've not talked about it, other than her acknowledgment when she saw me staring that first day, "Yep, it's a baby." That's all she said. Maybe now that I'm more clear-headed, we can finally get down to talking seriously. I'd like to know my big sis better. Once we were very close, and I'd like that again.

She puts the tray down, helps me out of bed, and over to the chairs. I look longingly at the fireplace, but it's too warm to build a fire. "Where's Sarah? I heard you two talking when I first woke up, but the house seems awfully quiet. Is she over at the Thompsons again?"

"No, she's in Dan's room, lying on his bed. She really misses him. It makes her feel close to him. I hope you don't mind—I was looking at some of his artwork. He's really talented. He may not talk much, but his pictures speak volumes. The one he gave Sarah for her birthday is amazing, so full of life, and the muted colors make it so dramatic. Have you ever thought of trying to sell any of them?"

"Do you really think he's that good? Of course we think he is, but we're his parents. They're our only insight into his world much of the time. I don't know if we can do anything with them—he knows if one is even slightly moved. Once in a while he gives one away. He gave a couple to our friend Carl." My heart clenches at the thought of that sweet man. Once more I wonder how Dan will react now that Carl's gone. Will he still want to go to the shop without him there? And what about Regina? How will he react to her being here?

"Lil, I think he's a natural. His eye for detail is astounding. I'd love to feature him in my new venture. Recently I opened a small gallery, and we're doing really well. I hope you and Mitch will at least broach the subject with him once he's home again."

"An art Gallery? I thought you worked for a group of lawyers? And yes, I'll talk to Mitch about it."

"I was, but that's a story for another time. Let's get you cleaned up. I bet you can't wait to get spruced up, and I'm the one to help you do just that."

It's not an easy task, but when it's over, I feel like a new woman. My hair is as clean as the rest of me that's not covered in cast—a cast that has survived without much damage. I want to hug her. "Reggie, you've made me feel human again. I don't know how to thank you." I wrap my good arm around her and hold her tight. "I'm so glad you came." I can barely talk around the lump in my throat.

"Me, too, Lil. Me, too." She squeezes me around the waist. "Now lets see what we can do with that hair before Mitch comes home. And I think I hear a Ladybug stirring. What do you think?"

Sarah is sneaking up on us, but her giggle gives her away. "Hey there, lady bug. Did you come to help Mama and your Aunt Reggie?"

"I did, Mama. I want you to have these." She hands me a colorful bundle of scarves. Reggie takes them, slips an opening over my arm and drapes the rest around me, knotting them together over the cast.

"Do you like it? I helped pick out the scarves. You look pretty, Mama." I hug her tight.

"Mama. Your cast is hurting me." She pushes back a little, but stays in the crook of my arm, watching Reggie fluff up my hair, letting my natural curl do what it will. Her sweet smile melts my heart.

Chapter 29

Being outside with the sun warming my face feels good—to relax and not have to do anything or be anywhere. *It's been too long.* Despite feeling helpless because of this broken shoulder, I will admit there are some benefits, too. I've learned to ask for help and then let it go. It's a relief to let someone else be in charge of everything. The best is having my big sister here. We've cheated ourselves by letting so much time go by, and I can't even remember what caused our divide. *Did something happen or did we choose different paths?*

Our backyard shows how much we've neglected it in the last couple of years. Once my haven, now the roses are overgrown, Danny's old pedal tractor sits abandoned, and his roads are filling in with weeds. But today I'm not worrying about it. Today I'm going to spend time with my sister, getting to know her again.

"Mind if I join you?" Reggie asks. "Sarah's off to the Thompsons for the day. What do you say to sitting back and being ladies of leisure?"

"I'd love that. I was hoping you'd join me. You've never said, and I was wondering, do you still like living in Cheyenne?" We start with small talk. She reveals why she likes living there—it's a city, but a small city. Although not far from the university at Laramie, the trip through Elk Mountain pass takes longer in the winter. Her new venture sounds like it's doing well. She has no regrets about leaving the lawyers, but doesn't divulge anything really personal. In turn, I share a superficial picture of our life without revealing anything about Dan's heartbreaking illness. Time slips away as we become comfortable with each other.

She's the first to broach the subject of Dan. "Lillian, would you like me to take you to see Dan tomorrow? I know you miss him, and I'm sure he'd like to see you, too. I think we can wrangle you in and out of my car. Besides, I'd like to see him—if that would be okay? He was a little boy when Mom died, and the trip here was such a whirlwind that I barely remember it."

The longing in her voice surprises me. She's never seemed to need family ties—her life always seemed so full. I hesitate to answer.

"Lil?"

"Sorry, I was thinking about your offer. I'd love to see Dan, but we should take Sarah, too. She'd like to see him, even though I hate that she has to see him there." I pause and take a breath. "I'm not sure how he'll react to you, that's why I hesitated. I don't want you hurt if he won't acknowledge you. He does that. Sometimes he won't even respond to us, but let's give it a try. The unit he's in is a good place to be if he gets upset. I'd really like to see him. Just remember, if he turns away from you—it's nothing personal. Sarah has a calming influence on him when he gets upset. She was the one who got him out of the storm the night this happened." With my hand I indicate the cast.

"I hadn't thought about that. I know I don't understand Dan's illness. If it will cause problems, I can wait outside for you."

"No, I think it's good. He could be discharged soon, and it would be good for him to see you before he comes home. I should have thought of it before. Thanks, Reggie. I don't know what we'd have done without you. I hope you're not overdoing."

I reach for her hand as she answers. "No, I'm actually feeling fine. It's good for me to be busy and active." A trace of sadness softens her voice.

"Would you like to talk about it? I don't want to pry, but I have so many questions. You've not mentioned the father or how you feel about this pregnancy."

She pulls her hand from mine, and I fear I'm overstepping an undefined boundary. She runs one hand across her forehead and stares into space. *Damn, just when we're getting close, I have to ruin it.* I'm about to tell her 'never mind' when she speaks.

"Lil, I've made a complete ass of myself and have only myself to blame. I'm afraid if I tell you, you'll not want me here around you and your family." She breathes deeply before she continues. "For over the past five or six years I had an affair with one of the attorneys at work. It's the same sad story. He fed me a line of bull that I swallowed hook, line, and sinker—his wife didn't love him, they'd drifted apart, stayed together for the children's sake, and me, the fool—I believed him for years. Six months ago I came to my senses and broke it off, quit my job, and moved to a new apartment. The only thing I didn't do was change my phone number. It took him a couple of months to track me down. I found out he doesn't like for people to leave him—he had to be the one to call it off. After a nasty argument when he showed up on my doorstep, it was finally done. I reacted badly, went out, got drunk, and made a fool of myself by picking up a guy in the bar. After a couple of wild days I pulled myself together and went home to sober up. The result of those two drunken days is pretty obvious now. I thought about abortion for a minute, but then I thought about you and your family—about how much you love your kids, Lil. I guess, at this time in my life, I really want a child. So I chose to keep the baby, and I'll raise it as a single mom. I just hope you don't hate me."

I have to admit I'm shocked. My 'all together' sister walking on the wild side doesn't match the picture I've constructed in my mind. Taking her hand, I squeeze it gently. "Oh, Reggie, I don't hate you. I'd be lying if I said I wasn't shocked or surprised, but hate you? No, I could never hate you for being human. I want you to be happy, healthy, and to have a healthy baby."

"That concerns me, too—a healthy baby. I'm a high risk. Because of my age, the chances are high for a Down syndrome baby. Maybe that's why I want to get to know Danny better and see how you deal with his problems. I know he's not a Down baby, but I know he's challenged."

"Challenged and challenging at times." I say with a chuckle. "But he's our Dan, and we love him. I know you'll be a good mom, no matter what. Have you let the father know?"

A flush reddens her cheeks. "No," she says sheepishly. "We spent the weekend in a motel room, and I never asked his name nor gave him mine or my phone number. I think he was a pharmaceutical salesman, probably passing through—but that's all I know. Besides, I don't want a complete stranger feeling obligated to either step up or reject this baby. It's mine." She puts her hands protectively over her baby bump.

"While we're getting personal, Lil, do you mind if I ask why you're taking addiction studies? I'm really proud of you going back to school with all you've got on your plate, but why addictions?"

The question surprises me. I give her essentially the same reasons I'd given Mitch. She watches me closely as I explain about my work at the Child Development Center, the families I've met whose lives had been touched by addiction. When I finish, she looks at me strangely for a minute, biting her lower lip.

"I thought it might have something to do with Dad and with me?"

I'm shocked. "Why would it have anything to do with you and Daddy? Neither of you had a problem. How can you even infer that, especially about Daddy?" My voice rises as what had been a nice day implodes around me. A sob catches in my throat. "Daddy was a good man. He loved us and took care of us. He was not an alcoholic. Why would you say that? How dare you, Regina. How dare you! And a wild weekend doesn't make you one either." As soon as the words escape, I want to say 'take them back, take them back' like I did when I was little and heard something I didn't like.

As I struggle to make sense of what I'm feeling, she studies me. She takes my hand in hers and gently massages it.

"Lil, do you remember how Dad died?"

"Yes, he was in a car wreck on his way home from work. I was eight. I remember hearing Mom scream, and it woke me up."

"Oh, Lil, yes. It was a car wreck. He was on the wrong side of the road and hit a truck head on. He was drunk, Lil. He was drunk—as he was most nights. He got off work at five, and the accident happened around one thirty in the morning. Honey, don't you remember how he and Mom fought, especially that last year? You'd hide in your room with your dolls. It wasn't always bad, though. You used to follow him when he was home. He'd carry you on his shoulders and dance around."

I'm too stunned to respond or process what she's saying, but a snippet of the truth in what she's saying resonates uncomfortably in my memories. I want to stop it, but I can't.

"You know that scar you have on your forehead, at the hairline? That happened when he ran you into the doorframe because he forgot to duck. After that he wouldn't let you ride on his shoulders any more. I know he loved us, but, Lil, he did have a drinking problem. Don't you remember why I left home when I was seventeen? I'd started drinking and partying. I almost dropped out of school. If it hadn't been for Mom's determination, I would have. As soon as I graduated she couldn't tell me what to do anymore, and I took off with a couple of my friends. The next two years are a haze of drugs and booze. I ended up in Cheyenne, alone. If I hadn't stumbled into a church and met a female pastor who helped me, I don't know where I'd be today. I hadn't been drinking or using drugs until the weekend I got pregnant. That weekend almost took me down the rabbit hole again. It took all I had to go to a meeting and tell them I'd thrown those years away over a married man—one I'd kept a secret from all my friends for years. We're only as sick as our secrets, and that secret was almost my undoing. Dad had a lot of good qualities, and I'm glad you have those good memories. I'm a good person, too. But I'm also an addict like our dad."

It can't be true, not my daddy. Yet, even as I'm denying it, I can see with clearer eyes and even smell the stale beer on his breath. *Is that why I don't like the smell of beer?* Is that why I became so upset when Mitch began drinking more—why I became so frightened? I look at my sister and feel the anger building. I struggle to get out of the chair. *God help me.* I want to run away. How dare she—how dare she say such things about my dad. I lurch toward the door and rush up the stairs to get away from her, from her words and lies.

Pausing at the top of the stairs, I look down at her standing there, tears streaming down her face. I'm torn. Part of me wants to run to her, but I steel myself against her pain. I can only think about what she's done to me. She's taken my childhood, my perfect childhood until Daddy died, and she's torn it apart. *I don't think I'll ever forgive her.* I need her out of my sight. Rushing to my room, the one place I feel at peace, I slam the door. *I WILL NOT believe her lies. I WILL NOT!*

∞

Chapter 30

I'm running down a hallway, a black cloud chasing me. My hands are over my ears to shut out the noise—so loud it vibrates our whole house. I have to hide—don't let them catch me. Quiet, I have to be quiet. I'll be okay. I'm safe in my room here on the floor between my bed and the wall with my dolls and Teddy bears. Oh, No! The door is opening. Holding dolly close to my chest, I whisper, Shh, dolly, we have to be quiet. I hum to her—

"Lillian. Lil, are you here? It's going to be okay. It's just Mom and Dad fighting again. You're okay. I'm here now. I came to take care of you, sweetie. Let me snuggle in with you." Slowly, she slides down beside me, wrapping me in her arms. "Shh, sweet sister. It'll be okay."

Why's Daddy yelling at her again? Why is he so mad? She made a nice dinner and even kept it warm. Reggie, make them stop fighting. It scares me when they fight. I want my fun daddy back. I wrap my arms around her neck as tears stream down my face.

A kaleidoscope of images flashes through my mind—people laughing, me playing in the yard, a shadow standing over me, jerking me out from between the sheets hanging on the line, Mama crying, and Regina standing between Daddy and Mama. A picnic at the beach, a happy family playing in the sand—there's only three? Where's Daddy? Then I'm riding on his shoulders. "You're going to drop her or fall with her. Please let me have her." Why doesn't Mama want me and Daddy playing our game? Why does she have to ruin it? Oh-Oh! Daddy's stumbling. I'm falling headlong to the floor, but Mama catches me. She's yelling at Daddy. He laughs, then scoops me away from her. I didn't know I could fly. So many contrasting images keep flashing—I'm looking for something, but I can't find it. I'm scared again, and the darkness is moving over me—

A hand touches my shoulder. I feel breath on my cheek, and I jerk away. "No! No!" I cry.

"Lil, wake up, honey. You're having a bad dream. Come on. It's okay." Mitch brushes the hair back from my face. "It's okay. Come on, wake up." His soothing voice pulls me from my nightmares.

"Mitch, what are you doing home?" It's not like him to come home in the middle of the day.

"Honey, it's eight. I was late because the crew and I cut up that tree branch and fixed the window at Carl's cottage. When I got home, Regina and Sarah were watching TV. Regina looked like she'd been crying. She said you were up here and that you were upset. She said it might be best if she left—she doesn't think you want her here anymore." His voice is thick with frustration. "For God's sake, Lillian, what's going on? I don't think I can take much more right now. We need her help. Can't you two get along for at least another week, until you're out of this cast and into a smaller one? She won't tell me anything, she said it was up to you."

The strain he's under shows in his face, and I feel guilty, but I'm also pissed. It's not his world that's been torn apart. He's always known his relationship with his dad was crappy. He's mentioned more than once how he envied what I had with my dad. Now I have to tell him it's all a lie? Damn Regina, why couldn't she keep her mouth shut. I open mine, but nothing comes out.

"Come on, Lil. Tell me. What did you and Regina fight about that's so bad she thinks you hate her?"

"S-she said our dad was a drunk, Mitch. S-she asked me if that's why I decided to be an addictions counselor. Why would she say something like that? Whyyy?" The last word escapes with a whine that shocks even me. I sound like a whiny child—not a capable adult. But right now I don't feel like an adult. Mitch cradles me as best he can and lets me cry.

There's a light tap on the door and when it slowly opens, Regina stands there, with tear-filled eyes, clutching a worn leather-bound book to her chest. "Can I come in?" Before I can tell her no, Mitch motions her in.

"Lil, I know you're mad and confused, but I didn't mean to hurt you. I thought you must remember some of what happened by now. I was sure that's why you wanted to be a counselor. I've been waiting for the right time to talk to you about it. That's what Mom wanted. She thought a time would come when it all came back to you—and we could be close again. I've hated keeping quiet about it all these years. I've always wanted a better relationship with you. If I'm truly honest, I'll have to admit that I've been mad that you're able to block out all the bad so that all your memories of our dad are good ones. I have some good memories, too, but they are few and far between those last couple of years before he died. Lil, I loved Daddy just as much as you. My heart broke just like yours when he died. I felt guilty because I was sad and I missed him, but I was also relieved that the yelling, screaming, breaking of furniture, and fear was gone. Mostly, I feel guilty because I screamed at him that night that I wished he was dead." She chokes back a sob. "Then he went out—h-he went out, and he d-d-died." She slides to the floor sobbing.

The agonizing wail of those last words and the pain that racks her body with tremors cuts through me. I need to help her somehow, but as I stumble to her, there's Sarah standing in the doorway gaping at her Aunt Reggie.

"Mitch?" I nod toward Sarah. He sees her and gently takes her out of the room, closing the door quietly behind them—and then I remember.

A loud crash jerks me awake. I'm afraid to move. Then I hear another crash. It's dark. I hate the dark. Bad things happen when it's dark. I turn on my light, gather my dollies and bears, then slide down by my bed and begin humming their favorite song. Now Reggie's here, telling me it's going to be okay. I keep humming, louder and louder. Then a scream pierces my ears. Mama screams again. I hum louder as the voices get louder and louder. A door slams. Reggie's holding me tight, telling me it's going to be alright. We both hear the scraping of furniture and Mama crying.

"I need to go help Mama, Lil. Will you be okay?" I nod, but I don't want to let her go. "It's okay, he's gone. He won't be back for a while." When

she leaves me to go help Mama, I crawl out of my hiding spot and quietly follow her. Mama is picking up chairs and setting them upright, but some are broken. Her favorite picture is lying on the floor with the frame broken. Everything seems to be turned upside down. I must have made a noise, because Mama stops and looks up at me, eyes wide, with a big, red bruise blossoming on her face. Her hands are shaking, and I see the big bandage on her upper arm as she reaches for me.

I have to go to Regina, but this damn cast is in my way. "Reggie? Reggie?" She looks like a broken doll sitting there. *Oh, God. What have I done?* She protected me from this all these years. Now when she thinks I've remembered and talks about it—I turn my back on her. "Regina," I say louder. "Please, Reggie, you're right. I do remember some of it now. Please get up. I can't come to help you. Please!" I plead.

The pain in her eyes when she finally raises her head breaks my heart. I struggle out of the chair and go to her, reaching down to comfort her as she lays her head against my leg. "Lil, I never meant to hurt you. I thought you'd remembered. I really did. I thought we could talk about it and maybe help each other. I'm so sorry. I'll pack my things and leave as soon as Mitch can make some arrangements for someone to come help."

"Oh, God, no, Reggie. You can't leave me now. I need you, and I think you need me, too. Please don't go, Reggie. Please." I'm on the floor with her, my good arm wrapped tightly around her. I won't let her go—not when I've finally found her again. I've found my big sister, the one who protected and cared for me, the one who let me have my 'reality' for years—who's kept the secrets for so long—the one I've missed all these years. "Please, Reggie, we need each other."

Chapter 31

Reggie and I talk into the night. She still has Mom's old, worn, leather-bound diary, and we read parts of it. The early years are happy ones, then things begin to change when dad's ankle is crushed in the oil fields—he can no longer do his job as a roughneck, a job he loves. Working as a mechanic for half the pay at a local garage is a blow to his ego. Mama writes about the building anger, the drinking, living with a stranger, and feeling like she's walking on eggshells. Her greatest fear is that he might hurt one of us when he's drunk. In her writing, she reveals the pain she's feeling, the hope she has when he tries to quit and they attempt to recapture the joy they once shared.

When she looks for a job so she can help, it makes him even angrier, although he admits they need the extra money. The realization that she worked so hard to protect us from the pain they were both experiencing hit me hard. She even talks about leaving him, but the thought of it breaks her heart. She loves him—at least the man he was before the injury and the drinking began—the man who was so thrilled at the birth of his girls. They had such hope for the future of their growing family. How my heart aches to learn she'd lost a baby three years after I was born. Then a year later she had an ectopic pregnancy that nearly took her, too. Because of the surgery they had to do, she was unable to have any more children.

"God, Reggie. How could I not remember any of this?"

"Lil, you were only eight when Daddy died. I didn't know most of it until Mom sent me this journal before she died. She always planned on getting us together to work through some of what happened. When the cancer spread so fast, she couldn't add more burden to what you already had in taking care of her."

"But Reggie, what about you? It wasn't fair to you. You had to deal with this when she was dying. How could she do that to you?"

"It was okay, Lil. A few years before she got so sick I talked to her about some of what I did remember. If you really think about it, we both tried to broach the subject with you, but you wouldn't listen to anything bad about dad—just like you didn't want to hear what I'd done. Every time we brought it up, you changed the subject."

"God, I'm so stupid. How could I be so blind? You must have hated me at times."

"Envy maybe, but never hate. I envied your ability to see our child-hood through rose-colored glasses, and I've envied your innocence. What I would have given for that innocence. I'm sorry I spoiled it all." A lone tear traces a path down her cheek.

"But I'm not a little girl anymore. I need to deal with this. Hell, if I can't deal with this, how can I deal with Dan? Every day I look real-ity in the face when I see our beautiful boy so cut off from the world. If that doesn't make me a grown up, nothing ever will. I must confess I've been hard on Mitch in my heart at times—blaming his side of the family for Danny's problems and being smug about our perfect little family. I feel like such a fool."

We sit quietly, both of us drained. Reggie breaks the silence. "Lil, do you think we could get off this damn floor? My legs are cramping, and I don't know how the heck we're going to get you standing. I might have to call Mitch to help me. We've got a lot more to talk about, but I'm here for at least another week or so, aren't I?"

In spite of myself, I laugh. I'm cramping, too, and I have no idea how long we've been sitting on the floor. Just then Mitch calls to us from right outside the door, "Do you mind if I come in?"

"Please do, Mitch. I need help getting your wife off the floor," she says, struggling to her feet, rubbing her legs. "Damn legs have gone to sleep." She shakes one and then the other as she reaches her hand out for me.

Mitch looks quizzically from me to Reggie. "Are you two okay? I didn't want to interrupt, but you've been up here for nearly three hours. I fed Sarah and put her to bed. I told her you'd be in to kiss her good night, and how in the hell did you get on the floor, Lillian?"

I giggle, "I have no idea, but would you please help me up? I'm a bit unbalanced." When he starts to say something, I swat at him. "And no, I don't mean in the head."

"I wasn't going there. It's good to see you can laugh, both of you. It looks like everything is okay now."

Between Mitch, Reggie, and the wall, we manage to get me up and standing.

Reggie and I look at each other. I reach for her hand. "I think everything is great now. What do you think big sister?"

"I think we're going to be better than ever. I feel like a weight's been lifted off my shoulders. God, I'm hungry. Do we have anything to eat?" Reggie hurries out the door on her way to raid the fridge.

Mitch watches me as I smooth my hair. "Lil, are you sure you're okay?"

"I'm good. I'll tell you all about it later, but right now I agree with Reggie. I'm hungry as a horse. Let's go, big boy. Take me to your kitchen." I grab his hand and kiss him as I drag him toward the door.

That night I slept better than I had in a long time. We decided to wait another day before going to go see Dan. We're both drained after our late night, but the emotional hangover is the worst. Sarah's happy to spend the day with us puttering around in the backyard. Regina pulls weeds, and I figure out a way to use the long pruning shears to prune the roses back. Sarah hauls branches and bags of trash in her wagon, chattering away. The yard work is cathartic, and by late afternoon we stand back, pleased with the work we've done. It wasn't planned which made it even better. We worked like a band in harmony, no sour notes, only smooth rhythm flowing throughout the day.

"Mama, I'm hungry."

Nothing like a hungry child to bring me back to reality. I check my watch and see it's after four. Mitch should be home before long. "Is that right, little missy? Do you think you've earned dinner?" I stand, hand on hip trying to look sternly at her, but a smile betrays my words.

"Yes, I do and so does Aunt Reggie. Don't we, Auntie?" Sarah tries to mock my stance and expression—with that I lose it laughing.

"Well, little one, we won't be eating in my kitchen with these dirty hands and clothes. What do you say to getting cleaned up and getting a pizza delivered from Me n Ed's Pizza? How does that sound?"

Reggie and Sarah shout in unison. "Pizza, pizza, we want pizza."

"That settles it, chicken it is."

"MAMA!" Sarah tries to stamp her foot, but loses her balance and falls into the sandbox. Regina flops down beside her, and we're all laughing. It feels so good, so freeing. I'm lucky to have these two with me right now. Live in the moment is what Mom used to tell me, but until right now I never really understood what she meant. For now, I'll savor this moment, before trying to tackle the next one.

Chapter 32

Sarah's excited that she's going with us to see Dan. She's a bundle of energy rushing to get us going. I hope she won't be disappointed. I hope he acknowledges her, and I hope he won't shut down when he sees Reggie. Dr. Landry says he'll be discharged soon if he continues making progress.

I'm so tired, I'm having trouble focusing, and at times I'm still having difficulty dealing with all I've learned over the last few days. After spending more time reading Mom's diary, I'm amazed I was able to shut it all out, giving me a new respect for Mom. She managed to pull back from her fears and build a good life for Regina and me. *If only I have half as much courage as her.*

Mitch and I talk into the early morning, and he is as shocked as me that my 'perfect' family is not really so perfect. In a way he's relieved, and he doesn't feel so guilty about his gene pool being responsible for Dan's illness. Although he said it jokingly, there is a grain of truth in it.

When I hear Sarah's footsteps running down the hall, I open the bedroom door and see her ducking into Dan's room. I follow to see what she's up to. "Hey girl, what are you doing in your brother's room? You know if you mess with anything he'll know, don't you?"

"I know. I'm taking his little blue truck to him." Reaching under his pillow, she pulls out a little, midnight-blue Matchbox pickup. "He likes to have it when he sleeps."

I didn't know that, and I wonder how she does. Is it possible he talks to her more than to us—or is she just more observant? Sometimes she reads in the playroom while he's working on artwork. They never say a word, yet somehow they communicate. She senses his moods and knows when he wants to be left alone. *Oh, for the wisdom of a child.*

The trip to the hospital is quiet. I notice a slight tremor in Reggie's hand when she shuts off the car. I take a deep breath as we enter the elevator. The only one who's relaxed is Sarah, holding Dan's pickup in her hand.

Dan's in his favorite spot in the Activities room, at the table by the window overlooking the park next to the hospital. His head's bent over the table, and I know he's drawing, lost in his own world, yet today he doesn't seem as lost. There's a subtle difference in how he holds himself—no tremors or tics—just a young man concentrating on his project. I pray our visit doesn't change that. Reggie hesitates as we approach the table. Sarah, of course, makes a beeline for him despite my cautioning her to stay with me.

"Hey, Dan. Whatcha doin'? See what I brought?" Sarah is all smiles and bubbling with excitement.

Dan raises his eyes and smiles slightly as he gently takes his truck from Sarah's outstretched hand, holding it close for a moment before carefully laying it on the table beside his art supplies. Then he surprises me by patting Sarah's head gently without saying a word, but that doesn't stop Sarah.

"Did you see Mom's big old cast, Dan? Mom broke her shoulder. Aunt Reggie came to help take care of us. Do you know Aunt Reggie?" And with that, Sarah hurries back to grab Reggie by the hand and pull her forward. "Dan, look up. You have to look up to see our Aunt Reggie."

I start to move between Dan and Reggie to slow down this introduction. "How are you Dan?" I ask.

He leans around me to look at Reggie, who is being pulled forward by Sarah. He looks at Sarah, then Reggie, then me, and back to Reggie, his eyes growing wide.

"Gamma?" he says quietly, reaching tentatively to touch her arm. "Gamma, you go way to heaven? You back?"

My hand covers my mouth, muffling a gasp. I'm so surprised that he even remembered Mom—what she looked like, let alone see Reggie's resemblance to her. This is the most he's said at one time in years. I want to grab him and hug him. Of all the reactions I'd prepared myself for, this wasn't one of them.

Reggie touches his cheek, tears pooling in her eyes. "No, baby, I'm your Aunt Reggie. Your gamma was my mama, and your mama is my sister, like Sarah is your sister."

He looks at her quizzically. "You not Gamma?"

"No, I'm sorry. I'm not. Can we still be friends?" She asked quietly.

He returns to his picture without a word. He's still painting lightning bolts, but he's added his old green pedal tractor sitting alone in the yard. I'm not sure he even knows I'm here. He hasn't acknowledged me. I pull out a chair and sit down next to him.

"I like how you made the tractor look old and worn like your real one." My voice is steady despite how I feel inside. "I miss you, Dan."

He puts a few more details on the tractor. "Miss you, too, Mama. An Ginna, you Sissy? Not Gamma?"

"Yes, Dan, she's staying with us for a while. Okay?"

He nods and continues his work. Sarah pulls up a chair and asks him for a piece of paper. Dan gives us all paper and scoots his colored pens, markers, and colors into the middle of the table. We choose our materials and begin drawing, though none look as good as his. Sarah chats easily as she draws. Dan seems relaxed and at ease, but his frequent glances at Reggie reveal his curiosity. He doesn't say much, yet because he's sharing, I know he's glad we're here.

Two hours with him goes by too quickly. When the nurse comes by to offer us milk and cookies, I'm surprised that Dan eats the chocolate chip cookies without separating out the chips. Then Reggie dunks hers in her milk, and he reaches over and dunks his, too. My heart is bursting with joy. This is the best visit with him in years. I hate to leave him.

When it's time to go, Sarah hugs him—and he doesn't pull away. He pats her on the back tenderly. I choke back tears when he then reaches out, puts his arm around me and allows me to hug him. Reggie holds out her hands when he looks at her. He hesitates for just a split second, then walks into her arms, letting her hug him, too. *I'm not going to cry!* Then, he really surprises me.

"Mama, I want go home. Can I go home soon?"

Although I long to wrap him in my arms and hold him tight, I muster every bit of restraint I have. "Yes, Dan. I think you can come home soon. Dad and I will talk to Dr. Landry tomorrow. If she says it's okay, we'll get you home. Okay?"

"Okay, Mama." He reaches for a colored pencil and turns back to his picture again.

I'm floating on air—*maybe this time.*

Chapter 33

Dan's return home goes smoothly. This time he's more willing to engage with family—Sarah or Reggie mostly. In fact, he appears to enjoy having them close by. His eyes, more than anything, and his mannerisms reveal he's so much more aware of what's going on around him. He even showed Reggie around the playroom, allowing her to look at and touch all of his pictures. The highpoint of their time together was just the two of them on an outing, a tour of the town.

Then, before we know it, it's time for her to leave us. She's postponed it twice, and what was going to be a couple of weeks has now been six. Besides the amazing change in Dan, my relationship with Reggie is incredible now. We're so comfortable with each other. She's opened up about her early years after leaving home and told me about the struggles she faced and overcame. At first it was hard to understand the depth of her descent into drugs and alcohol and the pain it caused, but I'm amazed at how willing she is to talk about it. I've gained a new respect for her. Once, I did believe she thought she was better than me, but in reality she feared rejection if I really got to know her. *Now I think Cheyenne is too far away.*

As she gathers her bags, with Dan helping her, I dread what might happen once she drives away. But Dan's been surprising me lately—maybe it will be okay.

"Dan, you know I have to go home now, don't you? But you have my address, and I want you to write me a letter, draw something, or send me a picture so I know how you are. Will you do that?"

As he puts her suitcase down, he nods. Seeing him making eye contact with her surprises me. Then from his pocket he pulls out a photo of them in front of the museum taken on the day of their tour. It's one of many photos he's taken with the new camera Reggie gave him. "I have this." He holds it out to her. "I miss you—I look at picture?" he asks. This is something they've talked about.

"Yes, Dan. If you start to miss me, take our picture out and remember our good times. Now, will you be a sweet boy and carry that heavy suitcase out to the car for me?"

As he lifts it and heads out the door, I'm struck by how tall he's become. Suddenly he seems like a young man instead of our little boy—a young man I'm not sure I know. For some reason, I'm reminded of the day of Carl's memorial last Saturday—the day we said goodbye to his friend. I'd needlessly agonized over how Dan would react, so I watched him. The memorial was wonderful. His friends held it by Clear Creek, not far from Carl's cottage, under the cottonwood trees lining the creek bank. As his friends talked about the kind and gentle man he had been, Dan stood back from the crowd, listening attentively as each shared their story of him. The music of the babbling waters provided a soothing background to the murmurs of friends joined together in grief and celebration of a life well lived.

While everyone was gathering for the potluck meal, Dan wandered off. We managed to search for him without causing a ruckus. Sarah found him a little further down the creek, asleep, curled up in the roots of a tree. He looked so peaceful lying there that we let him sleep while Reggie and Sarah stayed close by. As Mitch and I rejoined the rest of the group, I couldn't help but wonder *who is this new boy?* Being able to relax again felt so good. Let's hope I can learn to relax and appreciate his newfound sense of freedom.

My thoughts pull me back to what I've been avoiding—Reggie leaving. She hugs me tight in one arm, and with Sarah in the other, moves us toward the door after Dan. "Come on, my favorite girls, as much as I hate to leave, it's time I get back to my life. I can't expect my partner to run our new Gallery alone. And I need to get back to work so I'll be able to feed this little one." She rubs her growing belly.

As I start to respond, I see Dan has the hood up on the waiting car, and he's reaching into the engine. I gasp, concerned that he'll do something to sabotage the engine to delay her leaving. Reggie's hand on my arm stops me from calling out.

"It's okay, let me. Okay?"

I nod in agreement.

"Hey, Dan. Whatcha doin'?" She casually strolls up beside him.

He pulls out the oil dipstick and wipes it off with his fingers, just like I've seen Mitch do. "Checkin' oil." He pushes it back in and pulls it out again to show Reggie. "Oil's okay," he says, replacing it and slamming the hood, and then he pats it a couple of times. "Good car."

"Thanks, Dan, now I really do have to go. Can I have a hug?" He stiffens a bit, then awkwardly puts one arm around her as she envelopes him. He doesn't try to pull away even though she holds him a little too long.

Sarah is standing off to the side watching. I can almost see a storm cloud above our sweet little girl as she watches them. Over the past week or so Dan has usurped her place with Reggie without our noticing. Our once chatty Cathy is a bit quieter and more reserved around the two of them. I can relate, as I've witnessed the closeness building between them—something I've wanted for years. What I would give to hold him like that—yet I feel guilty. What kind of a mother resents her son liking someone—especially when that someone is her own sister? I move over to Sarah and hug her, then pull her toward Dan and Reggie, whose eyes are brimming with tears when she turns toward us. She wraps us both in a bear hug and holds on. Tears spill from my eyes as I hang on tightly—until my shoulder squawks, reminding me that it's still healing. I'm forced to drop my arm.

"Mmffff—"

"Oh, my God, Sarah, are we suffocating you?" Reggie releases us and kneels down, running her hand over Sarah's hair. "Are you okay, sweetie?"

Sarah nods, and she, too, is crying as she flings her arms around Regina's neck. "I don't want you to go, Auntie. Please, can't you stay with us? How will we see the baby if you aren't here?"

"Oh, sweet girl, I wish I could, but I have to get back to work. I've loved being here with you and the crip," she nods toward me. "I never thought I'd be grateful for your mom breaking her shoulder— but I am, because I've been able to spend time with you. But now your mom's healing, and thank God, she's out of the big old cast, and with your help she can take care of things. I hate to leave you, but I have to go—" She sings those last few words as she releases Sarah and stands. "Now let me go, sweet one. You have to write me and tell me all you're up to." She nods toward Dan. "Dan will send me pictures, I know. But I need you and Mom to send me words. Will you do that?"

"I will, and Mama will, too. Won't you, Mama?" She rushes to me, wrapping her arms around my waist.

Dan has the luggage in the car and is holding the door open. Reggie slides in, and ruffles his hair. He doesn't pull away, but gently closes the door after her, turns, and walks back into the house. Sarah and I stand waving as she backs out of the driveway. We watch until she's out of sight. Neither of us wants to go back inside. It's emptier now because Regina's no longer there.

⁓

Chapter 34

"Hey, Reggie, sorry I missed you. In fact that's why I called, I'm missing my sis. Plus I want to hear about little Timothy. Give me a call. Love you." *Damn, I didn't get it all in before the beep.* I grab my old gardening sweater, a cup of coffee, slide into my old boots, and head for the back deck—my favorite place on an early Sunday morning. I love the quiet time before the world wakes up—time for me and my God to commune, reflect, and hopefully, clear my busy mind.

• • •

It's been over three years since Regina came to help us after I broke my shoulder, and it was Dan's last hospitalization. The last few years have been good ones, with only a few hiccups and mini meltdowns. My college classes are about finished, and I am not interested in a Masters degree. When I start my new job as the family therapist at the New Hope Psychiatric and Addictions Hospital in a few weeks, I'll be developing a program for families. Despite the development of more addiction and mental illness treatment programs, the families of the addict often aren't included. I hope to make a difference in my new role. Knowing how difficult it was for us as a family to deal with Dan's illness, I understand the importance of providing the same support for the families that we give our patients. In our journey, we've lost friends who were frightened by what we were going through. They acted as though it might be contagious. A handful of close friends stood by us. They've been a blessing to us and a Godsend, especially for Sarah.

Dan is more outgoing, less reluctant to leave the house, and his fear of certain colors has subsided, but he remains resistant to much touching. He no longer spends all his time in his room or the old playroom—now called his studio. The new place he likes to spend time is not far from Carl's cottage at his old fishing spot. Several times he forgot to come home until Mitch found him there. The first time it happened, we were beside ourselves. We didn't know where to look and were about to call the police when Mitch remembered the fishing hole. He found Dan there, just enjoying the view—not even fishing.

Working on the early model 1955 Chevrolet pickup that Carl left to him is his other newfound pleasure. He's fascinated with it. It wasn't even running when first towed to our house and put in the garage. The paint was a mess, as was the interior. I was horrified. Dan walked around it repeatedly, muttering and touching it. The first month he put his sleeping bag in the truck bed and slept there in the garage. Mitch pulled the motor and created a workspace for them to work on it together.

At times I envy their closeness. I'd love to sit with him and have long conversations—not that he and Mitch do. His communication is still mostly through his pictures or by his actions, with little verbalization.

"Mom?"

"Sarah? What are you doing up early on Sunday morning?"

"I don't feel very good, Mom?" A tear traces down her cheek as she clenches her robe tightly closed.

I realize she's become a young lady. It seems to have happened overnight. I stand and gently wipe away her tears and feel her forehead for fever. There is none. "Where does it feel bad?"

"My stomach. I think I might be dying." The tears come harder. As she tells me what happened, it's obvious she's not my little girl any more; she's become a young woman. *When did she get old enough? Why haven't we had the 'talk' to prepare her for this moment?*

"Honey, you're not going to die. It happens to all young girls—some earlier than others." We go inside, and I take her to my bathroom to give her the supplies she needs, explaining as I show her what to do. At first she's embarrassed for me to see her sheets. When we strip her bed as we talk, it helps having something to do as I explain 'the facts of life' to my daughter. "You'll be fine, honey. You'll be fine."

"You promise?"

"I promise."

"Mom? We don't have to tell dad, do we?"

My little girl, standing on the edge of womanhood, is still her daddy's little girl. "I won't tell Daddy his little girl is growing up until you're ready. For now, if you don't have any more questions, let's fix breakfast. Are you hungry?"

"I am." She sounds surprised that she is.

"Why don't you make the pancakes while I fix the bacon and eggs? I bet by the time we get done the guys will be wanting to eat."

"I'd like that, Mama."

"I'm sorry I didn't notice how much you have grown up. But please don't grow up too fast."

"I won't, Mama, I promise. I'll always be your little girl, won't I?"

Her voice quivers, and I hug her tight. "Of course you will. Always and forever." I choke over that last word.

By the time we return to the kitchen, I'm humming. I'm relieved that our talk went so well. So is she—she's more relaxed, as am I.

She finds the Bisquick and studies the recipe as I suggested before mixing the batter. After warming the double cast iron grill on two burners, I fry the bacon, and try not to hover over her.

"Hey, ladies, are you planning on having breakfast without your men?" Mitch tussles Sarah's hair, but I sense her shyness with him.

Dan's right behind Mitch and stops to stare at his sister. "Sarah cooks? Oh no, will make me sick?" he asks with a faint smile. His new sense of humor is a blessing we're all enjoying.

Sarah slaps at him with one hand as she mixes the batter. "Keep talking like that, Dan, and I won't let you have any of my pancakes."

Dan retrieves his plate, silverware, and glass from the cupboard and places them on the table in 'his' place.

"Hey, Dan, are you the only one eating this morning? How about the rest of us? Don't we need some plates, silver, and a glass?" Mitch asks, winking.

Dan gives his dad a quizzical look, and then returns to the cupboard, gathering our breakfast dishes one at a time. Before suggesting that he stack them and carry them all together, I stop myself and simply say, "Thank you for helping, Dan." I'm rewarded with a slight smile.

The phone rings just as we finish cooking breakfast. Mitch takes it in the living room where it's quieter. Dan starts eating, not waiting for anyone, so I encourage Sarah to do the same, and I go to see what's taking Mitch so long.

When I enter the living room, Mitch is holding the phone to his ear, and tears are trickling down his face. "Mitch, honey? What's wrong?"

It doesn't seem to register who I am. Slowly, he covers the mouthpiece, "Dad died this morning." He chokes on the words. "It's Mom on the phone."

My hand flies to my mouth. We thought we were prepared for this day, but as much as we expected it, we really aren't prepared. Losing Mom should have taught me that.

Mitch's voice has grown stronger. "Yes, Mom. I agree, no funeral. I know he didn't like all that 'nonsense.' I'll call the prison to get word to Chris before I come down. Yes, I'm coming. You're not going through this alone. I'll call as soon as I've made arrangements. Is someone with you now? Good. Will she be able to stay awhile? I know you've been alone since dad's been in the nursing home, but this is different. Promise me you'll ask her to stay until I can get there. I'll call you in a few hours. Okay, Mom? I love you, Mom—and I'm so sorry about Dad." A sob escapes as he hangs up the phone and drops his head to his hands. I sit beside him, wrapping him in my arms. The kids find us like this when they finish eating breakfast.

"What's wrong, Daddy?" Sarah tries to hug us both. Dan stares for a moment, then turns and goes upstairs. Mitch tenderly seats Sarah between us.

"Papa Hawke, my dad, died this morning. I have to leave as soon as I can get a plane ticket to Nana's."

Tears well in her eyes, and her chin quivers, "B-b-ut, can't we go with you?"

"No, pumpkin. It's best if I go alone. I hope to bring Nana back with me to stay here for a while. Mama has only a few days left of her school, plus you and Dan are only a couple weeks away from the end of your school year."

"B-but, who's going to take care of you?" Our girl is saying what I'm thinking.

"Yes, Mitch. Who's going to take care of you? You made the trip alone last time, too, when your dad went into the home because of his dementia. I can't let you down this time, too."

"Lil, I've given this a lot of thought over the past year. We've talked about what to do when it happens. We don't know how Dan will react to a plane ride and a trip like this. Plus, you've worked too hard for your counselor's license. With only a few days to go, you can't leave now. If Dad were here and could, he'd say 'Don't be making no fuss, Lillian, you take care of those little ones and yourself.' I'm hoping Mom will come back with me, and we can have her with us. You'll be able to help both of us then. Okay."

"Okay, I feel like I'm letting you down though."

"No, Lil. You're not. In fact, it will help me, knowing you're here, carrying on with the routine we've established. I don't want to rock the boat." He holds Sarah and me close for a few minutes. "Now, I need to talk to Dan. Would you mind calling to see when the next flight is? That's something you can do to help me."

I hug him again. "Come on, Sarah. Help me get things ready for Daddy."

$$\infty$$

Chapter 35

"Mitch?"

"What?"

Following the sound of his voice to our bedroom, I find him staring out the window, his suitcase open on the bed with only a few items in it. The struggle he's going through is evident in the stooped stance of his body. My heart aches for him as I remember the pain I went through when Mom died.

"Hey, big guy." I slip my arms around his middle and lay my head on his back. "Is there anything I can do to help?"

He clasps my hands, "No, just the flight and that stuff. Well, maybe help me with my suitcase. My mind's a jumble, and I'm having trouble figuring out what I might need. Even the simplest things seem overwhelming right now." He turns and wraps me in his arms. "We've been expecting this for a long time. I know it's for the best, yet I can't seem to get over how shocked I feel. I also feel guilty that I don't feel more. If I'm really honest, I'm feeling some relief—and that makes me feel even more guilty. He was a son of a bitch to live with all my life, and he put Mom through hell. I realize now that his treatment of Chris was unconscionable. I want to love him—I really do. I want to be sad that he's gone, but I only feel sad for Mom because of all he put her through." He chokes and hugs me tighter. I understand how conflicted he must be and wish I knew what to say to soothe his anguish.

"There's nothing wrong with you. You'll be feeling lots of different emotions over the next few weeks. I did when Mom died—and we had a good relationship. But honey, guilt is the last thing you need.

He wasn't an easy man—and that's the truth, yet you kept trying in spite of that. That's all you can do, grieve for what you didn't have and always longed for." We stand holding each other until there's a knock on the door.

"Daddy, you didn't eat any of the pancakes I made. You've got to have some breakfast before you go see Nana." Sarah comes carrying a breakfast tray with a plate of cold pancakes topped with globs of unmelted butter, syrup, a cold fried egg, and a couple slices of cold bacon.

Mitch's eyes get big, and he stifles a groan. "Oh, baby, I'm sorry. I don't think it's a good idea eating a big breakfast before getting on the airplane." Knowing the effort Sarah put forward, Mitch adds, "It looks delicious, Sarah, but you know how you get carsick if you eat too much before going for a long drive? I don't want to do that on the plane. What time is my flight, Lil?" He's hoping my answer gives him the reprieve he wants.

Sarah's shoulders droop as she stands holding her offering to her dad. Gently, I take the tray and place it on the table. "Your flight doesn't leave for another four and a half hours, so maybe you could eat a few bites?"

He gives me that 'I'm gonna get you' look as he sits down and picks up his fork. "I see you even brought me a nice cup of coffee."

"I did, Daddy. Dan helped me make the coffee because there wasn't enough. I hope we did it right." She looks so proud as Mitch picks up the cup and takes a sip.

His eyes get large as he sips, but he shudders slightly as he extends the cup to me. "Mmm, that's good. It'll put hair on your chest. Here, Mama. Why don't you try some of this delicious coffee our children made for us?" He holds my gaze as I accept the cup.

How do I not hurt her feelings? From watching poor Mitch I know already it isn't going to be good. I swirl the coffee just a little. It's black as midnight. Slowly, I raise it to my lips and take a sip. *God help me praise this child*—and let me swallow this without throwing it up. They must have used a cupful of grounds. If I put a spoon in it, I bet it would stand on its own.

"My, that is good, isn't it? I'll have some later." I hand the cup back to him.

He cuts a big piece of pancake—good when they're hot—but cold with unmelted butter? I'm not so sure. "You've outdone yourself on these pancakes, young lady. Are you sure Mom didn't make them? Come to think of it, they taste better than Mom's."

She beams at his praise.

"Pumpkin, I don't think I can eat all of this. But thank you for bringing it up to me. I'm glad I got to taste your cooking before I leave." He manages to eat most of the pancakes and the bacon—good hot or cold, but he pushes the egg aside. Amazingly, he's drinking most of the coffee. Poor guy. I hope his flight is smooth, so the coffee can settle.

"Now, I'd better finish packing and get ready to go. Thank you, Sarah. Next time you cook, I'll be sure to eat while it's still hot."

"I'll take the tray back, check the kitchen, then I'll be back to help you. Sarah, do you want to stay with Daddy?"

"I can help Daddy pack. Do you want me to get you some socks?"

As I gather the tray and leave the room, they discuss what he needs to take.

He didn't have the best role model for a father when he was growing up, although the way he interacts with his own children, no one would guess. He deserves a gold medal for drinking that coffee without flinching. *What good memories he's making with our children.*

When I approach the kitchen, I hear clunking and banging. What the heck? Turning the corner, I see Dan with a sink full of dishes, washing away. The breakfast bar is clean, dishes are stacked by the sink, and the electric percolator is at the ready with its fresh brewed sludge. Our boy, who doesn't like disorder, is cleaning up for me. I pray this boy stays and that his problems remain manageable in the future.

Chapter 36

"Danny! Sarah! Hurry up, or you'll be late for school." *I can't believe I overslept.* "Come on, you two. Let's get moving." I push Dan's door open and find his bed empty. Hurrying to Sarah's room, I find her still snuggled in her bed. "Sarah, come on. Let's go. You'll be late for the bus. I have an early class today, so I can't take you." I pull her covers off.

"Mom! Let me sleep a little longer. I'm tired. I wish Daddy was here to take me." She tries to pull the covers back up.

"I do, too, but he's not. He'll be home in a few days, but right now I don't have time for this. Get your behind out of bed and get dressed. I've got to find Dan and make sure he's ready."

Where can that young man be? I check the bathroom and the rest of the rooms upstairs, and then hurry down the stairs to the garage where he's curled up in the front seat of his pickup.

"Dan, wake up! We're going to be late." I know better, but I reach in and grasp his arm. He flings his arm loose, hitting my head as he sits up looking confused.

"NO!" His eyes widen, and he begins to wring his hands, shaking his head from side to side.

I breathe deeply to calm myself, or this will accelerate into an episode neither of us wants. "It's okay, Danny—Dan. Take a deep breath." To show him what to do, I slowly breathe in a couple of times and blow it out as he stares. Then he, too, begins calming down—he can't be hurried. Yet today, with Mitch gone, I have to try if he's going to make the bus for school. I've relied on Mitch so much, but today he isn't here. I have to take care of all this by myself.

"I hit you? I sorry." He begins to crawl out of the pickup. He's not as accepting of Mitch's leaving as I thought. Change is still his Achilles heel.

"It's okay. You didn't mean to, but Dan, I'll be late for class, and you and Sarah will be late for school if you don't hurry. Why don't you change your clothes while I fix some toast with peanut butter for your breakfast. The bus will be here soon."

Wordlessly, he goes to the house and up to his room. I drop bread in the toaster as Sarah comes downstairs. When it pops, I slather on the peanut butter, put in more slices, and hand her the toast and a banana. Now I hurry to get dressed, leaving Sarah to fix Dan's for him.

The school bus is honking just as I finish dressing. Looking out the window, I see only Sarah running to catch the bus, no Dan. The bus honks again—still no Dan. The bus pulls away as I dash to his room. He's sitting on the edge of his bed, still in his pj's.

"Dan, why didn't you get dressed? Now you've missed the bus, and I don't have time to take you. What are we going to do?"

"I not go."

"What do you mean? You only have a couple of weeks till school's out, then you'll be able to work on your pickup all you want. If you hurry you can walk to school."

"NO! I not go to school. I go help Henry at the shop. He said I work for him, he help me paint my truck."

"Dan, that's a summer job. Remember?"

"No, I go today, not school. I walk there. Dad said I could walk there everyday. Only few blocks."

There's no time to argue. One last class, and I'm done, I am not going to miss it. When Dan and Mitch spoke with Henry at Henry's Body Shop and Junk Yard last week, I feared this might happen. Dan is supposed to sweep the floors, empty trash, and even sand some of Henry's old beaters—but it's supposed to be for the summer months.

"I'm not going to argue. I have to go, or I'll be late for my class. We'll talk about it when I get home. Stay here."

"I go to Henry's. You come there."

"Damn it, Dan," I say, my voice rising. "This time only. I'll pick you up at Henry's, and the three of us will talk. You still need to change your clothes. You can't go to the shop in your pj's."

I rush to my car to make it to the class on time. *What else can I do?* Part of the learning life's skills program is to let him have some independence. The goal is for him to learn to live on his own, but it's hard. Henry's the first person he's taken to since Carl died. He started hanging out at the body shop after he and Mitch went there looking for parts for Dan's pickup. Henry's patient with him and impressed with his knowledge of vehicles. He even had Dan taking parts off the junkers—that's why he offered Dan the job.

When I hear a siren and look in my rear view mirror, I slow down and pull over. I don't have to look down to know I'm speeding.

"Going to a fire, Mrs. Hawke?"

Gotta love living in a small town. "No, Sam, just late for my last class and a bit irritated. Sorry, I wasn't paying attention."

"Well, you were going fifty in a thirty-five—we can't have that, now can we? After all, what would those two youngin's do if something happened to you?"

"I know, Sam. But I'm late for the last class to complete my course, and if I don't complete it, I won't be able to take my new job and—"

"Okay, Okay. Far be it from me to be responsible for a hard-working woman not getting her education. I'll let you off with a warning this time. Don't let it happen again." He slaps the roof of the car and walks back to the cruiser.

My watch tells me I have barely fifteen minutes, so I pull out carefully, making sure not to speed. Sam's following, making sure, too.

I try not to think about Dan but it's so hard to keep those thoughts at bay. Every day that goes by without a meltdown is a blessing. Other times I just know that when that day comes, it's going to be a doozy. Big changes are coming to our lives.

The professor enters the room as I slide into my seat. For the next hour I focus on the course.

• • •

What the hell was I thinking? I had a part time job at the Child Development Center that I liked. My hours were great—allowing me to be home to get the kids to school and be there when they came home. *But no, that wasn't enough for me.* I wanted more. Now I'm standing on the precipice of having it all, and I'm overwhelmed. Thank God things have been on an even keel for a while, and now I'm done. I've completed the work for my Certified Alcohol/Drug Certification (CADC), plus my Social Work degree, and my new job begins in two weeks. *Why am I borrowing trouble?* Perhaps that's why I'm so concerned about the flash of rebellion in Dan this morning. *Why can't I just enjoy this, since it's my last class?*

Once class is over, it's time to clear up the confusion over Dan's new job. "Hey, Henry. Did you have an extra helper this morning?"

Henry wipes his hands on a shop rag and stretches one out to me. "Hi there, Miss Lil. He sure surprised me, but he did say it was okay with you. I tried to call but no one answered. I wasn't expecting him until school's out."

"I was late for class this morning, and Mitch is out of town for a few days. Dan was determined to come here instead of going to school. I need your help to make Dan understand that he won't have the job if he doesn't finish the school year. He can come in after school if you want, but not during the day."

"I like having him here. He's a natural. I'll be happy to tell him no school, no work. How's that?"

"That's great. I really appreciate what you're doing. Not everyone has patience with him—his idiosyncrasies are all they see. Where is he anyway?"

"Out back. There're some old hoods and doors I told him he could practice on. He has an idea he wants to try on his old truck. I gave him a small air gun and some paints so he can get the hang of it. Have you seen the drawings of his design? It's awesome." He walks over to a workbench, picks up a paper, and hands it to me.

I recognize Dan's work immediately—images of his old pickup with a mural painted on it. Four different angles are depicted. Down the sides are a creek with trees and foliage. The creek continues on the hood, widening into a quiet pond—Carl's fishing spot, complete with an eagle soaring overhead and a fish jumping as the sun sets. The creek flows to the tailgate where it disappears into a cluster of trees with another eagle perched on one. It takes my breath away. "Wow, that's amazing. But don't you think it's a bit much for a young man who's never painted a car?"

"He won't be ready for a while, but I do believe that one day, this design will be on that old pickup. As I said, I think he's a natural. Let's see what he's done in the short time he's been here."

We walk to where Dan's hard at work on an old rusty hood leaning against the fence. A little cluster of trees adorns the center of the hood with the sun a muted yellow, and the shadow of an eagle soaring high is beginning to show through. Henry gently taps Dan on the shoulder. He turns, looking like a bugman with the goggles on and a spray gun in his hands. He's already begun to master it, and at this moment, I, too, believe that design will be painted by Dan's hand on his truck one day. But first, we have to set some guidelines.

Although I want to explain—just one more time—the importance of school, he'll just shut down, so the ride home is quiet. His car door opens before I come to a full stop. He makes a beeline for the house, but his body is rigid as he walks determinedly away. A flush of sadness engulfs me. My knees almost buckle, and I force myself not to give in to gravity. I want to scream and rail at God at the unfairness of it all. *Why do we fight so hard to keep him in school?* I know the answer—but, why really? Do we do it for him or for us? Is it fair placing him in circumstances that remove his uniqueness and make him follow the norm—pounding the proverbial round peg into the square hole—to make him 'normal'?

Everyone's heart is in the right place. We create programs for these poor souls who see the world differently from us—programs that discourage the natural talents and force-feed them the blandness of our daily lives. What must it be like to live in Dan's world, where colors swirl, blend, and come to life with a few pencil strokes? He's not sidetracked by day-to-day events that take us on a ride to nowhere. His world is filled with his favorite simple things, TRUCKS. Trucks in all shapes and sizes—and nature that bursts forth in frenetic spurts—when the voices he hears aren't ruling his life.

He needs to be able to communicate, we say. But does he have to talk to be heard—or do we need to listen differently? If we take time to look at his art, he is communicating. If we want to know how he feels, we only have to look at his latest drawings—drawings sometime so bleak and full of darkness when he's troubled by his demons. Others are so full of colors, they take your breath away—some so defined you think you can walk into them—people so real you expect them to speak at any moment. Pictures of his sister are filled with the joy that is her, and from them you can tell how much he treasures her—though he rarely tells her.

He needs to learn the meaning of money and understand interactions with others so they don't take advantage of him. But will this really keep him safe from a predator or someone trying to cheat him? *Oh, God, I wish I knew.* How can I honestly say we know what's best for him? As his mom, it's my place to encourage him, to provide for him, to keep him on the best path to survive in a world that, for the most part, is hostile to him, to be his champion—even when he resists. When doing that puts him in the path of bullies and dims that special light that shines in him, am I really doing what's best for him?

I need to go in. It's not how I'd pictured the end of my schooling. I dreamed of a party to celebrate with family and friends, instead, I'm alone, and what I have is Dan—a possible runaway train—an absent husband dealing with his grief, plus a young lady who also needs me.

As if on cue, she's standing on the porch calling me. "Mom? Why aren't you coming in, I'm hungry."

I push away from the side of the car, raising my hand in a wave. "I'm coming. I don't think you're going to starve." I shake off the blue funk I'm in so she doesn't see it. "Come on, munchkin. Let's go raid the fridge and make some dinner." I put my arm around her shoulder, hugging her as I push through the front door.

"SURPRISE!!!" a roomful of people shout. Hanging from the ceiling is a sign spelling out "CONGRATULATIONS." I'm wrapped in a bear hug before I can see who it is, but I'd recognize the feel of him anywhere.

"M-Mitch, h-how?"

"Mom and I got in about an hour ago. I thought you'd never come in the house. Sarah planned it all. I'm so proud of you." It comes out in a rush.

My eyes fill with tears as I hold my husband tight, looking around at all my friends, family, and that special young lady I'm proud to call my daughter. I see my mother-in-law standing on the sidelines and make my way to her. "I'm so glad you're here. I'm sorry I couldn't be there with you."

"It's okay. It was good for us. I'm glad to be with my grandchildren and both of you. Sarah's a darling girl." A shadow appears in her eyes. "I tried talking to Dan when he came in, but he hurried away. I hope he's not upset with me being here."

"Oh, no," I reassure her. "Dan's upset with me, and he doesn't do well with crowds or people he doesn't know. Don't take it personally. He doesn't talk to us much either." Looking around, I can see how truly blessed I am. *Alone? No, definitely not.* All I have to do is look around this room to know that. And neither is Dan—he has us all—even if he doesn't know what to do with us.

Chapter 37

I always thought I could juggle chainsaws, but I seem to have dropped more than one. Here I am, all alone—surrounded by boxes packed with our most loved possessions. We're having to move out of our beautiful home. How could I lose sight of all that was precious and dear? I've been so busy keeping Dan out of trouble and protecting him that I forgot to nurture and take care of the others.

When the bottom fell out of the housing market, how could I not notice the toll it took on Mitch? Where was I when he laid off his crew, sold all of the heavy equipment, the shop, and part of the yard? At least he hung on to some of the yard and one storage building. He tried to talk to me about it at the time, but either my work or a problem with Dan interfered and postponed our discussion. As his mom got weaker, I did mean to visit her more. Even when he and Sarah were spending more and more time at Carl's cottage, I'd tell myself I need to be there with them, yet I kept putting it off. Then that call saying she'd passed, catching me totally off guard. *Was I even there for him then?*

When I wonder what happened to us, I have only to look in the mirror. All my efforts to save Dan from his demons didn't end successfully. Granted, for a few years it seemed as though we were going to be okay. Then the shop where he worked was sold, and he went off the deep end. He crashed his beautiful pickup through the front window, resisted arrest, ended up in the hospital with a broken arm, and when he was well enough, he spent six months in the state mental hospital.

If only that had been the end of it—but sadly it wasn't. He discovered the magic elixir alcohol. Drinking and refusing to take his meds led to more frequent interactions with the police. In fact, he's back in the state hospital. My efforts to save him, once again, wiped out our savings. We're selling our beautiful home and moving to Carl's cottage.

This morning as we finished packing the last of our things, Sarah let me know what a muck up of a mother I've become. In her anger she reminded me of everything I've missed over the past few years. She's now in high school. Thanks to Mitch and his support, she's a straight A student, on the school council, and singing in choir. She even starred in the school play of Romeo and Juliet, which she reminded me I'd missed. For the life of me, I can't remember what was so important that I'd place it over her. I've dropped the ball too often, and I don't know how I can make it right. I feel like I'm drowning, and I'm so numb I can't even cry. I feel like I'm about to blow away. I didn't hear anyone come in, so when strong arms wrap around me, I'm startled. "Hey, Lil. It's okay. It's only me. You look so sad—it breaks my heart. What can I do?"

How can I answer him? He's been a rock for us. I've been patting myself on the back for too long, thinking how strong I am, wearing my superwoman shirt so proudly only to realize the truly super one is Mitch.

"Honestly, I don't know what would help right now. My heart is breaking to walk away from our home—so many memories, mostly good over the years. I don't know if I can do it. I have to go back to work in three more days." I cringe as I say those words. *Has the job I've loved also become an escape—an escape from dealing with what's been going on at home?*

He takes my hand and leads me to the kitchen. He pours us both a cup of coffee then motions me out the French doors to the back deck where our Adirondack chairs sit. "Take a load off. We're going to take a break. Honey, I know you're upset about the move, but I can't believe what I'm hearing. Are you blaming yourself for all of this? You know that's not it, don't you? I know Sarah unloaded on you this morning. Now she's at the cottage feeling as miserable as you are. She told me some of what she said and regretted as soon as she'd said it."

"But she's right, Mitch. I haven't been there for her, or for you the last few years. I've let work and Dan take over my life. Now, knowing how badly I've hurt her, I can hardly stand it. I've failed her. How could I let that sweet, patient, funny, young lady down? And I've taken you for granted. Thank God, you've been here for her—and for me. You listened to me rant and rave, sat patiently when I withdrew or went wildly chasing after Dan, bound and determined to save him from himself. I couldn't even get that right—and now—" As great, heaving sobs wrack my body, Mitch gathers me into his arms and holds me.

I'm not sure how long we sat with him holding me. I feel him move and realize he's been crouched down, holding me all this time. When I try to pull myself up, he loses his balance, and we end up in a heap. Mitch is trying not to laugh, but a low, rumbling sound in his chest tells me he's not going to succeed. We both erupt in laughter, laughing until tears flow. I'm not sure if I'm laughing or crying again. Finally, we settle down, get untangled and slide back into our chairs.

"Oh, God, Lil. It's so good to hear you laugh. We've got some hurdles to overcome, but our home is where we are. It's not the building we're living in. This one served us well. But truth be told, it's a lot of house for three people and a lot to keep up. Honey, it seems that when you're not at work you're spending most of your time on housework, laundry, and shopping. How long has it been since you had a day for yourself? A day to kick back, read something that wasn't work related? Or a day out for you and Sarah? How long has it been since you two have had a girls' day out? Carl's cottage, our new home, will give us plenty of room with half the upkeep, freeing us to do more of the things we enjoy. I'm looking forward to that. We have that lovely property almost to the creek and, with my new riding lawn mower, it'll be easy to keep up. Mom really enjoyed it there, and I've done some upgrades to the house already. Would you consider something for me? Call work and see if you can get a couple more weeks off. You need it, and I know you have more vacation time coming, Lil. What Sarah and I need from you is for you to take care of yourself."

I start to say I can't, but he holds up his hand to ward me off. "No, Lil. Don't give me an answer until you think it over. If they can't get along without you for a couple of weeks they need to be paying you a lot more money. I've not asked you to take time off from work since you started there, but I've never been so worried about you."

"I'll think about it."

"Okay, that's all I ask. Now, how about we get busy. The guys will be here before long with the truck. We need to be ready so we can get this show on the road. We've got tomorrow to clean it and hand the key over to the new family the next day." He helps me out of the chair, dumps our cold coffee, and begins to gather the cushions.

With a deep breath, I square my shoulders, give him a salute, and an "aye, aye, Captain," feeling lighter and freer than I have in a long time. As for that two-week vacation—I reach for my phone before I can chicken out.

Chapter 38

My footsteps echo in the silence as I check the closets in Sarah's room. As I close my eyes, a kaleidoscope of memories of my baby girl squeeze my heart—the joys, the laughter, and the tears. In this room she blossomed from a sweet baby into a beautiful young lady. She transformed a little girl's room with a makeover using old wallpaper sample books from the paint store to create a diamond-studded wall with purple ribbon seams. Dan helped her cut the diamond shapes, each one a different design, and glue them next to each other to form an accent wall. Three weeks later soft lavender walls accented with deep purple completed the job. Pride glistened in her eyes when she saw our reaction as we took it all in. "WOW!" we said in unison to pay homage to her hard work. No wonder she was so upset this morning—knowing it would be the last time for her to enjoy her beautiful room.

It's hard to leave behind all that we accomplished here, but we will take the memories with us. It's time, not only for her, but for me—time to move forward, for new beginnings, new rooms to decorate, and new memories to make. But most of all, it's time for me to find Sarah and heal this chasm that's grown between us. I hurry down the stairs calling out.

"Mitch, I need to talk to Sarah. Would you help me put the plants in my car? Oh, I almost forgot. I did what you suggested. I called work and took another two weeks off."

Mitch's grin shows me how pleased he is as he wraps me in a bear hug. "Sounds good to me. Thanks, Lil."

In spite of how painful this move is, I know it has to be done. We have to let go in order to save even more. This is an opportunity, not a failure. With the money from the sale of the house we can pay our bills and have plenty left to take the pressure off Mitch as he grows his new business. Instead of building big projects, he'll do more home remodels, projects he can do either alone or with one part-time worker. This means he can focus more on building furniture, something he does so beautifully. Remembering the excitement I felt when I first went back to school to begin my own venture, I feel a twinge of envy. *Maybe it's time to think about doing something else again.*

Yet, why do I feel like my heart's being ripped out of me? The closer I get to the cottage, the slower I move. How can I make it right, reassure Sarah that I will do better? How can I make her understand how important she is to me and that I'm not angry about what she said? Because she's always so responsible, I sometimes forget she's still a child. She's a young lady trying to find her own identity and place, not only in the world, but in our family. She's never shown anger toward Dan, even through all the legal problems and hospitalizations. The anger she's experiencing is because she feels I abandoned her, and I can't fault her for that. Only my actions now can make things right again.

My heart's racing when I pull into the driveway of the cottage. I stop for a moment to say a prayer for guidance and compose myself and stop the tears that threaten to spill before pushing the door open. "Sarah? Sarah, where are you?" The silence is deafening. *Please, God.* Panic blossoms as I rush through the house. No Sarah. Where can she be? She was going to work on her room—but nothing's been touched since last night. I reach for the phone to call—Mitch? Her friends? But the phone hasn't been turned on yet.

Scurrying through the house, I open closets and cupboards, all the while knowing how ridiculous it is. She won't be hiding under the sink like she did when she was little. I have to find her. When it dawns on me where she might be, I rush outside and hurry down the path to the creek. I round the bend and see her sitting on the bench Mitch built for his mom—Mother Hawke called it her sanctuary. Sarah sits with her head bowed.

Her face is blotchy from crying when she looks up and sees me. Before she can run from me, I sit beside her and wrap her in my arms despite her protests. Sobs wrack her body, and my heart shatters.

"Sarah, my sweet girl. I'm so sorry. I'm here, and I'm not going anywhere. I promise. You've been so strong for so long. Sometimes I forget that you need me, too. I don't tell you as often as I should how much I love you."

"I love you, too, Mama." She clings to me, then she finds the words she needs to say to me. "I didn't mean what I said, Mama. But I hate feeling like I'm responsible for Dan. I know he's sick, but that's not my fault. I can't make him take his medication if he doesn't want to. I know you think he listens to me more than anybody else, but I'm still just a kid."

I want to interrupt her and say it isn't so, but she's right. I need to listen and really hear what she's telling me.

"I want him to be a normal brother, a brother who doesn't scare my friends. I want to have friends over to spend the night, to stay up late telling ghost stories, painting our nails, eating popcorn. The other girls talk about having sleepovers and all the fun they have, but I'm not even invited to them anymore. Even when he's not here, you're either too upset or you're not even here because you're working all the time."

What a mess I've made of things. "You haven't done anything wrong, Sarah. I'm so very sorry I've made you feel responsible for Dan. That isn't your job; your job is to be his sis, to be a teenager. You're the little sister, but we've been acting like you're the big sister, expecting you to take care of him." A cry of pain rips from her as sobs take her breath away. I hold her tight, and then I wipe her tears away as my own flow freely. *Please, God. Help me heal this wounded child and myself.*

Chapter 39

"Lillian! Sarah!" It's Mitch's frightened voice calling us. I've lost track of how long we've been here. Sarah's calm, but makes no move to pull out of my arms. I stroke her damp cheek and brush her hair back.

"Are you okay?" She nods as Mitch's panicked voice calls out again. "Lillian! Sarah! Where are you?"

"We're down here by the creek, Mitch" I call out.

His breath is coming in great huffs as he rushes down the path. "Don't you ever scare me like that again!" he shouts. When he reaches us, he pulls us both from the bench into an embrace so tight I can hardly catch my breath.

"Mmmum D-Daddd." Sarah pushes against his chest. "Dad! I can't breathe. We're okay. Take a pill."

"What was I to think? I pulled into the driveway, and Lil's car door's wide open—so is the front door of the house—and not a sight or sound from the two of you. I've been calling and calling with no answer. I was ready to call the police when your mother finally answered. I didn't know what the hell to think." He pulls us tight again.

"We're okay." I give him a quick kiss. "Can you give us a few minutes? Sarah and I need to talk."

He steps back, "What do you think Sarah?"

"I think Mom's right."

He smooths her damp hair, kisses her on the cheek, and does the same to me before turning to walk away. "Okay, fine. But don't think this gets either of you out of unpacking."

Sarah says with a slight smile, "Darn, and here I thought if I had a meltdown I wouldn't have to work."

God, I love this girl. "I'm so sorry. I've so much to make up for. I'm going to do better. I'm taking a couple more weeks off. Let's make them count. Tell me what you need from me."

"No, Mom. It's me who should be sorry. With everything you're going through, I didn't need to blow up on you. I know you do your best. I do understand that sometimes Dan needs you more. I really don't hate my life. Sometimes I feel invisible—and that scares me. I even wonder what would happen if I got in trouble. Would you be there for me like you are for Dan?"

"Don't go there. I do notice, but I've taken your spirit and independence for granted. Because of your maturity, I sometimes forget you're still a teenage girl. Your life is changing so fast, not only on the outside but on the inside. It can all be so confusing under the best of circumstances. I've placed burdens on you that aren't yours to bear and that's wrong. I won't make you a lot of promises this time—I've done that then neglected to follow through. I need you to remind me if I begin to do it again. Do you think you can do that?"

She takes a minute, looking in my eyes like she's searching my soul. "I'll try, but, Mom, you aren't always that easy to talk to when you're under stress. I—" she stops, not able to find the words.

"I know. You're afraid I'll tell you to remind me, but when you do, you think I'll be upset?"

She nods, starts to say something, but nothing comes out. Tears begin to pool in her eyes again. I reach for her hand and place it on my heart. "Sarah, I know we have work to do, but I give you my word— we're going to get through this. My heart to yours." I place my hand on her heart. "How about we try this, we'll write down some of the things that bother us and what we'd like to change. Today's Sunday. Let's make it a date for next Sunday to meet here at the creek and go over our lists. But, if I get really pissy between now and then, we could come up with a signal, something Gamma used to do in homage to our English ancestors. She would stop and have a cuppa when she felt stressed. She said it would give her time to recharge and relax the tensions of the day. What do you think? Should we try it?"

"Tricky, Mom, getting me to fix you a cuppa." Again a smile plays on her lips. "But I can work with that."

"So, it's a date, next Sunday, 5 a.m.?"

"5 a.m.!" She squawks.

"Okay, how about 9? That better, sleepyhead?"

She grips my hand, and we stand together, letting the gentle sounds of the water soothe us. I give her a quick hug. "Well, bug, we'd better get back to business before Dad docks our pay."

We hold hands as we walk back to the cottage. It's the first time I notice what a lovely day it is. My heart is lighter as we work to put a dent in all that needs to be done before we fall into bed to sleep, and for the first time in too long, to rest.

In only a few days, as it finally comes together, I find my frustrations once more beginning to dog me as I try finding places for everything I've brought with me—especially in the little kitchen. In frustration, I storm out to the yard, where I pull weeds in the flowerbeds. That's where Sarah finds me. She's carrying a cup of coffee as she approaches.

"Mom, I thought you looked like you could use a cuppa."

For a moment I almost reject her offer, but catch myself as I remember our talk by the creek. I stand and brush the dirt off my knees. How can I resist this? As I reach for the cup she extends to me, I see the hot tamale candy she's put on the saucer. Grinning, I look from it to her face.

"Thought you might need a chill pill," a tentative smile plays on her lips. "How about coming up on the deck with me?"

"You think you're pretty smart, don't you, Sissy?" I can't help but chuckle.

We're quietly enjoying our coffee when the door opens, filling the air with the smell of fresh bacon. Mitch places two plates of bacon, eggs, hash browns, and toast in front of us. He returns shortly with a tray holding his full plate, a thermal carafe of coffee, and jam for our toast.

I didn't realize how hungry I was until I start to eat. I shovel it in as though I'm starving. "Oh, Mitch. Thisissoogood."

Sarah bursts out laughing. "Are you the same Mom that's always telling me ladies don't talk with their mouths full?"

I throw my napkin at her and keep on chewing—enjoying our family and our time together. I'm feeling so lucky, and I find the tension sluffing away.

"I have an idea." Mitch says, "Do you have everything you need unpacked for now?"

"I think so, why? Do you want to have a bonfire?"

"No," he chuckles. "I was going to suggest we put the rest in the extra bedroom for now so we can get the house straightened up. You know, out of sight, out of mind."

"I think that's a marvelous idea. I can't believe I didn't think of it." He pitches the napkin I threw at Sarah back at me.

"Would you two children leave the napkins where they belong? Can I put some in there, too?"

"That would be fine. Make sure you put your name on them."

I start to stand. "Let's get started shuffling boxes." Mitch puts a hand on my arm.

"Not so fast. I've got another brilliant idea. After we put all the boxes away and put our house in order, how about we get cleaned up and go to the movies? Then we can go out to dinner. We've been going ninety miles an hour for months. It's time for a break. Who's with me?"

With little hesitation we both raise our hands, shouting, "Me, me, me." *This is what I've been missing, family!*

Working together, we make short order of stacking boxes in the extra room, straighten up the furniture, and get ready to take in a movie. We have no idea what's playing but we're going and looking forward to a fun evening.

When we get to the theater, we find "Viva Las Vegas" starring Elvis Presley. I try not to laugh. Sarah is beside herself, and poor Mitch, he rolls his eyes. Yet he's game and buys the tickets. In spite of himself, his toes tap along with the music. He'll never admit that he's enjoying it. When it's over we opt for take out. We're tired and anxious to go home. Just as we make the decision, it dawns on me that I thought of it as *home*, not Carl's cottage.

Chapter 40

When Sunday morning arrives, I'm feeling more relaxed than I have in a long time. I'm looking forward to my 'girl' time with Sarah. I'm sure she will remember, although neither of us have mentioned it since last Sunday. To get things ready, I mix up a batch of popovers, pour it into muffin tins, pop them in the oven, and set the timer. While they bake, I fry link sausage, break some eggs to be scrambled, pour whipping cream into an aluminum bowl, and place it in the fridge to chill. Chilling makes the cream whip better, although Mitch thinks I'm full of it when he sees me do it. With a little searching I find the insulated cover for my Corningware casserole dish—it was one of Mom's that I only use on special occasions. The oven timer buzzes, and the popovers are golden brown—perfection. I put the casserole dish in the warming oven to heat before I'm ready to place the eggs and sausage in, praying that the popovers will cool quickly so I can fill them with whipped cream. Once I add the skillet of sausages to the warm oven, I carry a cup of coffee out to the picnic table to join Mitch reading the Sunday paper.

"You're up early. Would you like me to fix you some breakfast before I meet Sarah?"

"I thought I smelled sausage, and of course I'd love some, since I'm not invited to join you ladies." he pushes his lower lip out in a pout.

"Aww. Poor baby." I pick up the funny paper to read.

"What are you doing out here if you have breakfast to fix? Where's Sarah? Is she up?"

"I'm letting the popovers cool so I can make cream puffs. Other than that, I have eggs to scramble, then I'll pack it all up. No to waking

Sarah up—she asked me not to. She wants to do it on her own, but I've not heard a peep. Have you seen the picnic basket with the plates and silverware in it?"

"I found it, washed up the dishes, and took it down before starting to read the paper. I thought it'd be one less thing for you to worry about."

"And here you were pouting about not being invited. I think you might be as excited as I am about our ladies' morning. I'd better quit lollygagging and get busy." The sound of his laughter follows me.

I'm singing as I whip the cream, fill the popovers, and dust them lightly with powdered sugar. Mitch helps by scrambling the eggs, ladling them into the warmed casserole dish, snuggling the sausages alongside, and putting it into the thermal cover, then placing it in the insulated carrier he brought in earlier.

"You can't put the cream puffs in with the warm items, so let me carry those down for you."

"I'd appreciate that. I want to be ready when Sarah gets there. I haven't heard a sound out of her room though. Oh darn. I forgot. We're going to need the little table from the workshop. Would you bring it out after we get this all carried down? I want everything to be special today. I'll give you an extra cream puff—and maybe something else sweet later." I wiggle my eyebrows. We both start to laugh.

"God, how could I resist that awkward attempt at seduction, though the whipped cream on your cheek is kind of a turn on."

"What?" I swipe my hand across my cheek and sure enough, whipped cream. But then I never claimed to be a neat cook.

We walk in easy silence. Just before we get to the turn in the path, Mitch motions for me to go on, "Go ahead. I think I've got a stick in my shoe."

I walk on ahead. I'm speechless when I see tea lights twinkling on the branches of the quaking aspen and the bushes by Nana Hawke's bench. Her lace tablecloth over a burgundy cloth covers the table. The centerpiece is a crystal bowl with colored rock on the bottom, covered with enough water to float candles with flames dancing. My darling daughter's face is beaming as she looks at me shyly. When she sees my delighted surprise, her pride is obvious. She and her dad have been up much longer than me, and they have been very busy. Tears fill my eyes as I open my arms for her. Mitch hugs us both tight, then kisses us both before he steps away.

Sarah and I eat, we talk, and even shed a few tears. Time slips quickly away. Before we know it, we've been here over two hours. We talk of many things, good and bad, what bothers us, and what we want to do differently. I'm tickled to hear her hopes and to hold her hands as she tells me about her confused feelings where her brother's concerned. For me to admit to some of the same concerns is a big step, especially the frustration and fear I feel when he stops taking his meds.

"Sometimes I want to kill him—not dead—but that part of him. Then I'm afraid that something will happen to him, and I can hardly bear it. It's not fair, Mom. It's not fair." The pain she's feeling shows in her eyes, and I want to take it away. I remind myself this is my time to just listen.

"When he's taking his meds, he's so sweet. Then, when he goes off them, he turns into this scary guy and starts trashing everything. Last time he almost cut up my picture—that first one he painted for me. If I hadn't stood between him and it, I think he would have. I was so scared. His eyes were so wild. He was breathing hard and mumbling, like he was talking to someone else. Then he started hitting his head and shouting, 'Shut up! Shut up!' He wasn't talking to me—it was like he didn't even see me. Then he threw down the knife and went running out of the house. It wasn't long after that you came home, and the cop pulled up to tell you he'd been in an accident." Her eyes are glazed, and I know she is reliving that moment.

"I thought it was my fault, Mom. I should have let him have my picture. But I couldn't, Mom. I just couldn't."

The horror of her words grips my heart like a vise. My first impulse is to reach out and stop her. Her words dredge up my worst fears. I am so goddamn angry—at Dan, at that damn illness, at God—who allowed it to happen. Yet more than anything, I'm scared to my soul that in an instant I could have lost them both. My mind is inundated by the what if's that are taking over, but I can't let her know. She needs to tell me—and I need to know. I need to hear it as much as she needs to tell it. Yet, inside, part of me is yelling, "No-no-no-no-no!"

"Oh, my God, Sarah. Why didn't you say anything? I've always told myself he wouldn't hurt any of us, especially you. You must have been so scared. Honey, don't ever keep anything like that from us again. We need to know. We not only have to protect you, but we have to protect him from himself when he's like that. Promise me that you'll never hold anything like that from us again. When you notice even the slightest change in his behavior, we need to know. Okay? He's our Dan, and we love him. We'll do whatever we can for him, but not at your expense. Ok? Deal?" I don't realize how tightly I'm holding her until she moves, trying to break away. I let her go, yet cling to her hand—I need the connection to her for a few more minutes. Once she relaxes, I do, too.

"It's a deal, and thanks, Mom. Thanks for this morning and this past week. I feel a lot better." A smile plays on her lips. "Do you think we should get the worker bee back down here to clean up this mess? Then, maybe we can talk about painting my room."

∞

Chapter 41

And just like that, it's time to go back to work. Before I know it I'm pulled back into the whirlpool that's my life—fighting to keep my head above water. All of us are running in different directions, but we work to maintain the closeness we rebuilt over the past few weeks. Mitch has picked up a couple of big jobs. Sarah started a new job at Dairy Queen. And me—same thing, different day.

Dan's doctor has asked us to come up next weekend for a staffing—where all staff members involved in his treatment will report on his progress. If all goes well, we can spend time with Dan, but we're undecided about taking Sarah.

Arriving home to an empty house once in a while can be nice, but every night this week? Instead of feeling sorry for myself, I decide a treat is in order. Sarah won't be home from work until after nine, and Mitch called to say he's finishing the job he's on before calling it a day. I draw a bath, light some candles, sprinkle in bubble bath, and pour a tall glass of iced tea. Just as I dip a toe in, the phone rings. Thinking it might be Sarah or Mitch, I hurry to answer, grateful we installed a phone in the bedroom. As I answer, I hear a click. "Damn!" I mutter. I go back to the bath. The phone rings again, and I decide to ignore it. I'm about in the tub when it rings again. Whoever is calling is persistent, so I rush to grab it. "H-hello?"

"Lillian, thank God. Why didn't you answer before? I've been ringing and ringing."

"Reggie? I know. I was about to get in the bath. What's so urgent? Is something wrong with Timmy?"

"No, nothing like that. I received a note from Dan today. He didn't say much, only that he's painting again. He asked if I would be interested in looking at some of his pictures—said it was his doctor's idea. Does this mean he's better, that he'll be coming home?"

"I don't know, Reggie. It seems you know more than I do. We're going for staffing next weekend, and hopefully, we'll be able to visit with him. We've stored some of his paintings—the angry, raging ones. It breaks my heart when he destroys his paintings, especially those that depict such beauty and joy."

"You know, Sis, the dark art might sell. Would you consider letting me sell them?"

"Reggie, I can't. It's not my choice to make, and I'm not sure when or if Dan will be able to give his consent. I'm glad he's reached out to you, though."

"I know, Sis, but keep it in mind. The money could be put in a trust for him and help with his expenses. I know how difficult it's been for you guys. This could help him to be more self-sufficient when he gets better."

"I'll talk to Mitch, and maybe we'll bring it up at the staffing. The doctors can address it with him when they think it's time. Why don't you write to them and explain what you can do. Maybe you could include a short summary of how well his art has sold over the years."

"I'll do that. I have the address—all I need is the doctor's name. Would that work?"

"That would work for me. His name is Randolph Sinclair, Psychiatrist. I know I sound hesitant, but I appreciate what you're doing. Now, how are you? And my nephew Timothy?"

We spend some time catching up before I bring the call to an end. "Reggie, I love you to pieces. I'm glad you called, but I'm sitting here in a towel while my bath is getting cold."

So much for my bath. The candles are melted, the bubbles are gone, and the water is cold. I pull the plug and drain the tub. A shower it will be.

The phone is ringing again when I step out of the shower. I can sit here all night with no calls, but when I try to take a bath or shower, it rings off the hook. "Hello."

"Mom? Are you okay?"

"Sorry, Sarah, I was rushing to get to the phone. I just stepped out of the shower. What's going on?"

"I've been asked to work till closing and help with clean up tonight. That means I won't be home until about midnight or a little after. Can I, Mom? Mr. Simmons will give me a ride home."

"I guess. Wake us when you get home."

"K, thanks, Mom. Love ya. I have to go. I've a customer."

I slip into my pj's and wander to the kitchen for a snack, wondering what's taking Mitch so long. I glance out the window and see his pickup in the driveway. I call out to him, thinking he might be in the other bathroom, but there's no answer. A light is on in the work shed, so I fix two cups of coffee to take out and see what's going on. Something pressing must have happened to take him there without coming into the house.

As I approach the shop, I hear strangling sounds. The door is ajar, so I push it open. I'm about to call out when I see him hunched over his desk, shoulders heaving. The sounds I heard are his anguished cries. My guy, who's been so strong, a pillar for us to lean on over the last few months, is sobbing his heart out. In his hand is a picture of Dan on his third birthday, dressed in a cowboy hat and boots, his pistols strapped on, and Leo by his side. He looks like he could take on the world. We had such high hopes for Danny that day.

I set the coffee cups down. "Mitch?" I whisper as I embrace him. "Shh, Mitch, it's okay." He turns to me and holds on like a drowning man to a life raft.

"I don't know, Lil. I don't know how we can keep going through this. I thought when we moved it would be easier. At the old house, everywhere I looked were reminders." He stirs in his chair. "Damn it. I've been fighting to hold it in for so long, but knowing where he is, that he's safe, has made it easier. Then we get the call to go to the staffing, and hope begins to falter. We've been here before, and look at what happened." His chest heaves as he draws a ragged breath. I've not heard the anguish in his voice in ages, and I don't know what to do. Before I can comfort him, he stands, kicks the chair, and begins to pace.

"Today, the Wilson's son, who's about Sarah's age, came to see what I was doing. His folks have been divorced for years, and he rarely sees his dad. When he asked questions about what I was working on, I offered to let him help me. Lil, he was so happy, and he's a quick learner." He looks at me with tears shimmering in his eyes.

His voice is so low and strained that I can barely understand him when he continues. "On the way home, it hit me. This is what Dan and I have been cheated out of. This is what I thought our future would be when he was the shining boy in this picture." He shakes it, and I'm afraid he's going to throw it. Instead, he draws in a ragged breath, staring with empty eyes. "Once more I have a glimmer of hope that we might do something together, a project, maybe, when he comes home that will bring us close together. Then I remember how it's gone in the past. What's going to be different this time?" Again, he chokes and can't continue. He stops pacing and looks lost, standing there, holding the picture, looking around like he's searching for the answer.

"When I got home, I wanted to come in, grab you, and hold you. I wanted to reassure you that everything would be okay, at the same time reassuring myself. But I couldn't face you with that lie. We know how this movie ends, Lil. We know the cycle will continue if he quits taking his meds. History tells us he will quit. Why is it, Lil? Why does he quit them? Does he miss the voices? They seem to be his only friends. He doesn't relate to people, so he remains isolated, even to us. With Sarah, it's a bit different. She seems to understand better than we do, but it's so unfair to her. What are we going to do? I love him so much. If only I could rip those voices from his head." His hand clenches—he throws his arm up, releases his grip—like throwing a ball. "I want a do over." Those words are spoken so quietly I can barely hear them. He's run out of energy. We hold on to each other. I have no answers, and he doesn't expect any.

Slowly, he pulls away, wiping his face and blowing his nose. Looking at the picture one more time, he brushes his fingers to his lips, and touches that little bright-eyed boy and gently lays the picture down.

"Let's go in the house, Lil. I need a hot shower. Isn't it about time for Sarah to be home?"

I tell him about her call as we walk to the house. I see a flicker of disappointment. He's been looking forward to seeing her.

While he showers, I make a pot of coffee and take a couple of cups to the bedroom. He's just coming out of the bathroom in all his glory, his skin pink from the hot shower, toweling his hair dry. When I hand him his cup and trace my fingers down his chest, I'm rewarded with a salute from the nether region. He puts his coffee down, drops his towel, and reaches for me. Our lovemaking is frantic as we share our pain and assure each other with our bodies. Once we reach our peak and beyond, we lie spent, holding each other.

Mitch turns to me. "I love him so much. Sometimes I wonder if we're being punished, and I'm afraid we might lose him." A tear drops on my breast where his head is lying. "The thought of losing him rips my heart out. I'm afraid that my anger at his illness is telling God that I don't appreciate Dan. But I do. Yet every day that fear is with me in the good times and the bad. The challenge is learning to enjoy the day that he's having a good day—not live in anticipation of when it's bad again. Can't we kill the illness and save the boy? We have to love and appreciate the whole picture. Just think, if he didn't have the voices, maybe he wouldn't have the talent. I'd not want that. Our life would be missing the beauty he sees." He strokes my arm.

While we lie holding each other, I tell him of the call from Reggie. He's as surprised as I was. We discuss it, then I offer to fix him something to eat. I'm rewarded with a gentle snore. I snuggle close and join him in sleep.

Chapter 42

Although we arrive early, bringing Sarah with us, by the time we sign in and we're taken to the conference room for the meeting, it's almost 10 a.m. Even as I gaze out the window overlooking the well-tended hospital grounds where a few people are enjoying the sun, I feel the tension creeping into my muscles. The door opens, and Dr. Sinclair enters with four others following him. He reaches out a hand to Mitch.

"Welcome. I'm Dr. Sinclair." He motions to his left, "This is John Marlow, the charge nurse on Dan's ward; Mari Jewell, case worker; Lawrence Scott, occupational therapist; and Mick McBride, community liaison. Mick will be bringing Dan for home visits and making arrangements in your community when it's time for discharge. If you don't mind waiting a few minutes, I've arranged for some refreshments that should be arriving any minute.

Everyone shakes hands, but when Dr. Sinclair comes to Sarah; he takes both her hands in his and pats one lightly. "I'm especially glad to see you here, Sarah. It's important to have the whole family involved. If you have any concerns, please feel free to share them." His eyes crinkle when he smiles at her. She nods, and I see her begin to relax.

A cheerful lady rolls a trolley in with carafes of water, a pitcher of juice, and two pots of coffee on a hotplate. She arranges them all on the credenza, along with a plate of sweet rolls, cups, glasses, saucers, and napkins. "Enjoy," she says as she leaves.

My stomach rumbles. Damn. We should have stopped for breakfast. Mr. McBride reaches for the coffee pot. "Grab a cup if you want coffee, and I'll pour." As we enjoy the sweet rolls and beverages, we share small talk with the staff, and I begin to relax—nothing like breaking bread together to bring people closer.

When everyone has finished eating, Dr. Sinclair says, "Let's get started. I know you've come a long way and are anxious to know how Dan's doing. John, our charge nurse, will go first as he has the most day-to-day contact with Dan."

Mr. Marlow shuffles a few papers, clears his throat, and begins. "When Dan first came to my ward he was withdrawn, with flat affect—meaning he didn't reveal any emotions. He followed directions, but did not initiate any interactions with staff or co-patients. He showed no interest in television, jigsaw puzzles, or any of the items for patients to enjoy in the patient lounge. In fact, we had difficulty getting him to come out of his room most of the time. I am happy, however, to report that in the last few weeks he is more animated, especially when high-speed chases are a part of a TV program. When we saw his reactions to anything vehicle-related, we brought in magazines, jigsaw puzzles, etc., with that theme. He blew through the puzzles in record time. About that time, he began asking for art supplies. He is more outgoing, cooperative, and even began initiating conversations with a few of the staff and a couple of the patients. Although he still tends to isolate himself, he's more willing to join small groups of three or four. If there are more than that, he withdraws. He enjoys being outside and takes a sketchpad with him wherever he goes. His overall physical health is good at this time. He enjoys weight lifting, using the treadmill, and he exercises when he is on his own, but he won't participate in games of basketball or any group sports." He pauses, and then asks if we have any questions.

"I don't at this time. How about you and Sarah?" Mitch asks. We both shake our heads.

The rest of the staff give similar reports. I was hoping for something different. What I'm hearing fits the pattern of his previous hospitalizations. As much as I know better, I still hope for that miracle cure. I want them to tell us he's fixed and will be a normal young man.

We take a short break after more reports. It feels good to move around. Sarah and I visit the ladies room. I jot down a few questions I may ask to clarify some of what's been said. Dr. Sinclair is the only one who hasn't given his report. When we return to the conference room, the coffee has been refilled. I pour myself a fresh cup. Mitch is talking to Mr. Scott, the occupational therapist, who told us more about Dan's talent for art and his knowledge of vehicles. He stated what we already knew, that he should pursue any type of work related to art or vehicles once he is well enough for release.

"Let's take our seats again," Dr. Sinclair says. Once everyone is re-settled, he starts. "When Dan first came to us, as I'm sure you remember, he was experiencing violent outbursts, responding to voices un-heard by others, and he was uncooperative and had to be restrained. In reviewing his past records, we found a prior diagnosis of schizoaffective disorder with possible bipolar. The recommended course of treatment was Haldol for schizophrenia and lithium for the bipolar. These medi-cations appeared to work quite well as long as he kept taking them. According to reports since his last discharge, he did follow up for about three months with his local psychiatrist and was taking his medica-tions. Apparently, he was doing well until friends encouraged him to drink with them. He quit his meds, and his drinking increased. His behaviors became more and more erratic and out of control. When he was arrested for being drunk and disorderly, he resisted arrest, and the local police, who knew his history of mental illness, transported him to the psychiatric hospital in your town. I understand that his first hos-pitalization with us was the result of a similar experience, but he drove his newly restored pickup through the front of the body shop where he worked. He was upset because the shop had sold, and he couldn't work there any longer. I recall that he did most of the work on that pickup. It was a work of art. Is that right?"

Memories of that night come rushing back. "Yes, that's right. The first hospitalization happened when he crashed his pickup into the body shop, totaling it. He's lucky he only broke his arm and wasn't hurt worse. I wish I could show you a picture of the mural he painted on that truck. We've recently found out something more about that night that concerns us even more."

"What is that, Mrs. Hawke?"

"He went to the house that day and only Sarah was there. He was about to cut up a picture that he'd painted for Sarah years ago." Her hand is gripping mine.

"Why wasn't that in the chart?" Dr. Sinclair asks, a bit sharply.

"I didn't tell." Sarah's voice is barely a whisper. "I didn't tell anyone until a couple weeks ago. I didn't want him to be in worse trouble." A lone tear trickles from her eye.

Dr. Sinclair looks at her with compassion and says softly, "That had to be so frightening for you, Sarah. Is there anything we can do for you?"

"No, Dr. Sinclair. Mom and Dad have been really good. We've talked a lot about it and how I feel about what happened."

"Are you concerned it will happen again?" he asks quietly.

"Yes," she whispers, clutching our hands while fighting back tears.

"I can understand that, Sarah. While we can't promise you Dan will never have another breakdown, I will promise you that we'll do everything we can to help him. Hopefully, he'll stay on his medications this time. Okay? I also recommend the three of you get some counseling before his discharge and continue after he comes home." He says it firmly, looking from me to Mitch and back to me, holding my eyes.

"You do know that Lillian works at the psychiatric hospital as an addictions counselor, don't you?"

"Yes, Mr. Hawke. I am aware of that. I also know that those of us who work in the field are some of the worst at taking care of ourselves. We tend to assume because we have the book knowledge and we help others, we should have all the answers. That's one of the biggest lies we tell ourselves and the biggest disservice to our families. What do you think, Mrs. Hawke?" He stares into my eyes, leaving me no place to hide.

"You're right, Dr. Sinclair." I say, fighting back tears that choke my voice and threaten to spill. I grip tight to the arm of the chair, willing myself not to let the tears fall—afraid if I start I'll not be able to stop. I take a sip of water to settle myself. "I agree. I definitely think we need to get some counseling. So much has gone on this past year, and it doesn't all pertain to Dan. We need to make time and quit waiting for when we have the time." I look at Mitch and see that little frown that appears when he doesn't want to talk about something that makes him uncomfortable. I look at Sarah. She's pulled her hands away and is sitting quietly looking at them. "Mitch? Sarah? Will you go with me?"

"I-I think I'd like to go, Daddy. There are things I don't say because I don't want to make more problems for you and Mom. Sometimes I feel so angry I want to throw things or break things. I'm afraid that maybe something like what Dan has is happening to me. Please?"

For a minute I wonder if he's even heard her. He stares straight ahead. Finally, his shoulders slump, he puts his arm around her shoulder, and pulls her close. "If you want, pumpkin. We'll go." He kisses the top of her head, and she rewards him with a smile and a big hug.

"Good, I'm glad you agree. Would you like a recommendation, or do you have someone in mind?"

"I don't want it to be someone Lillian works with every day. I'd rather it was someone who doesn't work at her hospital or even knows us."

"I agree with Mitch. We'd like a referral, even if we have to drive to Sheridan. If you could give us a call or have someone call with the information, we'd appreciate it. Now, can we get back to Dan?"

Dr. Sinclair instructs Mr. McBride, and he agrees to handle it.

"As for Dan, he's not ready for discharge even though he's shown marked improvement. The plan is to continue on the same course of treatment that was successful up to a point last time. What we will do differently is develop a more structured aftercare program for him. He'll have daily support, not just by you, but by professionals. There's a new halfway house there in your town. We'll get his name on the waiting list, but this will work to our advantage as he's not ready anyway. Are you familiar with it, Mrs. Hawke?"

"Yes. Serenity House. We've used it a couple of times, and I'm impressed with their program."

"We'll start with a home visit first." He then lays out the plan of treatment for Dan to be admitted to the halfway house, with the length of time determined by the staff there, then to independent living. At that time, he'd need to be self-reliant and have some kind of work. A case manager will assist with this and help him with money management, grocery shopping, and meal planning, as well as to supervise him as he accepts responsibility for his medications, and in building a foundation for him to live on his own.

I'm so overwhelmed that I almost forget about Reggie's phone call when Dr. Sinclair asks if there are any questions. When I bring it up, I discover that he had suggested Dan write to her.

Everyone agrees it would be good for him to sell his art if he wants to, because it could be a way for him to be self-supporting—as long as he has someone looking out for his interest. We assure them that his Aunt Reggie will definitely do that.

Finally, it's time to wrap things up so we can see Dan. As we're gathering our things, Ms. Jewell goes to fetch Dan. Mr. Scott asks for a moment.

"I want you to know I've not seen a talent like Dan's before—it seems to flow from him. We say he's non-communicative, but his art speaks volumes. One picture he did last week took my breath away. It's of a young boy pulling a wooden wagon with a little girl holding a Raggedy Ann and Andy, with a blue bunny rabbit sitting in front of her and a scruffy little dog alongside. It's amazing."

Sarah gasps, "That's my picture. The one he was going to cut up that night." Eyes wide, she looks from Mr. Scott to her dad and me.

"That makes sense. He told me he broke it, and he has to fix it. I think it will help if you let him know it's not ruined. His memories are jumbled, and he doesn't know what's real and what's not. It's been a pleasure to meet you. I've seen your faces in his works. He's a special young man. We're going to help him learn to navigate life."

The door opens, and Dan walks through.

Chapter 43

Dan stands hesitantly in the doorway, glances toward us, lingering on Sarah's face for a second before his eyes look down at the floor. As much as I want to rush to him and hug him, I know I don't dare. When Sarah steps forward, reaching for his hand, I hold my breath, knowing how difficult this has to be for her.

"Dan?" she says quietly, "I'm glad to see you, big brother. Please, won't you look at me?" Her voice is choked.

He raises his eyes to her, searching her face. "Sissy? I sorry." He lets her take his hand.

"It's okay. You don't have to be sorry."

"Did Dan hurt his sissy?" He's becoming agitated.

"No, Dan. You didn't hurt me." She smiles easily. "I miss you, big brother."

"You miss me?" He asks, like a child needing reassurance.

"Yes, and so do Mom and Dad. Won't you say hi to them?"

"It's good to see you, Son." Mitch holds out his hand. Dan takes it, and they shake. "You're looking good. I hear you've been doing some exercises."

"Good to see you, too. I been lifting weights and use the treadmill. It helps me when I get upset."

My heart leaps as I watch him. He's certainly not my little boy anymore. He's taller than Mitch, who stands 6' 2". I can see the muscles on his arms—he's filling out from a boy to a man. Other than what they call the flat affect and his dull eyes, he looks like any other young man.

"Dan? Would you mind if I give you a hug?" Hesitantly, I approach him.

"Hi, Mom." he says shyly, moving to meet me. "A little hug, please?" I give him a small hug. He steps back, pulls out a chair, and sits down. I wonder if it's to protect himself from more physical contact. He pulls out a chair beside him. "Sissy, do you want sit by me?"

She takes him up on his offer while we sit across from them. She tells him about her job, and he asks if she gets free ice cream. Dan loves ice cream. I know we don't have much time, so I ask him about Aunt Reggie.

"I did write An Reggie. Dr. Sinclair say to. Does she want paintings? I do that?"

"Yes, you can. Dr. Sinclair and Mr. Scott think it's a good idea, and we agree. If you want, you can pick some to send to her. Maybe Mr. Scott can help you with that."

"I like Mr. Scott. He help me. He like to paint, and he like trucks. We talk bout trucks. I tell him bout my pickup." He stops, looks around, takes a deep breath. "I think I broke my truck. I not member. It like a dream. Dad? Did I break truck?"

"I'm afraid you did, Dan. I'm sorry, Son."

"His shoulders droop, "It not bad dream. Can we fix, dad? Can we?"

"No, Dan. But maybe we could get another old one to fix up."

"Don't want to. Might break it, too. Don't need no truck."

He sounds defeated, and it breaks my heart. "Dan, we don't need to make that decision today. I know you're sad it's broken. Maybe you and Mr. Scott could talk about it?"

"I do that. Mr. Scott good to talk to."

Ms. Jewell reminds us it's about his lunchtime. Dan stands up, ready to go. We're able to walk with him to the reception area, and it's then I see some of his paintings on the walls. I wish I'd taken more notice when we came in. We'll be parting ways in reception.

He doesn't want to stop to say goodbye. He's only interested in lunch, but we all manage to get in another quick hug. As he's about to leave, I see a painting on an easel—a breathtaking picture of a 1955 green Ford pickup with the most beautiful mural running down the sides, over the hood, and wrapping around the tailgate. Mesmerized, I feel like I could reach out and open the door. It's standing in front of a two-story Craftsman home with a wrap-around porch—our home, Dan's truck.

"Dan? This is beautiful." I manage to say before he leaves the room.

He pauses, "Yes, I try to fix." Then he walks out without a backward glance.

Before leaving, we tell Ms. Jewell that the picture is the exact image of Dan's truck. She'll tell Dr. Sinclair. They've asked Dan, but he never said.

Although short, it was a good visit. We're on our way before I realize we didn't mention our move to the cottage.

"Mom, why don't we take some pictures and send them to him to let him know. We can tell him how happy we are to be close to the creek and his favorite fishing spot."

"That's a great idea. We could be sitting at a table by the creek and having a picnic when we take pictures. We can write, wish you were here. What do you think, Mitch?"

"I like the idea. Hopefully, he'll be prepared for the cottage when he comes home. I've got another idea." He slows the car down and pulls to the side of the road. "I think Sarah should get some wheel time and let the old man kick back."

She's beside herself as she settles behind the wheel, adjusts the mirror, and slowly pulls back on the highway. With almost 400 miles to go, the winding Wind River Canyon and the Cloud Peak Mountain pass to navigate at slower speeds, we have a long trip ahead of us. But, with all three of us taking turns we'll sleep in our own bed tonight.

∞

Chapter 44

The week in Casper was exhausting, and I'm glad to be heading home. These in-services are necessary to keep my certifications, but I've never really enjoyed them. The session on Dual Diagnosis that I'd been looking forward to was a rehash of what I've already learned, and I was disappointed in the low turnout for the Family Therapy Workshop. Although we need to include families more, insurance doesn't cover it, so it's becoming increasingly more difficult to keep these programs in place. Sadly, we seem to be losing ground instead of moving forward. While many changes have been made since I began in my field, they've not always been an improvement. I'm more frustrated than ever, but now's not the time for me to consider a change of career—I do love working with clients. It's all the other administrative crap coming from the home office in California that gets to me.

I'm almost home—home where Mitch and Sarah will be waiting to welcome me. Hopefully, with a pot of coffee or hot chocolate, then a good night's sleep in my own bed. As I pull into the driveway, music is blaring from the house. It's a good thing we don't have neighbors who live closer. All the lights in the house are on. There's no one to greet me or help with my luggage. *Nobody! Nada!* Only rock and roll—loud enough to break an eardrum. I yank my suitcase out of the backseat, stomp toward the house, and jerk the door open.

"Sarah! Mitchell! What the hell's going on?" When I finally find the source of the music, I turn the stereo off. Glancing in the kitchen, I'm appalled to see that it looks like a bomb's gone off. Where there was once a wall and a door is a gaping hole, the table and chairs are pushed against the wall, and the counters are covered with dust.

"Hey? Who turned off my music?" Sarah rounds the corner from her bedroom. Paint spatters cover her coveralls and smear her face. There's even some in her hair. *What color? Black?* "Oh, hi, Mom. When did you get home? I didn't hear you come in."

I tell myself not to yell. *Don't yell 'how the hell could you hear me?'* Breathe. "I could hear that music blaring before I opened the car door. What have we told you about that, young lady? You're not only going to blow out the speaker but also your eardrums. And what color is that? Black? Tell me you're painting a piece of furniture and not a wall. And where the hell is your father, and what has he done to my kitchen?" My voice goes from calm to a full-blown yell as I watch her morph from the excited, pleased, young lady to a deflated little girl.

"Dad said I could pick my color—my room, my colors. And this mess? He wanted to surprise you, but he got called away for a job. Sorry I had the music so high. I wanted to hear it while I'm painting. I'm sorry you came home to such a mess. I'm sorry Dad and I are such a disappointment." She swipes a tear off her cheek, smearing more paint, turns and stalks toward her bedroom.

I'm left standing there, wavering between shame, justified anger, and self-pity. I start to go after her, stop, then decide to find the damn coffee pot and make myself a cup. I glance through the hole in the wall toward the workshop. Mitch talked about making a studio for Dan—looks like he's made progress. A scar across the yard shows where sewer and water lines were laid. Sunset reflecting with shades of orange, red, and violet on new windows is breathtaking. The knots in my shoulders begin to loosen as I see all Mitch has accomplished in a short week.

I walk toward the workshop, and see Sarah's contribution there—a wooden plaque, DAN'S STUDIO, burned with her wood burning set, and a picture of an old pickup stained a rich mahogany. As I trace my fingers over the letters, there isn't time to look inside. There's something more important I need to do. Returning to the kitchen, instead of coffee I decide to fix hot chocolate, enough to fill two large mugs, pile them high with marshmallows and carry them to Sarah's room.

"Sarah?" I tap lightly on the door. "Sarah? I'm sorry. Can I come in?" I wonder if she'll answer.

Finally I hear her say, "Yes."

"Honey, could you open the door—my hands are full."

A chair scrapes. She sniffles slightly, and then the door opens. She stands back, watching me with apprehension.

Keeping my eyes focused on her face, I offer her a mug. "I made us cocoa with lots of marshmallows. I even dug out your favorite mug, so I had lots of room for them. Peace offering?"

"Peace offering accepted." She takes a ragged breath and looks toward the walls.

Keep calm, I tell myself, *no matter what, keep calm.* Breathing deeply, I look around. The wall with her big window is painted high gloss black, with glossy white on the window frame. The rest of the walls in the room are white with black trim. It's beautiful. In the corner a small table is marked off with squares that she is painting in alternating colors of black and white—a checkerboard. One of the wooden chairs is painted black, the other white. My clever girl. How can I be upset about this?

"Mom? Are you mad?"

"Oh, no, Sarah. It's beautiful. What a wonderful job you've done." I can't stop smiling. "Even if you have as much paint on you as you do on your walls. I'm sorry about my reaction when I first got home. I'm really tired, and it was all a shock. I was feeling a little sorry for myself, thinking about the week I had. I didn't even consider you and Dad and what you might be doing while I was gone. I hope Dad hasn't bitten off a bit too much to finish in a week. Do you think we'll have deer in the kitchen when we wake up?"

Finally, a smile from her. "Yeah, I guess he might have. Maybe I did, too? I'm not sure I can even find my bed." I have to agree—her room is a mess.

A door slams. Mitch is home. He rushes through the front door just as we reach the living room.

"Oh, God, Lil. I'm so sorry. I thought I'd have it finished before you got home." He speaks so fast all the words run together.

"Slow down, dad. You missed the fireworks, and you can be thankful that you did. I've already calmed the beast, so you're welcome."

"Was she really mad?" Mitch grins at Sarah.

I answer for her, "Mad might be too small a word for it. I'm afraid I was over the top. In my defense, I expected to come home to my loved ones waiting, coffee ready, and a nice dinner to feed the hungry worker, home from the hills. Instead I got—"

"No one waiting? Music blaring? Your kitchen a disaster. No coffee. No dinner. No love."

"That about covers it, Mitch. What do you have to say for yourself?" Although I try to sound stern, I can't help but smile.

He holds up a large, brown, paper sack. "I bring dinner, my lady, if you'll follow me to the patio. Sarah, will you bring the best china and some silverware and try not to get paint on things."

"About that, Mitch. What were you thinking? Letting our daughter turn her room into a black dungeon?" Sarah bursts into peals of laughter, and we can't help but join in.

∞

Chapter 45

Summer morphs into fall, and the morning air turns cool. The trees are dressed in hues of gold, orange, and reds. School starts, and we're as scattered as the leaves in the wind. Sarah is starting her senior year, Mitch's handyman business is keeping him busy, and my job changes with each program we revamp. We're down to one full time A/D Counselor—me, and one part time. Our family program is a thing of the past, and I miss it. I love working with families.

Since shortly after our meeting at the state hospital, we've been going to counseling. I look forward to the sessions. Mitch dragged his feet at first, but he's more relaxed since we began. In the beginning, it was difficult for me to relax and not take over the sessions. Mr. Bacon reminded me gently that I was a client and not a facilitator. When I realized how much harder it is to take a long, deep look into myself, I felt pretty sheepish. We've been encouraged to keep a journal, and it's all I can do to keep from asking Sarah and Mitch if they're doing their assignments. It's much easier to see what they need to do than it is to look at myself.

Mr. McBride called to tell us Dan's coming for a visit next weekend. They will be flying. Ms. Jewell, it turns out, is a pilot with a small plane. They took Dan to see the plane and gauge how he would react to flying before they solidified the plans. He loves it. Mr. McBride said he might love planes now as much as he loves his trucks. He will still be coming with him. The rest of the plan is for him to spend time at Serenity House as well as with us. I'm excited, yet apprehensive—new territories are being explored.

"He said Dan liked the plane? And he wasn't scared?" Sarah asked when I explained the plan to her and Mitch.

"That's what Mr. McBride said."

"That makes sense though, don't you think? It has wheels and all. You said we meet them at the airport? Maybe they'll give us a look at the plane?" Mitch sounds as excited to see the plane as to have Dan home.

"You want a plane ride, don't you?" I ask, laughing.

"I wouldn't turn it down. But think, Lil, this is a new adventure for him, and it sounds like he's embraced it. That's progress, don't you think?"

"Definitely progress."

Friday afternoon arrives quickly. Dan will be landing soon. He'll spend the night at Serenity House tonight, then all day Saturday with us—and possibly the night—then fly out early Sunday morning.

We arrive a half hour early, and Sarah keeps fiddling with the radio. I reach out to stop her. "Are you okay?"

"I'm a little nervous. Is that bad?"

"No, I'm nervous, too. I want to see him, but I'm not sure how to treat him. I guess we'll have to take our cue from him. You were amazing with him when we saw him at the hospital. If you approach him like that again, I think it'll be fine. I am concerned how he's going to act once we get to Serenity House and the new people he'll have to meet."

"But Mom, he's had to mix with more people at the hospital, hasn't he? If he wasn't able to handle it there, they wouldn't bring him to Serenity House, would they?"

Before I can answer, Mitch calls us, pointing to the sky. "Here they come!" He's like a little kid.

We watch as the plane circles and lands. Dan is sitting by one of the windows, a big smile on his face, and he's waving to us. I almost forget to wave back in my shock at how animated he looks. I think this plane is a good thing after all.

Dan is the first one out of the plane. He hurries across the tarmac in his stiff-legged walk. "I fly, Dad. You see me? I fly! I love planes, Dad! Planes good as trucks, maybe gooder." He grips Mitch's extended hand, pumping his arm up and down. "Dad, come see Ms. Mari plane." He pulls Mitch toward the plane.

Sarah and I follow, waiting for him to notice us, and maybe feeling a little jealous as we watch father and son walk around the plane.

"Ms. Mari, can Dad go in plane?" She agrees, and they are almost to the plane when Dan turns abruptly. "Sarah, Mama, you come see plane?" They wait for us to join them before following Ms. Jewell into the plane. It's smaller than I expected.

Once inside she shows us the cockpit and explains the instrument panel. I'm surprised when she asks if we'd like a short ride. I'm not sure, but Sarah, Mitch, and Dan are all for it. So, as Mr. McBride goes into the airport to arrange a rental car, Ms. Mari takes us up, presenting a breathtaking bird's eye view of our little town, the lake, and the mountains. Like the others, I don't want to land. How I wish I could bottle Dan's exuberance. He's practically shivering with excitement. Our concern that he would be frightened was wasted energy, as is most worry.

Dan rides with us to Serenity House. From the back seat, Sarah and I listen as he and Mitch talk about planes all the way. He explains that it's a 1958 Apache 160 and tells more about it—much I miss as he's speaking low to his dad. It's only when we're almost there that he begins to run down. He notices familiar places, and he begins naming them.

"JCPenney, where Mom buys our clothes, Dairy Queen, Sissy work there, Gatchell Drug have good ice cream sodas and Mom's favorite broasted chicken," he continues as we drive through town.

Ms. Jewell and Mr. McBride are waiting for us when we park in front of Serenity House. Dan hesitates before joining them on the covered porch where they have a pitcher of iced tea and glasses ready for us. Mr. McBride asks the two house managers to join us, so they can meet Dan before we go in to meet the residents. Xandra is a motherly woman, with graying hair pulled up in a messy bun. She's ample in stature, with deep laugh lines and sparkling dark-brown eyes. She extends her hand to Dan in welcome. After a moment's hesitation, he takes it. She explains she is the house manager, in charge of daily operations. Douglas is the night manager. He spends nights at the facility to make sure all rules are followed and takes care of any problems.

All residents are assigned duties, as well as being responsible for keeping their rooms neat, doing their laundry, and any personal needs. Residents and staff care for a big garden in back. She explains that the rules of no drugs or alcohol are also a part of the contract Dan will sign if or when he comes here to stay. He relaxes as she and Douglas answer our questions—until a bell rings suddenly.

I want to yell "no-o-o," when Dan jerks, looks around, and his hands begin to flutter. Sarah reaches out to him, patting his arm to calm him.

"Hey, Dan. Shh, big brother. It's okay. I think it's the dinner bell?" She looks to Xandra for confirmation. "Yep, dinner. Dan, are you hungry?"

"Yes, Sissy, I hungry. We eat now?"

Xandra leads us into the large dining room where the residents are gathering for dinner. Dan chooses a chair at the head of the table so he doesn't have to worry that someone will touch him. Introductions are made as we join them to share the meal. Served family style is a large bowl of spaghetti and meatballs, green salad, and garlic bread. Dan reaches for the spaghetti when Xandra stops him.

"Sorry, Dan. We say Grace here before we eat. Okay?"

"Okay." He folds his hands and bows his head as the prayer is said.

The meal is delicious, and the atmosphere is quite pleasant. Seeing the environment he'll be staying in after his release is a relief. He eats heartily, but I can tell the excitement of the day is catching up with him. He knows he'll be staying here—we've barely finished eating when he asks to be shown his room.

"Ms. Xandra, Mr. Douglas, I stay here tonight? I tired. I go bed? Dad, I need suitcase from pickup." As he and Mitch go to get his suitcase, Sarah and I help to clear the table and give our compliments to the cook.

Douglas gives us a short tour before taking us upstairs where the bedrooms are. Dan will be sharing the room with another resident,

Sam, who's been there for three months, and will be moving into his own place soon. He shows Dan where to put his suitcase and clothes, where the bathroom is, and his bed.

"Thank you, Sam. I be a good roomie. Not bother you. I go bed now?" He looks at us expectantly.

"Is that our cue to go?" laughs Sarah.

"Yes, Sissy. You go. I sleep. I glad you here, and you, Mama, I glad you, too. But I tired. See you tomorrow?"

We've been dismissed as only Dan can do. At least he allows us all to give him a quick hug as we arrange to pick him up at eight the next morning.

Chapter 46

We're up early, ready to get Dan. We want to be there before breakfast—I'm planning to make his favorites, pancakes, bacon, and eggs. He's always loved his pancakes with lots of peanut butter.

When we get to Serenity House Dan is pacing on the porch. There's no place to park in front so Mitch has to park a few car lengths away. Dan's standing, still staring at us, when we get out of the pickup.

"I thought you not stop. I thought you change mind."

"No, Buddy. I needed room to park."

"Hey, Dan. I hope you haven't had breakfast yet. Have you? I thought I'd make my special pancakes. You still like pancakes, don't you?"

"Yes, I like pancakes and peanut butter. I can have peanut butter?"

"Of course, you can. Let's get you signed out so we can go home."

I notice he has his suitcase with him. "Aren't you going to sleep here tonight?"

"I told Mr. Doug I want to sleep home. He said I could after he talked to Ms. Mari."

As we go through town, he points out the businesses he recognizes again. When we pass the old construction yard, he points to our name on the side of the old shop. The new owners haven't done much with it. Mitch now has the smaller shop. "Hawke Construction" is also painted on the side of it. We don't talk about the sale. Now's not the time. The closer we get to the cottage, the more nervous I become.

As we turn toward the cottage, Dan shifts uneasily in his seat. Sarah grips my hand tighter. Mitch tries to distract him by talking, but it doesn't work. By the time we pull in the driveway, Dan's hand begins the flutter, the signal of his growing agitation.

Mitch turns off the ignition. "Here we are, Dan. Home and Mom's good cooking."

This is when we face our biggest fear, the reality of our move and how Dan will react. Although we anticipate his reaction, we hope for a different outcome. Instead of becoming angry and defiant, he reacts like a confused child. I want to reach out and comfort him as I do Mitch and Sarah when they're in pain. Without thinking I reach toward him, but Mitch shakes his head. Not now—it would be like touching a frightened deer. *I must not startle him.* How we handle the next few minutes will set the tone for the success or failure of this trial visit. I can barely breathe.

"Dan, didn't Dr. Sinclair tell you we moved and about the changes we've made?"

"I think so. I don't know. I don't understand. But, dad, I don't want that old lady to yell at me. I do remember—she not like me." Poor Mitch, he's fighting to keep calm, but I know how those words hurt him. He was upset with his mom for the way she treated Dan. She even called the police one night when Dan was only retrieving the fishing pole he'd left by the creek. She saw him walking on the path to the creek and reported him as a burglar, then denied knowing it was him. We wanted to believe her, but we were aware that every time she looked at him, she saw Chris, Mitch's brother. All the anger and pain she carried spilled over on Dan.

"Dan?" Sarah said quietly. "Nana Hawke doesn't live here anymore. She died, remember? She's in heaven. She can't yell at you any more. Please, Dan, we want to show you our new home. Won't you come and see?"

"She in heaven, with Gamma, Leo, and my friend Carl? Gamma talks to me, Sarah. She not tell me. Gamma won't let her say bad things to me."

"Does Gamma talk to you often?"

"Not in long time. Dr. Sinclair make me take medicine, makes my voices quiet. I miss hearing Gamma voice. She help me be good. Why can't medicine leave good voices and take bad ones?"

"I wish they could, Buddy. I'm sorry my mom, your nana, wasn't as kind as your gamma. But like Sarah said, she's not here, and this is our home now. We all miss the old house, Son, but we had to sell it. Tell you what, why don't you and I take a walk down by the creek while Mom and Sarah start breakfast. Lil? Do you think it's warm enough to have it on the deck? We'll take it a step at a time." He opens the pickup door and gets out, not waiting for an answer, and slowly begins to walk down the path. Dan hesitates before opening his door and joining him.

Sarah and I watch them walk away, father and son, strolling down the path. Dan's a good inch or two taller than his dad now, all grown up—on the outside. When I see them like that, it's a bitter pill to swallow because his mind will never catch up. Their relationship will never be an easy one, nor will Sarah or I ever have that with him. Once more, I'm pissed at the lot in life Dan's been given. He looks so normal. People expect him to behave in a manner appropriate to the age he appears. When he doesn't, many react in frustration and anger, just as Mother Hawke had done. Angrily I wipe a tear that's escaped in spite of my attempt to hold them in. I need to be strong for Sarah, and for Dan.

I feel her head on my shoulder and a hug holding me tight. "Mom, it's not fair, it's not. He looks okay, but he's always struggling to be okay. Is he going to be all right this time? Do you think he'll be able to come in the house? Do you think he'll like his studio?"

"I don't know, pumpkin. I don't know." I square my shoulders and give her another quick hug. "But what I do know is Dad's right, we take it one step at a time. I also know if we don't have pancakes started by the time they come back, we will have a crisis." I find a couple of Kleenex, hand her one and use one to wipe my face and blow my nose. "We're going to make this work with patience, understanding, and love. This is our Dan, and this might be the best and brightest version of him we're going to get. Remember how excited he was yesterday. We've never seen anything like that before, and I'm not going to be sad about it. So, let's get this party started."

Sarah gives a choked laugh, wipes her tears, and takes a deep breath. "Yes, today we're going to follow his lead, aren't we? And you're right. If we don't have those pancakes ready, we're going to have a problem—not only with Dan, but Dad, too." It's good to see her smile.

I start a fire in the barbeque, and while I'm gathering everything I need to fix breakfast, Sarah cleans the new workstation Mitch built around the barbeque/fireplace, as well as the table and chairs. We'll use the cast iron griddle for pancakes and the skillets for bacon and eggs.

Using the indirect heat from the fire on one side to heat the griddle and skillets, I start cooking the bacon, using one piece to grease the griddle. There's nothing like the smell of bacon cooking. It's like the siren song calling the sailors, and it worked.

"Dan and I smelled the bacon and thought we'd better get here for our breakfast. Right, Dan?"

"Yep."

"Coffee's on in the kitchen? You want some, Dan? Well, come on. Let's get it. The ladies are busy." Mitch goes into the kitchen. Sarah and I hold our breath as Dan hesitates, then follows his dad into the house. I breathe out. The ice has been broken.

Chapter 47

A stack of pancakes, eight eggs over easy, and a pound of bacon disappear as though inhaled, and I've barely sat down. We sit in easy silence on the deck, watching birds flit back and forth between feeders. I don't want to break the spell by speaking. Having us all together is such a joy, but I notice Dan begin to squirm and look around.

"What's wrong, Dan?"

"I need bathroom." He looks toward the creek.

"Come on, big brother, follow me," Sarah says and walks into the house. He looks at me first, then follows her. Mother Nature wins this battle. She chatters to him easily as they go in the house—another step taken.

"That went pretty good." I hear the relief in Mitch's voice. "You outdid yourself with breakfast, Lil. Let me help you clean up. Do you think I should put another log on the fire first, so we can hang out here instead of in the house?"

"Why don't we ask him what he'd like?"

"Sounds good." He hugs me, then we stand holding each other, listening to the sounds of our children's voices. It's mostly Sarah, but once in a while we hear Dan's low rumble. She must be showing him around.

We've finished cleaning up when they make their way back to the kitchen. Poor Dan looks a bit shell-shocked. Sarah didn't leave him much room to object to the grand tour. At first he stands shyly by the door taking in the kitchen. The only thing similar to the old house is the island and the bar stools. He pulls one out and sits down with his elbows on the counter. "My place." He's picked the second stool. He seems much more at ease, as though this feels like home for him for the first time since we arrived. And he's right—it is his place, the same stool he's used since he could crawl up on it.

"But Dan has no room? No bed?" Confused, he looks from his dad to me and back.

"Yes, you do, Dan. We have something special for you. Since you're a young man, you'll need your own place. We've made one for you. Dad's worked really hard to finish it by the time you came home for a visit. Let me get the dishwasher going, then we'll show you. Okay?"

"Okay, I want some water."

"Sarah, why don't you show him where the glasses are so he can get a drink without having to ask every time." When she does, he fills his glass and follows Mitch out to the deck where Mitch asks him about keeping the fire going.

"Yes, dad. I like fireplace. You don't have in house now. I like this one. Mom can cook on it. It's cool."

Hearing him use the phrase, "it's cool" brings the biggest smile to both Sarah's face and mine. It's so out of character for the Dan we've known. Once the dishwasher is started, I dry my hands. "Let's show our young man his room, so he knows he does have a place with a bed here at home."

When Dan sees the plaque Sarah made for him, he stops and studies it, running his fingers over his name. "Dan's Studio?" Only he says study-o.

"Sarah made it for you," Mitch tells him.

"You did, Sissy? For me? I like it. Thank you, Sarah." He opens the door and enters his new room. He walks around, taking it all in.

Mitch did a wonderful job on his remodel. On one end he put in a small bathroom with a shower, commode, and sink. The sleeping area has a walk-in closet, Gamma's bed with a new mattress and springs and a new dark-gray comforter. On each side of the bed are matching nightstands with lamps. A wicker room divider separates his bedroom from the rest of the room. His chest of drawers stands between the window and the doorframe, with a doorstop in the floor to keep the door from knocking into it. Built-in shelves hold some of his little trucks and cars. Another shelf runs the length of the room two feet off the ceiling with his older and more fragile toys and prized possessions.

On the other side of the room divider, we've placed a small, round table with two wooden chairs. A four-drawer dresser holds a coffee maker and a tray with cups and glasses. Inside the top drawer are coffee, snacks, small paper plates, and some silverware.

The rest of the room is his studio, with large windows on the end and on both sides of the room. A drafting table and easel are ready for him to use. Shelving, some vertical to hold canvases, and the rest horizontal, hold a variety of acrylic and water paints, paper, different sizes and kinds of brushes, along with his old ones, and assorted art supplies we think he might use. Open and airy, the large room has window shades that pull down at night or whenever he might want to block some of the light.

Dan wanders from one thing to the other, picks up some of his favorite things and holds them for a few minutes before going on to the next. He runs his fingers over familiar furniture and makes his way to where the various-sized canvases are stored. He selects one and places it on the easel.

"I paint now."

"Does that mean you like your room?"

"Yes, dad, I like. Now I paint. I come talk later."

We watch as he puts some water in a container, picks out some colors, places them on a pallet and, with a flick of his wrist, he sends us off.

"Guess that's it for us, then." Mitch laughs as we return to the house.

"But he likes it. Don't you think, dad? He seems to really like it."

We all agree that he does. We could tell by the way he went from one thing to the other, taking it all in. And if we can't be with him, thanks to the windows, we can see him at work. Contented, Mitch and I sit on the deck enjoying ourselves, while Sarah goes to her room to do homework.

Chapter 48

Mr. McBride and Ms. Jewell join us an hour later. We've been expecting them, since they need to observe Dan while he's here. The purpose of this trip, as Mitch says, is to see us all in our natural habitat. Because things have been going so well, I'm hoping the transition to Serenity House won't be needed. Once they see the arrangements we've made, maybe they'll consider having him come home—if not right away, at least when he's ready to leave the structure of the halfway house.

Spending a few hours together will give us all a chance to get to know each other better. After all, they hold our fate in their hands. Even though it's their job, I'm already feeling defensive. While Mitch takes mugs and condiments out to the deck, I make a fresh pot of coffee and slice some zucchini bread.

Just as we finish getting everything ready, they come around the corner from the front drive. "Welcome to our home," Mitch says. "We thought we'd sit out here if you don't mind, unless you need to see the house first and how Dan will fit into our new life?"

"No," Ms. Jewell laughs, "we're not here to inspect your house, only to see how Dan's doing. We know you only want what's best for him."

"Have a seat then, would you like coffee, tea, milk or—?"

Both choose black coffee. "What a lovely deck and backyard. I love the fire to take the chill off. And please, while we're here at your home, please call us by our first names. I'm Mick, and I believe Ms. Jewell would prefer Mari." She nods in agreement.

"Only if you'll call us Mitch and Lillian or Lil." I reply and feel myself relax. "Now that that's out of the way, what can we help you with while you're here?"

"Not much, really. Just treat us as you would any guest. We try not to be intrusive, and we're prepared to answer any questions you might have. But first, Dan missed his meds this morning, so I need to give them to him. I can see he's already hard at work." Mick nods towards the studio.

Mitch describes how he remodeled his workshop into a studio apartment for Dan. Mick responds enthusiastically from a lay carpenter's point of view by sharing his own love of working with his hands in his time off to help him relax. Mari asks about the plaque and is impressed when we tell her Sarah made it.

Mitch taps lightly on the door to the studio before opening it. "Sorry to disturb you, Son. You have visitors who need a minute of your time." He ushers all of us in without giving Dan a chance to respond.

Dan continues to work, with his head down, not acknowledging us. "Dan," I say, "you have visitors."

He holds up a finger and continues to work. Quietly, we show them around the studio while Dan completes what he's doing. Finally, he raises his head and appears confused to see us all. "Mr. Mick? Ms. Mari? Did you come see my study-o? Dad build it for me."

"We came to see you, Dan, but I really do like your studio. You're a lucky guy. Your dad did a great job. But, we came to see how you're doing and to bring you the meds you missed this morning. You need to take them now."

"But, Mr. Mick. I not in hospital."

Although we can still hear them talking, we turn our backs as Mick patiently explains why Dan has to take his medicine every day, whether he's in the hospital or not. He reminds him of conversations they've had, and how it will be a condition for him to come home. When Dan gets a glass and takes his pills, Mick mentions that he has everything he needs except, perhaps, a kitchen.

Dan overhears the remark, and says, "I don't need kitchen. Mom cooks good food. She make me pancakes with peanut butter for breakfast. Mom's the best cooker." My cheeks redden with pride.

"Dan, why don't you show them around?" I suggest.

He waves his hand around, "This my study-o. My trucks up there, my gamma bed, and my paints. Don't have green tractor or big yellow truck." He frowns when he mentions the truck.

I bite back a laugh at the grand tour in a capsule.

"The tractor is in storage if you want it, Dan. I wasn't sure. It's too big to have in here, but we can put it outside by the door if you'd like. It could use a new paint job though."

"Yes, I want tractor, Dad. You wait. I help paint, okay? But not big yellow. Don't want big yellow. Makes me do bad things." He becomes restless just thinking about it.

Quietly, Mitch replies, "No, no big yellow. We sent it away, remember? It won't be coming back. And I'll definitely wait until you're here to help me paint the green tractor. Okay, buddy?"

Mick and Mari are watching them closely. She asks me, "Are they talking about THE big yellow? It's a, what?"

"A big yellow Tonka truck, his favorite childhood toy, until he was about eight. Then it became one of the destructive voices, the driving force behind his first fit of destruction of many of his toys." I tell her quietly. I can see the awareness register.

"That's right, I remember now. Thanks."

Dan has settled down and is returning to his easel, "I need to paint now."

"Can we see what you're painting before we go?" Mari starts to walk toward him.

He holds his hand up. "No, Ms. Mari. I show you later, not now." When he returns to his work, we know it's time for us to leave him to it.

We stroll down to the creek. Mitch invites them to come fishing anytime they're in the area. Both are easy to talk to. Any apprehension I may have leaves me as we talk about Dan and the plans for him. Mari and I rest on Nana's bench while Mitch and Mick walk further down the creek. We discuss Dan's aftercare plan, how they will use the halfway house to transition him back into the community and give him more independence. They agree the studio is a possibility for his independent living. Although I think about discussing him coming home without the halfway house, something makes me hesitate.

They have other business to take care of in this area, so before they leave we arrange to meet them at the airport for their return flight at eight thirty the next morning. Mari cautions me not to feed Dan a big breakfast before the flight, maybe just scrambled eggs and a piece of toast. He's not been airsick, but heavy food and flight aren't a good mix.

Around noon, Dan comes looking for lunch and stays with us on the deck for an hour or so before going back to his studio. He's more relaxed with us now, and he and his dad talk about painting the tractor next time he comes home. Sarah talks him into a walk with her to the creek. When they come back, he goes back to his studio, but surprises us by asking Sarah if she wants to bring her schoolwork there to finish it. She, of course, jumps on his offer. Mitch and I take advantage of the nice weather to do a little yard work. For the first time in a long time, I feel complete and content. I'm not worried about tomorrow, just living for today—enjoying my family. It feels like I'm buying insurance—making good memories, enjoying life, and living in the moment—filling my emotional bank up an hour at a time.

Dan and Sarah return to the house about five, looking for food. Their timing is good as Mitch has just returned with our dinner, our favorite, take-out fried chicken, smashed taters, and gravy. I make a salad to go with it. We spend the evening watching television, "The Walton's" and "Rockford Files," two of our favorite programs. Dan especially likes Rockford. I think it's the Firebird he liked the best. Before it's over, we're all struggling to stay awake.

"Do you want me to walk you to the studio, Dan?" I ask, though the path is well lit by our porch light and the one on the studio that comes on automatically at dusk.

"No, Mom. I do it myself." He's almost out the door before his sister stops him.

"What? Just get up and walk off, no good night? Nothin'?" She grins at him to take the sting out, but I can tell she's upset.

"G'night Sissy, Dad, Mom. Sleep tight. Don't let bedbugs bite. And Mom, can you bring me some hot chocolate? Sissy? Would you and Dad come out, too? We drink hot chocolate in my room before I go asleep?" And he's gone before we can answer.

I start the cocoa, made from scratch, of course—no instant for this bunch. And topped with whipped cream. Sarah changes into her pj's, then comes to stir the cocoa while I whip the cream. Mitch retrieves Dan's mug, and they finish up while I go put on my pj's. Then we join Dan in his new digs, our hearts light with another positive step forward.

Chapter 49

When something wakes me around midnight, I lie listening. It's only the wind brushing a branch on the window. I roll over to snuggle up to Mitch but he's not there. "Mitch?' There's no answer, so I crawl out of bed to look for him and see the lights on in the studio. Hurrying across the yard, I tap on the door and enter. Dan and Mitch are sitting cross-legged on the bed engaged in conversation, each focused intensely on each other.

"Mitch? Dan?" I mean to say it quietly, but it sounds sharp instead. Dan jerks back, looking around wildly. I hold my breath as Mitch reaches out and takes his hand.

"It's okay, Son. It's Mom. It's okay."

Dan shakes his head, looking at his dad without understanding. "It's Mom? Mom gave me bad dream?"

"No, Dan. Mom's come to check on us. See?" He points to me standing in the doorway.

"Hey, Dan. You had a bad dream?"

"I did. Big yellow comed back. Told me do bad things. Don't want do bad things, Mom. I don't."

"It's okay, Dan. It's only a bad dream. We're here, and you're safe. Do you want to come in the house with us?"

"I-I think I do want to come in the house. I sleep there? I can do that?"

"Sure you can, Buddy. Mom can make up the sofa in my office. You can sleep there. Why don't I get it ready. Mom can walk back to the house with you when you're ready."

Dan looks from Mitch to me. He's a young man, but right now he looks like our little boy. "I walk back to house with Mom."

Sarah's up when we get to the house, and Mitch has told her about Dan's bad dream. "Dan, you can sleep in my bed tonight, and I'll sleep on the couch."

"Okay, Sissy. I sleep in your bed. Can I go sleep now? I had bad dream. Mom, Dad, tell me it a dream, and I tired now."

"Come on, big brother." Sarah takes his hand and leads him to her room while Mitch and I make up the sofa for her.

"Sarah, that was a very nice thing you did, letting him have your bed."

"It's nothing, Mom. Tomorrow's a big day, and he needs his rest. We know what he's like when he's overtired."

The rest of the night's uneventful, but we all oversleep so we have to rush to be at the airport at 8:30. I fix Dan toast and peanut butter while he gets his suitcase from the studio. He returns with it and a crudely wrapped package.

I'm glad I haven't mentioned anything to Mick or Mari about him coming home instead of to Serenity House when he's discharged. His nightmare shows me he's not ready. The treatment plan they have in place is what's best for him. I wanted to rush things, based on just a few hours.

Mick and Mari are already at the airport when we arrive. Dan's eyes light up when he sees the plane. He grabs the package and hurries across the tarmac to them. Mitch carries his suitcase as Sarah and I rush to catch him. That's the fastest I've seen him move in years—usually he's slow and steady.

"Miss Mari, Miss Mari. I made for you." He extends the package to her with a broad grin.

She looks at him, confusion in her eyes, then at Mick as she tears off the paper and hands it to Dan. Staring at the picture, she cradles it in her hands like something precious. "Oh, Dan, it's beautiful," she says softly with a catch in her voice and turns it for us to see.

A white plane with red striping rests on an old airstrip with spikes of grass and weeds poking through the pavement beneath its wheels. Nearby, a tattered, red windsock hangs at half-mast, and behind the plane an old Quonset hanger stands, spots of rust showing on its metal door. What catches the eye is a beautiful blue bird on the wing of the plane, the details so vivid the plane looks as if it could take flight. Mari's eyes fill with tears.

"How did you do that Dan? It's my plane and Dad's old hanger." She turns to us. "That's where we keep the plane. It's my dad's, but he can't fly anymore. Dan's only been there a few times. I don't understand how he can remember and replicate it in such detail. He's even included the old windsock." She tries to hand it back to him. "It's beautiful, Dan."

"No, Ms. Mari. I paint it for you. It yours." My heart is nearly bursting with pride, not just for his artistic ability, but his thoughtfulness.

She looks helplessly at Mick, "What do I do, Mick? I can't accept presents, especially one like this, from a patient."

"You don't like? Did I do wrong?"

"No, no, Dan. It's beautiful, I love it."

"Mari, you can hang it in your office. A lot of his paintings hang in the hospital. They can't object to one more."

"Thanks, Mick. I think you're right." She beams. "I love it, Dan. I'm going to hang it in my office where everyone can see it. Is that okay with you?" She places a hand on his arm. "I could almost hug you."

"No, no hug. Let's fly the skies." We all laugh.

"When I frame it, I'm going to add a little plaque engraved *Artist Dan Hawke, Date: Sept. 27, 1980; 1958 Piper Apache owned by Howard Jewell and daughter Mari Jewell.* I want it to be commemorated."

We say goodbye quickly. Poor Dan's impatient and anxious to board the plane, but he lets us hug him before we leave. As he gets on the plane, Sarah yells, "Later Gator" and is rewarded with, "While Crocodile."

He's waving from a window as they pull out on the runway, a huge smile lighting his face. He loves to fly.

• • •

The following week Reggie calls, concerned regarding the ownership of Dan's paintings. The confusion is over whether the hospital or Dan owns them since he allows them to be hung throughout the hospital. She's retained an attorney, and they'll be flying to the hospital to prepare appropriate contracts. I trust her, knowing she has Dan's best interest at heart. In lieu of payment, the attorney requests one of Dan's paintings. He's a Dan Hawke fan who purchased a couple from Reggie's gallery before. He's convinced Dan's work is going to increase in value. I'm glad she's handling the legal end of it. She thrives on that kind of thing, and I only get frustrated.

"I hope you realize how much I appreciate what you're doing for Dan."

"You know it isn't only for Dan, don't you? I do make a few bucks on each one, too. But mostly I want the world to know his talent. Paintings like his don't come along every day. Under other circumstances, I'd have him here and do a whole show with him in attendance signing autographs. By the way, how's that girl—and the hubby? And you, Lil? How are you?"

"That girl's all grown up, straight A's, part time job, and a beau hanging around. I'm not ready for that. She's still my little girl. Mitch is taking on more and more, and it worries me. He's like a man driven. I think he blames himself because we had to sell the house and the business. But it wasn't his fault; it was the economy. Anyway, that's us—running and running. Say, Sis. Why don't you come for Thanksgiving? Dan will be home by then. Plus I'd love to see you and the kid."

"I'll think about it. And speaking of the kid, I'd better go. I need to fix him something to eat. I'll call after we meet with the hospital board and their attorneys. Love you."

A few days later, Reggie calls me back to say the deal's done. "We worked out an agreement after first meeting with Dan. All proceeds from any artwork generated by Dan while he's in the state hospital will go to defray the cost of his stay. A copy of all bills will be submitted to our attorney. A percentage will go for supplies to keep him in paints, canvas and sketchpads, and for my commission. The remainder will pay his bill. Any excess over the costs will be put in his trust fund.

That's the gist of it. Of course, there was a lot of lawyer talk."

"That sounds great. Dan didn't have to sit through all of that did he?"

"No, thank goodness. Ms. Jewell was there; however, Dan was brought in to sign the paperwork once she and I explained it to him. He only had one problem, and he wasn't shy about telling them."

"How did he tell them?" I ask, praying he had his say without getting upset.

"He told them that Ms. Jewell's picture of her Piper Apache was not painted at the hospital, and it belonged to her and no one else. There was some talk about staff not receiving gifts from patients until our attorney spoke up, saying it was payment to Ms. Jewell for flying him home in her plane—just like they receive the proceeds of his works done while in the hospital. That shut them up."

I couldn't help but laugh. "I'm sorry I missed that."

"Me, too, Lil. And before I go, we'll be there for Thanksgiving. I'm planning on staying a week, but we'll stay at the Zbar Motel. It's reasonable, and I know you don't have extra room.

I want to argue, but know I'd lose. "See you at Thanksgiving, Sis. Love and thank you. Gotta run. Can't wait to see you."

Chapter 50

Dan was released from the state hospital early in October. His stay at the halfway house went smoothly. According to the staff, he participated in the required programs, took his medications with little resistance, cooperated in doing his assigned house duties, and followed all their rules. He handled social situations best in smaller groups, but overall did well. When he was released from the halfway house, he moved into his studio.

For now, we give him his meds to insure that he takes them. Working part time with Mitch, he's cleaning reclaimed barn lumber for the new workshop they're building in the far corner of our property. Most of his free time is spent either painting in his studio or down by the creek. Mitch built a portable easel he straps to his backpack that carries his paint and other supplies.

Work's been busy—the federal audit went smoothly. We passed with flying colors. My community presentation on "Surviving the Holidays with Family" was well attended. The highlight for me was the question-and-answer segment. I can tell when the message has been received by the interaction with the audience. And that night I answered a lot of questions. This type of presentation is one of my favorite parts of the job—giving the frustrated actress in me a chance to shine.

Mitch keeps busy with his handyman business and personal projects. With Sarah working and the time spent with her boyfriend, we seldom have time together—so it's nice Mitch and I find a few hours mid-week for breakfast together. I work late on Wednesday nights and go in mid-day on Thursdays, so Mitch tries to schedule his Thursday mornings to match mine. When it does work, we enjoy a leisurely breakfast and catch up.

Now, Thanksgiving is almost here. We're looking forward to Reggie's visit. I'll be off for two weeks to prepare before and rest after her visit. I'm looking forward to the time off with family. Sarah's taking two days off work, too. She wants to be home to greet Reggie and Timmy. They'll arrive the weekend before Thanksgiving but they need to leave the day after. Sarah's asked if she can invite her boyfriend for dessert after Thanksgiving dinner. Our main concern is how Dan will react since he's very protective of her, but we don't want to borrow trouble. She'll want to be the one to tell him about her friend when the time is right.

As we sip our coffee, Mitch tells me that he's glad I'm taking some extra time at Thanksgiving. "We don't spend much time together lately. You hardly see Dan, and on the weekends you're so tired it's hard for you to enjoy him." His eyes brighten, and he smiles. "He's really coming along. He even made a joke the other day, sounding like Sarah when she's kidding around." He leans back in his chair and grins. "I was pounding in a nail and almost dropped my hammer. He stopped what he was doing, and in that monotone of his, says, 'What's the matter, old man? Did ya butter your fingers? I call you butterfingers.' Lil, I wanted to hug him. He never cracked a smile, just went back to carrying lumber. The rest of the day he called me butterfingers. I don't want you to miss moments like that."

I smile at the image he's created for me. "I know. That's why I'm taking the two weeks now. Of course, it means I'll only have a couple days off for Christmas because I traded some time to make it work." I pause before broaching another subject. "Something that bothers me is that we've let our counseling slide. I'd like us to go back. I'll be calling Mr. Bacon to schedule an appointment. I hope you and Sarah will consider it, but I'll leave that up to you."

He clears our breakfast plates and pours us another cup of coffee before responding. "I did fight it in the beginning, but I agree—it helped. I'll make the time whenever you get an appointment. As for our social butterfly, let's talk to her and see what she says."

Pleased with his reaction, I tell him I'll set up an appointment.

When I call, the earliest available appointment is the first of December, but I feel better knowing we'll be working on us, rather than focusing so much on Dan.

"And now, about Thanksgiving. I want to get the big shopping done before Reggie gets here. What are we having besides turkey?"

"Weell," he drawls. "Don't we usually have mashed potatoes, gravy, sweet potatoes with gooey marshmallows, green bean casserole, hot rolls, cranberry sauce, and that green salad you insist on that nobody eats. As far as I'm concerned, we can leave off the sweet taters, green beans, and salad, but I like all the rest." He laughs as only he can when he thinks he's funny.

"You silly goose." I slap his arm with my notepad. "I mean ham or something. I want to make sure we have enough."

"A small ham might be nice. I hope Dan doesn't decide he wants a p butter n jelly sammie. Remember the Christmas when you went all out and all he'd eat was his p butter n jelly?"

"If that's what he wants, we'll let him fix it. After all, we're working towards his independence, aren't we? Isn't that why he now has his own toaster, bread, peanut butter, and jelly in his studio?" I can't help but laugh, picturing Dan with his sammie while the rest of us gorge on turkey dinner. "Now, I need to get busy. I've lollygagged around with you long enough. I have a shower to take before I leave for work. I'll make the grocery run Saturday morning before Reggie and Timmy get here—and you're coming with me." I plant a noisy kiss on his buttered-toast lips and head upstairs to get ready for work.

I'm singing in the shower when I feel a draft. I didn't hear the bathroom door open, but an arm slides around my waist. "I thought you could use some company, little lady," Mitch whispers in my ear. *I might be late for work after all.*

Saturday, I'm up early and prod a reluctant Mitch out of bed so we can go shopping. He grumbles as he follows me through the store, though the twinkle in his eye tells me he's not serious. Both our grocery carts are almost full, and we're heading to checkout when I'm waylaid by a lady who was at my presentation. This kind of situation, when I'm on my own time and someone wants a private counseling session in a public place is always awkward. Once I reassure Ms. Woodchuck that she's not responsible for her brother and give her a little encouragement, we check out.

Mitch is frustrated by the encounter. As we leave the store, he checks to see that she didn't follow us out of the store. "I can't go anyplace with you in this town anymore, can I? Someone always recognizes you and needs to bend your ear. Aren't you the one who always says 'no' is a real word, and we all have the right to use it?"

"I know, but I can't be rude, and I do try to keep it short. You know that. Let's not have it ruin our day. We have celebrating to do, family to enjoy, and food to cook. And, let's hope someone is home to help us carry in the groceries."

With Sarah and Dan's help, we just finish when Reggie's car pulls in the driveway. We scurry out to greet her and Timmy, who are still in the car deep in a serious conversation. Slowly, she opens her car door, glaring at him with one last, ferocious look while he slouches with arms crossed, jaw tightly clenched.

Reggie, dressed smartly in stylish slacks and a trendy blouse, smiles broadly when Sarah is the first to reach her. She engulfs her in a bear hug. As he waits for his turn, Mitch says, "What did you do, see us schlepping the groceries in, so you waited till we got them all in and wouldn't have to help?"

"You bet," she says. "I'm on vacation. I didn't come to work." She hugs him tightly. "It's good to see you, you big galoot."

I push in. "Okay, leave my sister alone. Come here, Reggie." She holds me close. "I've missed you so much, and I'm glad you're here," I whisper.

"Me, too, Lil. Me, too."

"You're earlier than we expected, the roads must have been clear."

"They were, Lil, and nothing like a sullen eight-going-on-sixteen-year-old to make me want to have the trip over. I'm hoping that his spending time with Sarah might help mellow him out. He's not taking the move to a new neighborhood very well, then when he finally makes a friend we leave. You'd have thought we were going to be gone forever."

Her attention returns to Timmy. She marches back to the car and pulls open the door on the passenger's side where he's sulking. When she jerks her thumb toward the house, he lurches out of the seat and storms into the house, ignoring us all. He's a head taller than the last time we saw him. "He wanted to stay in Cheyenne with friends, so he's pouting," she explained.

Dan is in the kitchen, eyeing his cousin warily, when we walk in. "There you are, Dan. Come here, and give your favorite aunt a big hug."

"No, no hug, An Reggie. Dan don't give hug." He pats her outstretched hand.

Timmy opens the fridge door and begins rummaging around, much to our dismay. "What the hell do you think you're doing?" Reggie screeches at him, "Shut that door right now." She grabs him by the collar of his shirt. "You know better than that. You haven't even bothered to say hello, yet you think it's okay to help yourself to the fridge?"

"Low, Aunt Lil, Uncle Mitch," he mumbles and plops in a chair.

"Sarah, why don't you take Timmy outside and show him around?"

"Come on, squirt," Sarah says, "I'll give you the grand tour." Reluctantly, he follows her.

"What's there to do out here in the sticks? Let's go to town. You've got a car, don't you?"

She stops in her tracks before they even reach the door and turns to face him. She's slow to anger, but I believe I can see smoke coming out of her nostrils. "Let me tell you something right now, little cousin. You're here for barely ten minutes and manage to offend everyone already. You're going to be here for a week. I can make sure it is the most miserable week of your life or one of the best. It's your choice. I do have a car, because I work hard at my job, make good grades, and treat my parents and others with respect. If you want to sit here and pout, fine with me. I have other things to take care of." Leaving him standing there with his mouth open, she marches out of the room.

Dan watches Timmy carefully. He wants to go to his studio, but he's hesitant to walk past Timmy.

Mitch breaks the mounting tension. "How about I stoke up the fire outside while you rustle up some coffee and hot chocolate, Lil?"

By the time everything is ready, Mitch has Timmy helping him while he explains how he built onto the deck and remodeled Dan's studio. He has Timmy carrying an armload of wood for the fire. Sometimes I think Mitch could charm the rattle off a snake. *This little boy is obviously in need of a strong father figure.*

∞

Chapter 51

Enticing aromas fill the house as Reggie and I begin preparations for Thanksgiving. Apple, pumpkin, and chocolate pies cool on the counter as spiced apple cider warms on the back burner. Ingredients for some of our favorite childhood recipes are at our fingertips. We're making cranberries two ways, homemade sauce simmering on the stove and Mama's special cranberry relish: fresh cranberries ground with oranges, apples, walnuts, and sugar to taste. It has always been my favorite.

Timmy's lost some of his attitude and shadows Mitch's every move. Dan and Tim haven't really spoken, but when they're in the same room Dan's eyes seldom leave him. Timmy gives Sarah a wide berth since she told him so eloquently when they first arrived something he didn't want to hear. He watches her as warily as Dan watches him.

A couple of days into their visit, Reggie asks to see Dan's studio. "Lil, do you think we could take a break and visit Dan in his studio? I don't think I'm going to get an invitation."

"I was just going to suggest that same thing, Reggie. If you wait for him, it'll never happen." When Timmy sees us heading there, he falls in behind us. He's been watching Dan at his easel through the window where he can see all the pickups and toys on the shelves, and he's curious.

Dan isn't very receptive to company when we arrive. "I busy. I have picture to paint."

"But Dan, I want to see where you create the masterpieces I sell in my gallery. We won't be long."

"Okay," he says grudgingly, wiping the paint off his hands. He stops when he sees Timmy, points to him and says, "Do not touch my things."

Shocked at his reaction and disappointed by his rudeness, I call out, a bit harshly, "Dan!"

"Don't want to touch your old junk anyway." Timmy plops down in a chair. His eyes travel around the room, lingering on the collection of trucks and cars before his eyes go wide when he focuses on the collection of Hot Wheels. For a moment his charade fails. "WOW, look, Mom, look!" He can't help himself. "Dan, you've got some really nice cars."

"Yes, I do. An Reggie? You and Timmy want hot chocolate? Mom say always offer drinks to company."

"No, we won't take up much of your time." She and Timmy stroll around the room admiring his collection. Temptation finally gets the best of Timmy, and he picks up a red pickup and opens the doors.

"Ti-mo-thy! You do not touch. You leave, NOW." His hands begin to flutter. He steps towards poor Timmy who stands stock still, holding Dan's beloved toy pickup.

"I don't want to look at your stupid pickup anyway." Slamming the toy on the shelf, he darts out of the studio, breaking into a run when he clears the door. Frightened, he runs to the new workshop where Mitch is working.

Reggie's torn between anger and sadness. "Daniel, I'm disappointed in you. I know Timmy can be a nuisance, but he's a little boy. He loves cars and trucks just like you, and he wasn't going to hurt your damn toys." Before he can respond, she follows Timmy.

Dan doesn't understand. His shoulders droop, and his chin drops to his chest, no doubt concerned that he's in trouble. Then, he looks at me. "I paint Timmy a picture of red pickup."

"No, Dan. A picture won't work with a little boy. You need to use words to say you're sorry for scaring him."

"But, I not—" He tries to protest.

"Only words will make this right. You need to find some right now. You don't want Aunt Reggie mad at you." I leave him to think about what he needs to do.

Reggie and Timmy are talking to Mitch when I enter the workshop. She's upset, and I don't blame her. My first instinct is to make excuses for Dan, but that would only make matters worse. He's frightened her little boy, and she has every right to be upset.

Folding Reggie in my arms, I tell her, "I'm so sorry, Reggie." Then I tell Timmy, too. "I'm really sorry about what happened, Timmy." I hug him, but feel him stiffen when he sees Dan walking toward us. Unconsciously, we all draw closer together, Mitch and I standing in front of Reggie and Timmy.

"Mom, Dad, I need talk to An Reggie and Timothy." Reggie steps forward holding tightly to Timmy's hand, both apprehensive. Dan's holding two little boxes. He holds them out, one to Timmy, the other to Reggie. "Timothy, I sorry I yell at you. That was bad for me to do. Want you to have this." He turns to Reggie, "An Reggie, I sorry, I not want you mad with me. I will be better to Timothy. He little boy. I not. I want you to have this. It not a picture." He looks at me as if to ask. *'Did I do okay?'*

When Timmy looks from the box in his hand to his mom, she gives him a nod, and he opens it. His eyes grow large as he pulls the little red pickup out of the box. "I-is this for me?" he's asks quietly—in awe. "Really? I can have it?"

"Yes, Timothy. I should not yell at you for touch. Mom and Dad teach me share."

Timmy rushes forward, wrapping his arms around Dan's waist. Dan freezes but doesn't pull away. He pats him awkwardly on the head. "Thank you, thank you, Dan." Then he hurries to show Mitch.

Dan watches Reggie as she opens hers, revealing a deep purple miniature 1966 Mustang. I bite my lip so I don't laugh. "Why, thank you, Dan. I'll treasure it. I accept your apology. If Timmy upsets you again, I want you to take a deep breath, use your inside voice, and let him know what he's done wrong. Will you do that?" She touches him gently on the arm.

"I will do that, I will." He pats her hand and walks back to the studio.

• • •

Thanksgiving arrives without another crisis. Wonderful aromas fill the house, and all is well. The table, covered with Mom's precious lace tablecloth, our best china, and Mom's silver, set a formal tone. Shedding a tear or two as we share our favorite childhood memories of Thanksgiving, Reggie and I work in harmony to pull it all together.

Mitch leans in to steal a kiss when we meet in the hallway as Sarah's coming out of her room. "Eww, you guys, child present." She laughs, thinking she's funny. "Ronnie Dean's going to be here about four, will that be okay?" What can we say but yes?

When we sit down, the table's overflowing with foods tempting us to overindulge. Even Dan changed into nice clothes, and he surprises me by asking if we are going to bless the food. Mitch says the blessing, then we fill our plates and enjoy the meal. We're almost finished when I notice Dan watching Timmy, a pensive look on his face. He lays his fork down and clears his throat.

"Dad, I want to ask Timothy something, is that okay?" All conversation stops—everyone looks at Dan. Timmy looks up, startled. "Timothy, would you like to see my pedal tractor? It not here. It at storage, but I think Dad will take us after we done eat. I too big to ride, and you too big too. You like my cars. I think you like see my pedal tractor, too."

That's quite a speech for Dan. Timmy looks at his mom, and she nods. "I'd like to see it. That would be cool. Did you keep all your toys from when you were a little boy?"

"Most all, but they not toys to me. They my friends. That why I don't like people touch them. You can touch tractor, just not get on. Dad, will you take us?"

Mitch's eyes, like mine, are filled with tears. "Sure, I'd be honored to escort you young men to the storage unit. Maybe we'll bring the tractor back with us so we can get it painted before the weather turns any colder."

"Dan?" Timmy asks, "Why do you call me Timothy instead of Timmy or Tim?"

"You don't like I call you Timothy? Timmy is little boy name. You not little boy. Tim is okay for young boy or Timothy. You want I call you Tim?"

"No, I kinda like you call me Timothy. I don't like it when people call me Timmy, but I like Tim. I like that you're the only one who calls me Timothy though." He looks at each of us to make sure we get the message.

"Before we go, we have to bring some wood from the wood pile for the fire. I think we're going to have our dessert out there later."

"Okay, Dad. Timothy, you help carry wood with me?"

They walk off the deck before anyone moves. "What the heck just happened? First, someone who looks and sounds like my big brother invites Tim to see his tractor, using almost full sentences. Then he answers Tim's questions and touches him on the shoulder when it's time to do a chore. That's the most I've ever heard him say at one time. Talk about having something to be thankful for." Sarah's eyes, like the rest of ours, are filled with tears.

⚮

Chapter 52

While the guys are gone, Sarah and I put turkey, cranberry, stuffing, and mashed potatoes in containers and take care of the dishes. *I shouldn't have to cook for a week.* Sarah's watching the clock, waiting for Ronnie Dean to join us. We're on the deck when Mitch and his followers return with the pedal tractor. Dan places it by the door-stoop of his studio. Without a backwards glance, he goes inside. I'm not about to object. I'm too proud of him. The shuffle in his walk is more pronounced, a clear indication that he's tired, and rest is vital to him. He heads straight to his easel—painting is where he finds respite.

Mitch, Reggie, Tim, and I are relaxing on the deck, enjoying the fire and the beautiful day when the doorbell rings. Sarah had to be waiting in the living room as I heard her voice immediately.

"Time to welcome the boyfriend." Mitch mutters. We stand when Sarah brings him outside and introduces him to Reggie and Tim. A stocky-built young man, he's barely as tall as Sarah, and he's a top wrestler on the high school varsity team. He stands with his shoulders back and his head held high. His hazel eyes twinkle, and he looks directly at each of us as we greet him. He wears his brown hair in a mullet, currently in style—much to Mitch's dismay. *Please, Mitch. Don't make a comment about his hair.*

"I'm glad you could join us, Ronnie. Did you and your family have a nice Thanksgiving?"

"Thank you for inviting me, Mrs. Hawke. It's Ronnie Dean, by the way. Our Thanksgiving was okay—just Dad, my older brother James, me, and Mom. She's upset with us all, so she kinda put a damper on the day. She thought we should all eat at the table, but the football game was on—so we guys filled our plates and ate off TV trays in the living room."

He grins and lowers his voice. "Mom got pissed and hid out in the bedroom. Don't know why she got upset. It's just another day and another meal. That's her job."

His lack of consideration and disrespect for his mother is a shock. I start to say something, but out of the corner of my eye, Sarah, who's standing a little behind him, mouths "No." My girl knows me too well. I let it slide, but a sliver of worry prickles a bit too much. *What does she see in him?*

The ladies serve pie, and as we talk, the less impressed I am. Sarah seems to fade in his company, as though he's sucking the life out of her. He's big into sports—that's the topic of his conversation. He has a football scholarship to the University of Wyoming, and his goal is to have one in wrestling. Tim hangs on to his every word. After we finish dessert, he offers to teach Tim some wrestling moves.

Sarah follows them off the deck into the yard. Tim's practically bouncing with excitement. Ronnie Dean grins broadly, obviously enjoying the limelight. He's gentle when they start. From the deck, we can't hear what they're saying. It's like watching a pantomime. They crouch, circle around, moving closer together, Tim eager to learn the moves. Suddenly he grabs Tim, slams him to the ground and flops down, his body alongside, holding Tim's shoulders flat on the ground. Tim cries out. He can't catch his breath, and he's trying not to cry.

We jump up, and Reggie's halfway down the steps. Ronnie's on his feet, his hand out to Tim as if he's trying to apologize. Tim swats the hand away, fighting back tears. Just as suddenly, Dan appears from nowhere, grabbing Ronnie Dean and slamming him to the ground. It's like watching a car crash in slow motion. He towers over Ronnie Dean, face red, chest heaving, and fists clenched.

"You not hurt Timothy. He not big like you. You hurt him, you bad man!"

By the time Reggie, Mitch, and I reach them, Sarah is already in her brother's face. Her face is red, eyes are glaring, and her fists are clenched as tightly as Dan's.

"DAN! Dan, he didn't mean to hurt Tim. Tim wanted Ronnie Dean to teach him how to wrestle. You didn't have to do that." She points to Ronnie Dean struggling to get up.

Dan looks wild-eyed from Ronnie to Sarah and back to Ronnie, who's gotten to his feet. "He not teach Timothy. He hurt Timothy. That not nice." He turns to where Ronnie is standing, beyond arm's length. "You 'pologize to Timothy, then you leave."

"No, Dan. He's my guest. Go back to your studio if you don't want to be around him. He is NOT going anywhere!" She moves to Ronnie's side, but when she tries to put her arm through his, he shakes her off. She's crestfallen.

"Tim. I'm sorry, bud, I didn't mean to hurt you. Are you okay?" The smirk on Ronnie's face doesn't matach his words.

Reggie's brushing Tim off, making sure he's not hurt. He pushes her hands away, dashes the tears away, blushing a deep red.

"Mom! Mom! I'm fine. I forgot to take my pickup out of my pocket, and I landed on it." He showed her the red pickup, the wheels broken and one door hangs loose.

I pray Dan doesn't see it, but of course he does. His eyes go wide. He looks from the broken toy to Ronnie and back again. When he takes a step toward Ronnie, Sarah holds her hand up.

"Stop right there."

"B-but Sarah, he broke red truck. He broke Timothy's present."

"I know. But you stop it." She deflates as she looks at her brother. "Dan, please, he didn't mean to. He's my friend, don't ruin it for me." Unshed tears fill her eyes. Again she tries to put her arm through Ronnie's, but he shakes her off again.

"Sarah, you're a nice girl and all, but I don't need this shit. My friends warned me about your crazy brother. I thought he was supposed to be better. I guess I was wrong. He's still batshit crazy. Good luck on ever finding a boyfriend with him around."

I tense, moving toward them just as Mitch does. A loud crack, like a bullwhip snapping, fills the air. Sarah stands in front of a stunned Ronnie, her chest heaving, tears gone in an instant, replaced with lightning rods of anger. The side of his face sports a bright red handprint. "Why—you—jumped-up little muscle-bound pea-brained idiot." In a huff, she takes a deep breath. "I don't know why I gave you the time of day. You strut like a little banty rooster, like you're God's gift. But you're not. My brother may have problems, but he's worth ten of you. Go back to your brain-dead muscle-bound buddies. I deserve better than you. Now get the hell off our property!" She steps aside and points him toward the driveway.

He squares his shoulders and struts away, making a wide swath away from Dan who's staring open mouthed at his sister. She yells out as he goes, "Oh, and you're a horrible kisser." Standing stiffly, she watches his retreating back until he's out of sight.

Looking slowly at each of us, she laughs. "Well, that went just flipping fantastic, don't you think?" Then, she drops to the ground, covers her face, her body racked with heaving sobs.

In two strides Mitch scoops her up and carries her to the house, murmuring soothing words. Dan is confused as he follows them with his eyes. "I make Sarah cry? Sarah mad with me?"

I'm torn between staying and reassuring Dan or going to Sarah. My heart tells me my daughter needs me. Thankfully Reggie steps in and tells me to go—she'll stay with him. Dan surprises me when I say that Aunt Reggie will stay with him and I'm going to go to Sarah. "Sissy need Mom now to make it better. I sorry Mom. I screw up, didn't I? Should I go find that guy and 'pologize more so he'll like Sarah again?'

"No, Dan. Sissy will be okay."

"Come on, Dan. Let's go back to your studio." Tim takes him by the hand and reaches for his mom's hand. The three of them walk toward the studio as I go to comfort Sarah. *And a little child shall lead them.*

⌯

Chapter 53

When I get to the house, Mitch is at the kitchen table sipping a cup of coffee. "Where's Sarah? Is she okay?"

"She said she wanted to take a shower."

"And you let her? You left her alone when she's miserable?"

As I turn to go to her, he grabs my hand, pulling me up short. "Lil, I simply did what our very mature daughter asked. She'd quit crying by the time we got to the house. She said she didn't know if she was crying because she and Ronnie were done or because she was—and I quote, 'so damn mad she wanted to rip his face off and feed it to the dog, if only we had a dog.' I snorted and she laughed, wiped her eyes, gave me a big hug, and said she wanted a shower. What did you want me to do? Hogtie her and insist she continue feeling horrible?" His voice had risen, and he looked away.

"Mom, Dad, stop it. I'm fine. I don't need you two fighting on top of everything." Sarah came out of her bedroom when she heard us. "Yes, I'm upset, Mom, but I'm not devastated. I've thought about breaking up with him for a while—but it was nice to have a boyfriend. He can be a real pain in the neck, and he was getting possessive—demanding, wanting to know what I was doing and who I was talking to. He even threatened a couple of boys from my biology class last week—told them if they didn't stay away from me they'd be sorry. We're assigned a project together—so that will be impossible. I told myself it was because he cares so much, but I don't think that was it. Then today when I heard how disrespectful he, his dad, and brother sounded toward his mom, I knew I was ready to break up with him. I was sorry I pushed to have him here for dessert. The tears felt like a release valve popping off, like a pressure cooker." She sighs, then squares her shoulders. "Now, if you two don't mind, I'd like that shower. Can I trust you children to play nice?" A small smile lets me know she really is okay.

"So? How do you know he's a bad kisser?" Mitch asked innocently "Dad!" she turns bright red, pulls the belt on her robe tight as she leaves. "Behave yourselves. And wouldn't you like to know?"

We're both still laughing when Reggie and Tim join us. She looks at us as though we've lost our minds. "Pray tell. What's so funny? I'm getting whiplash from the changing emotions. We're happy, we're sad, we're mad, totally pissed, remorseful—and now we're happy?! It's enough to make a drunk want a drink." Then she laughs, pointing at the shocked look on my face. "It's okay, Sis—just a bit of recovery humor. I have no desire to numb any of what goes on in my life today. I'd miss all this excitement."

By the time Sarah finishes her shower we're back out on the deck, bundled from the cool air with the fire going. She's wearing flannel pj's, a heavy terry robe, and Sherpa-lined boot slippers to ward off the chill.

"Nice to see you dressed up for the occasion," Mitch says as they banter back and forth. *She's putting on a good face for us all.*

"How ya doin', kiddo?" Reggie hugs Sarah and kisses the top of her head.

Her eyes fill with tears. "I'm doing okay, Auntie. Like I told Mom and Dad, I've thought about kicking him to the curb for a while. I kinda wanted to hold out until after prom." She rolls her eyes and makes an attempt to smile. "What kinda loser does that make me?"

"Not a loser—just a girl trying to navigate the pitfalls of her teen years. It means you're human. It's gonna hurt for a while, even when you know he's a jerk—but in the end you'll be okay, that's all I'm saying."

"Thanks, Aunt Reggie—I think." She rewards us with a small laugh. "Did someone say pie?"

Reggie and Mitch go to fetch pie—and whipped cream, of course—muttering good humoredly about being expected to wait on everyone. For once Tim doesn't follow Mitch. He's slumped in a chair, looking dejected. It's been a tough day for him. Mitch checked to see if Dan would join us, but he's peopled out for the day. *I'll take him dessert later.*

Tim devours his pie, then pulls out his broken pickup and tries to get the door to stay closed. Mitch takes it from him gently. "Why don't you let me keep that tonight? I'll see if I can fix it. I might have some old pieces I can use. It might not be as good as new, but it'll still be something special. Okay, bud?"

He attempts to hide a yawn when he agrees to leave it with Mitch, but his mom notices. "I can't believe how tired I am." She yawns dramatically and stretches. "I'm sure Tim would be okay longer, but not me. It's been a full day for all of us. How about we go back to our hotel, Tim?"

• • •

After cleaning up the kitchen, I cut a big piece of chocolate pie, heap it with whipped cream, and carry it out to Dan. The lights are all on, so I know he must be awake. When he doesn't answer, I knock harder and try the door, but it's locked. My heart thuds as I pound on the door. Suddenly, the door jerks open. Dan's standing there in his robe, shampoo in his hair, and water dripping.

"I am taking shower, Mom. Okay? I take shower, then go to bed. I tired, I told Dad."

"I'm sorry, Dan. I brought you pie and wanted to make sure you're okay."

He takes the pie from me and says, "I talk you tomorrow." Then he closes the door in my face.

Shocked, I almost knock again, but drop my hand and walk back to the house. He has the right idea—a shower and bed sound inviting. In the morning Reggie and Tim will be here early to say their goodbyes. Mitch will fix the little pickup before coming to bed so it'll be ready for Tim, but I'm not going to stay up with him. It's shower time for me. *All in all it's been a very good week.*

Chapter 54

In late February brave crocuses are the first colors to herald spring as they push through the snow on the sunny side of the house. Carl's wife planted them close to the foundation soon after they bought the cottage, along with daffodils, tulips, and hyacinth. The trees begin to bud after a warm spell, and the warmer weather signals the earth's renewal after a miserably cold winter. Spring finally arrives in May, and blooms burst forth in an abundance of colors. All the hard work Carl's wife did that brings the yard to life lifts my spirits and fills my soul with gratitude.

Dan has become a wanderer, sometimes staying away overnight on his treks. We try not to worry about him. When he's here, he still spends time with us and works fervently in his studio. Some of his landscapes reveal many of the areas he loves. His huge backpack is his portable studio, including the portable easel Mitch made him. He sees Dr. Nelson weekly, walking to his appointments now that the weather is nice.

Sarah graduates at the end of the month. She's busy with school, work, and end-of-school-year tasks. She's torn between wanting Dan to come and not come, knowing how the noise and excitement in crowds affects him. We'll simply ask him what he'd like to do. She has a new guy in her life who is the complete opposite of Ronnie Dean—not only physically, but in attitude and behavior as well. Tall as Dan, he's soft-spoken and very respectful of her and of us. Because he's in Laramie at the University of Wyoming, he won't be here for her graduation or to accompany her to the senior functions. She's disappointed though she doesn't complain.

Mitch's business is doing well. He's enjoying his new workshop, and building furniture keeps him as busy as home remodels. He's hired someone to help with it all. Dan was his first choice, but he wanted to spend more time on his art. He considers his art as his job—his paintings are selling well in Reggie's Gallery.

• • •

After another long week, it's good to come home to a pot of fresh coffee and to find Sarah busy on a school project. Pictures are scattered all over the table for her last assignment in Health and Science—building a pictorial family tree. We reminisce for a few minutes as we look at pictures from Thanksgiving.

"That was a crazy week wasn't it?"

"Yes, it was—one of our best Thanksgivings, don't you think? Your dad worked his magic and turned a pouty boy into a fan. Dan came out of his shell a bit. And, oh yeah, you called Ronnie Dean a banty rooster and a bad kisser."

"I did, didn't I?" We both laugh remembering it.

"Now here you are, a couple weeks from graduation, and you have a new beau who towers over you. I'm assuming he's a good kisser—since I've caught you at it often enough."

"Mom! Stop it." She swats my arm with the picture in her hand.

"I'm not going to sit here and be accosted by my daughter. I'm off to the shower. Have you seen Dan since you got home?"

"No, but remember he's a big boy, and Dr. Nelson said to let him have his independence. That's the only way we'll know if he can do it or not."

"I know. Good luck with your project. Will we be able to find the table for dinner?" I leave before she has a chance to answer.

The hot water feels so fantastic I want to stay forever, letting it flow over my tired body. I'm lost in thought till I hear footsteps in the bathroom. "Hey, Lil? How about saving some hot water for the hard working man, home from the salt mines."

As I step out of the shower, he wraps a towel around me. "Mmm, you smell good," he says as he nuzzles my neck.

I'm tempted to snuggle against him, until a whiff of sweaty, greasy, body odor changes my mind. "Whew." I pull back and wave my hand to clear the air. "I might smell good, but buddy, you don't. Hold that thought until tonight." Quickly I reach back, turn on the shower, spin him around and push him in fully clothed. He's cursing me as I hurriedly pull on my sweats and rush out of the bathroom before he grabs me. He won't drip all over the bedroom carpet, and I'm lucky he's not wearing his new boots—I'd hate to ruin them. I'm still laughing when I reach the kitchen.

"You know you two are weird, don't you? What did you do? I could hear him yelling in here."

"I helped him into the shower—without giving him time to undress."

"Weird, definitely weird." She hands me a stack of pictures to check so she doesn't cut and paste any on the poster board that I might want to keep.

• • •

The next two weeks rush by. Sarah gets an A on her project—and in all her classes. She and I are on a shopping spree to find "the" dress to wear under her gown for graduation. It's a pale-gold sheath with a fitted bodice, and it skims over her hips, showing off her curves without clinging to every line. *Our little girl is all grown up.* After we come home, she's modeling it when Dan comes in, looking for something to eat.

"You look nice, Sarah." He watches as she twirls like a runway model.

"Thanks, Dan. It's my graduation dress. Now, wait right there. I want you to see me in my gown."

She returns in a flash, snapping the top fastener on the black gown. The Peter Pan collar on her dress shows at the neckline. She places the mortarboard on her head with the gold tassel hanging down the right side. She strides across the living room, stops in front of him, and mimes receiving a diploma. When she reaches her hand out, Dan hesitates—but takes it. She shakes it firmly, thanks him, and transfers her tassel to the left side of her cap.

"See Dan. That's what I'll do at my graduation. Will you come with Mom and Dad?"

"No, Sarah. I will go to family dinner tomorrow night, but no graduation. Okay?"

"Okay, Dan."

She's still conflicted that he won't be with us for her big day. And so am I, because I'm relieved—and yet I feel guilty for it. Her graduation needs to be about her. I want to focus on her—not worry about something upsetting him.

• • •

The big day's a bevy of activity, beginning with a last-minute change to a simpler hair style that makes getting ready easier. The local flower shop delivers a delicate orchid corsage for Sarah to wear on her wrist, ordered by Phil, her beau. Many pictures are taken in various poses, some of Sarah with both Mitch and I, some with each of us, and lots of just her. Dan is included in a couple of the pictures, but he stayed mostly in his studio. He's watching us as we get in the car. I wave for him to join us, but he shakes his head no. He waves as we back out of the driveway.

Mitch and I swell with pride as Pomp and Circumstance plays, and the graduating class files in. Sarah searches the audience for us, and her face lights up when she sees us. When it's time for each student to cross the stage, Mitch bites his lip and wipes a tear as Sarah appears. I won't remember the speeches, but watching Sarah, so poised, is burned into my memory. Then her tassel gets caught in her earring, and she can't switch it to the left side of her cap.

The principal says, "Well, perhaps we'll have to take back that diploma, Sarah, since you can't move the tassel to signify that you've graduated."

Laughing, she hugs the diploma to her chest, squares her shoulders, and looks Mr. Patton directly in the eyes. "Just try to take this from me. Don't forget, I excelled in my self-defense class." The audience erupts in laughter along with Mr. Patton.

When the last diploma's given, he presents the graduating class and dismisses them for the last time. Caps fly, and the kids come running, looking for loved ones and friends. Sarah's pulled into hugs as she makes her way to us. With tears in our eyes, we finally hug our darling girl. It's not quite perfect without Dan.

We mill around, congratulating her classmates and visiting with other proud families, but Sarah's anxious to go home to see her brother. The studio's dark when we arrive, but the light's on in the kitchen so we expect to find him there. Sarah runs ahead, anxious to show him her diploma. In the kitchen we find her staring at a painting propped on a chair of her in cap and gown. Her face radiates light, and a glow surrounds her head. She's standing in front of the studio, holding a long-stemmed, red rose. In the studio window behind her is the shadow of a man. On the table is a note in his child-like print. "Dan loves his sissy." But Dan is gone.

∞

Chapter 55

As much as Sarah loves the painting, she's disappointed that Dan's not here to share her joy. She's also torn about going to the graduation party without Phil. He did call and encourage her to go, hang out with her friends, have fun, and celebrate her accomplishments.

"I know he says I should go, but what's the use of having a boy-friend if I'm still doing things by myself. I don't know about these long-distance relationships."

Mitch wraps his arm around her shoulders and pulls her close. "That's what you get for dating an older man. He's off to college, and you're stuck here. I tried to warn you the age difference was going to be a problem." He tries to look serious, but can't stifle a chuckle.

"Dad, a year older doesn't make him 'older.'" She laughs, using air quotes. "I should change into something comfortable. Tammy's pick-ing me up in a half hour." She pauses, studying herself in the painting. "He's so darn talented. I only wish—" She wipes a tear as she turns to go change.

Mitch and I admire the beauty of Dan's creation. He tugs me into an embrace. "I'm with Sarah, I just wish—oh, so many things."

"I know. I try not to worry, but some days—" I shake my head and sigh. "At least he's keeping his appointments with Dr. Nelson, taking his meds and not drinking."

"I hope you're right. I do, but I thought I smelled booze on him after he was out all night last week. When I asked him about it, he said he'd taken some cough medicine—and he's not good at lying—"

"Unless he's hearing voices?" I finish for him. Surely I'd have noticed any significant changes. *Wouldn't I?* "Why didn't you say something?"

"Because I want to believe him. I've been keeping an eye on him, and it hasn't happened again. Plus, it's Sarah's time, and I want us to focus on her. God knows how often we haven't because of Dan."

When a horn honks, Sarah rushes in, giving us a quick hug and kiss on the cheek. "You guys are the best. Thanks for everything."

The party's being held at the little Clear Creek park. We repeat the standard instructions; home by one, no drinking and no riding in cars with anyone who's been drinking, and make sure she has change so she can use the pay phone at the park to call us if she needs or wants a ride home. The horn blares again and out the door she flies.

We have a bite to eat, and then we're off to bed, though I doubt I'll sleep.

• • •

"Wha—what the hell?" The shrill ring of the phone rips through my sleep. I fight blankets trying to answer, but Mitch beats me to it. This can't be good—the bedside clock says it's a little after midnight. I tell myself to relax—it's probably only Sarah wanting a ride home. Then I hear Mitch.

"Whoa, slow down, Sarah. I can't understand you. What? Ronnie Dean did what? Dan did? No! Tell me he didn't. Where is he now? The cops, what? Hold on, Sarah. Are you okay? Is someone with you? A lady cop and Tammy? It's okay, baby. Mom and I are on our way. You're still at the little park, right? We'll be right there." He hangs up the phone, rubs his hands across his face, takes a deep breath, and slowly lets it out.

"What the hell's going on, Mitch?" I try to stay calm, but panic creeps into my voice. "Something to do with that jerk, Ronnie Dean, cops, and Dan? What about Dan?"

"I don't really know. She wasn't making much sense. We need to find out, so let's get going."

• • •

Three police cars are at the park with lights flashing. A bonfire glows in the background, and a subdued group of teenagers mingles nearby when we reach the park. Sarah is sitting on a bench talking with an officer. I'm out of the car before Mitch comes to a complete stop, rushing to our girl. I pull her up into a hug. I don't care if I'm interrupting something.

"Excuse me, ma'am. Who are you?"

Before I can answer, Mitch speaks up. "Look, we're Sarah's parents, and we need to know that she's okay. Please give us a minute, Officer."

"It's Officer Amy Shorcroft. I'll give you a minute, but I do need to ask her some more questions so we can wrap this up and let everyone go home." She steps away to question another teenager.

"Sarah? What happened?" Mitch asks gently.

"I—I'm not really sure. It's all so confusing. We were having a good time when Ronnie Dean and his bunch showed up—they'd all been drinking. They brought beer and were trying to get everyone to drink it. Some of the kids did, but not me and my friends. He got upset when I wouldn't pay any attention to him. He grabbed me by the arm and tried to drag me off—"

"He did what?' Mitch bellows, heads turn in our direction—including Officer Shorcroft's.

"Are you hurt?"

"I think I might have pulled something when I jerked away, but I'm okay. The paramedics checked me, and I'm only bruised. Anyway, he kept saying we needed to talk. My friends told him to let me go, when all of a sudden someone came out of the trees, grabbed Ronnie, and threw him to the ground, yelling. 'You bad. You leave my sister lone. You hurt her. I warn you.' I realized it was Dan. Then, just like that, he was gone. How did he know I was here? Did you tell him? Did he come back home? Anyway, somebody called the cops. Ronnie's threatening to sue, and he's demanding the cops find Dan and lock him up. I don't think they will. I think they've arrested Ronnie and his buddies. They were drunk as skunks, and they all had beer. Plus, I heard one of the cops say, 'There's a couple cases in Ronnie's pickup.' I want to go home."

I'm in shock. "Dan was here? Are you sure?"

"No, Mom. I lied," she says sarcastically. "Don't you think I know my brother even if he did look like a wild man. Cripes, Mom. Give me a break."

"I wasn't doubting you, Sarah. It's all so bizarre. I'm sorry, baby." I wipe a tear from her cheek.

"You should have been here. It was just as bizarre up close and in person. The scary thing is how quietly he moved. He was like a shadow. If Ronnie hadn't been screaming about it, I wouldn't have believed my own eyes." Her lip quivers, and her body starts to shake. Mitch and I wrap her in our arms, trying to reassure her everything will be okay.

Officer Shorcroft asks her a few more questions, takes pictures of her bruised arm, and tells us we can go home. The imprint of Ronnie's hand shows on her arm, and by the way she's holding it, it's hurting her. I wonder what would have happened if Dan hadn't shown up. Would her friends have protected her as well?

"You might want to have that shoulder checked out. It looks like Ronnie Dean had quite a grip on her, and I know she was fighting against him. I'll need to talk to your son. Do you know where I might find him?"

"I'm not sure if Dan will be home tonight or not. He has a studio room behind our house, but he comes and goes without telling us. What's going to happen to Ronnie Dean?"

"For starters, Mrs. Hawke, Ronnie and his friends will be guests of the county tonight. They'll be charged with underage drinking and public drunkenness. Ronnie will be charged with assault on your daughter. Now, I suggest taking this young lady home to get some rest. I'll stop by tomorrow to talk to your son. He's not in trouble—I only want his side of the story."

As we're leaving, I notice Ronnie Dean in the back of a police car, pounding on the window with his cuffed hands. Thankfully, I can't hear what he's saying—but when he flips me the bird, it's pretty evident. I pray we'll find Dan at home when we get there.

But he doesn't come home that night nor the next. Mitch goes to all the places he thinks Dan might be, some based on the pictures he painted. We talk to Officer Shorcroft about filing a missing person report on him, but since he's an adult, she doesn't think they will do much until he's been gone longer—even when we explain he's an at-risk adult.

We're all a mess. Sarah blames herself, saying if only she hadn't gone to that damn party. Mitch is driving himself crazy trying to find Dan. *And me?* I'm lost. I'm on the phone calling everyone I can think of, jumping every time the phone rings. When I talk to Dr. Nelson, I find out he hasn't seen Dan in over a month. When I'm stressed, I clean—so the house is spotless. Next, I'll work on the garden we decided to plant for some reason—like we don't have enough to do.

It's been almost a week, then one evening I see a light in the studio. The coffee cup I'm holding slips from my hand, shattering on the floor. I step over the glass and run to the studio to make sure he's okay. I jerk open the door. "Dan!"

But it's not Dan.

∞

Chapter 56

Mitch is sitting on the side of Dan's bed, a notebook in his hands. His eyes are glazed—he looks as though he's not sure where he is as he holds the notebook out to me. When he chokes on my name and seems to shrink in front of me, I freeze mid-stride. He waves the notebook at me. "Read."

What could possibly have him so upset? Our Dan's not one for writing much. He hated it in school and struggles with it to this day. Reluctantly, I reach for the book. What does it say that could do this to my husband—he looks like a broken man. He shakes himself as if to toss the burden of it away. He waves the book at me again, and what he says chills me to the bone. "They're back."

At that moment my legs nearly collapse beneath me. I know what Mitch means without reading it. "They're back? The voices? B-but how? Why? He's been taking his meds. How could they be back?" Then I remember he's not seen Dr. Nelson for over a month.

"Read, Lil, just read. It doesn't tell us everything, but it tells us enough."

I take the notebook and crumple on the bed next to Mitch. Holding it to my chest, I pray, "God help me." Slowly, I open the book, half expecting something to jump out and grab me. Dan's name is printed on the front cover. On the first page he's written:

> **doctor nelson gave to me, said to rite what i feel. How i do that i don know, sarah rite in her book tell me it help so i rite.**

The first two pages aren't too bad. I look at Mitch, confused. "Keep going."

So I do. There are no dates, so I have no idea when he started it, but soon little pictures of gargoyles appear in the margins.

> i here gamma today i miss her and carl talk me help me i need tell doc but i like here them he want them not talk me.

I riffle through the pages. Looking ahead, the border pictures become more distorted. A chill runs up my spine when I see the only capitals in the book:

> BIG YELLO BACK he say i need leave no one tell me wat i do i man now

My hand is shaking as I turn the page.

> big yello say i not leave mom dad sarah will be hurt i not want them hurt i will leave i will watch no let big yello hurt.

I hurl the book away from me, scrubbing my hands on the blanket as though to remove the words I just read. My first impulse is to run screaming from the studio. No, what I really want is to wipe away these last few minutes and create a different ending.

We cling to each other, neither of us wanting to be here, but we can't move. I convulse in tears, mine mingling with his. We've lost. We've lost the battle, and I'm afraid we've lost our son. It was such a hard fight last time. I'm not sure either of us can face another. But we have to. We can't give up. As long as Dan is breathing, we have to believe there is hope.

I take one more shuddering breath and pull back, running my hand down his cheek. "We can do this. We have to—if not for Dan, for Sarah. But we can't help Dan until we find him. Sarah's still here, and we need to be here for her. I just don't understand why the medicine quit working?"

"You didn't read it all. You skipped to the end and missed it. Big Yellow told him not to take it—to hide it under his tongue if someone was there and then throw it away. Or get rid of a dose every day. Our Dan wouldn't know how to manipulate people or lie, but when Big Yellow talks to him, he does. How does that happen, Lil? Tell me, 'Counselor,' how the hell does that happen?"

I jerk back as though he slapped me. The way he said 'Counselor' held so much anger, like I should have all the answers. "I don't know, Mitch. All I know is that it's his illness." I'm on my feet, pacing, looking around the room and notice the difference. Dan's little trucks, his paints, sketchpads, and most of his canvases are gone, along with his backpack and portable easel. He's taken some of his clothes from the closet and his dresser, and in the bathroom his toiletries are gone.

"Mitch, doesn't Dan have a duffle bag?"

"Yeah, he's got my old one, why?"

"Look around. He's taken almost everything with him. He must have planned it for when we'd be gone. I never thought he'd be so devious. He must have done it while we were at graduation. He waved goodbye when we backed out of the driveway—he rarely ever does that, but I never thought anything about it, until right now."

He looks and realizes what I'm saying. When he checks the food storage drawer, it's empty—along with his utensils, cups, and little plates. His electrical appliances are still here because he won't be able to use them. The tin in the bottom drawer where Dan keeps his money is empty. He never spends much. Anytime he sells a painting for cash or gets paid for work, he puts it in the tin, keeping only a few dollars in pocket change. There was over three hundred dollars in it, so at least he'll have money for food for a while, but not enough for a place to stay. Maybe he'll go back to the halfway house—he seemed to like it there.

I want to leave—it hurts too much to see the empty spaces in what's supposed to be Dan's safe place. I turn and look away, trying to make sense of it all. That's when I notice it.

"Mitch? Did you see this?"

"What?'

"On the easel. Look." We move closer. On the easel is a painting of our family on the deck including Dan, though he sits separate from us. Everyone's laughing but him. He's watching us as he always does when we're being silly. Over his shoulder is a yellow-shrouded figure with red-glowing eyes and malevolent features.

The rest of the day, we wander like zombies, struggling to make sense of it all. I'm still annoyed over Mitch's snide counselor remark, in part because it's easier to be mad at him than give in to the pain of imagining Dan out there all alone. I want to grab a hammer and beat the crap out of something—anything, like Mitch is doing in the backyard chopping wood. He must be exhausted, yet he keeps chopping. At this rate, we'll have enough wood for two years. I can't call the hospital, police station, Salvation Army—I've done all that. When I call the Serenity House, they say he's not been seen nor heard from since his discharge. All I get when I call Dr. Nelson is the answering service. What can I expect from him? He's already told me Dan quit going over a month ago.

Sarah's gone to work today, despite her black and blue arm. Bless her—I don't know how she manages it. She insists her shoulder's okay and refuses to have it checked at the ER. For a girl usually meticulous in her appearance, she pulled her hair into a simple ponytail, swiped on a smear of lipstick, and slid into a long-sleeved blouse to cover her bruised arm. She doesn't seem to care today. I dread telling her what we've found. Once more, what should have been a high point in her life is blemished by something out of her control.

To burn off energy, I dump whipping cream into a bowl and with a whisk whip it to stiff peaks. With every stroke I curse God, the universe, mental illness, the doctors, and even Dan. If I could find him, I'd reach inside and rip out the voices and inject him with some of his sister's compassion, understanding, and self-confidence. She's never met a stranger and gets along with everyone. She seems to have a double dose of everything Dan's lacking.

The phone rings and I grab it, hoping it's good news. It's Dr. Nelson. I tell him about the journal. He, too, is surprised at Dan's deviousness and asks to see it. I agree to take it to him this next week and promise to call if we hear anything, feeling even more defeated when I hang up.

Mitch finds me holding the bowl of whipped cream, staring out the window. He reaches around me and scoops some on his finger. "Mm—that's good. What are we having?"

"I'm not sure. I needed to beat the crap out of something, so I picked on the cream. Did chopping wood help you?"

"Yeah, it did. And Lil, I'm so sorry for my snarky remark. I know you're just as confused and upset as I am. I had no right to take it out on you." He slips his arm around my waist and pulls me back against him.

I relax into his embrace, an island in the storm. "I know, Mitch, I know. What hurts is the only time you acknowledge what I do is when you're upset, and then you throw out 'counselor' like it's some kind of bitter pill. My head tells me you don't mean it, but my heart aches—like today, when I'm holding on by my fingernails. Don't you think I kick myself all the time because I'm supposed to know things? I'm supposed to help people navigate the minefields of life, and I can't even fix my own son? Don't you realize when I see you and Sarah in so much pain, I know I let you down? And Mitch?" I turn and cling to him. "I don't know if I'll make it through this time. I'm afraid if I let go I'll be so shattered the pieces won't fit back together again. I'm scared, Mitch. I'm so flippin' scared." My sobs garble those last words. He holds me as I cry.

When the tears slow, he steps back, holding me at arm's length so he can look in my eyes. The pain I see in his face breaks my heart.

"Oh, Lil, sweetheart, you've never let me down—nor Sarah and especially not Dan. You've worked so hard all these years trying to find the answers to help him. I've watched you throw yourself into classes to learn all you can. I'm overwhelmed by your knowledge, and I feel like a dunderhead when I listen to you giving a presentation. Maybe I'm jealous. Let us down? Never, you're the glue that holds us together."

I hug him tight. "I don't want to be the glue. I'm too tired. I can barely hold me together. It's like I've got a big bottle of super glue, but keep gluing parts in the wrong place—and it all turns into a muckin' fess." We're holding each other as the tears dry—that's how Sarah finds us.

Standing in the doorway watching us, she scrubs her hands over her face, runs her fingers through her hair, and clears her throat. Tears glisten in her eyes. She looks exhausted. "You two are a mess—you look like hell. Can't I leave for a few hours without you falling apart?" Her smile is shaky, but she straightens her shoulders. "I don't know about you guys, but I need to claw myself out of this well. We're not doing Dan any good. I've been to see Mr. Bacon, and I feel better. I'm sad Dan may be having another breakdown, but, dammit, I'm not going to join him in hell." She slaps at a tear escaping down her cheek, daring any more to fall.

She hugs us before spying the bowl of whipped cream wilting on the table. "I see dinner's ready. Where's my spoon?" She succeeds in enticing a chuckle from us both, and I relax in spite of a splitting headache.

Chapter 57

A few weeks after we found Dan's journal, Mitch is heading toward the studio, but stops suddenly. "What the—?" He rushes out the door, with Sarah and me close behind. We're almost there when I see it—the plaque Sarah made is gone. In its place is a piece of driftwood with "DAD STUDIO" carefully painted on it, along with the image of a man bent over a drafting table.

• • •

Mitch doesn't do anything with the studio for a couple of months. Once in a while he walks up to the door, looks at the new sign, and rests his hand on the pedal tractor—but he never reaches for the doorknob. At least we know that when he took his plaque and hung one for his dad, Dan was still thinking of us—bittersweet knowledge at best, but it gives us a flicker of hope.

Summer turns to autumn. Mother Nature dresses the trees in her finest hues of gold, oranges, reds, and some green. Our garden has produced well. We enjoy the fruits of our labors, and the overflow we give to the Serenity House, hoping he'll show up there. When some of the veggies I targeted as almost ready-to-pick come up missing, I suspect a visitor to the garden. Because it continues over the summer, I'm convinced it's Dan. Mitch sometimes stays up late, sitting in the dark hoping to see him—but he never does.

Over the summer Sarah agonizes whether to go to the Junior College in Sheridan or to the University in Laramie. She decides to take some classes in Sheridan, because she isn't sure what she'll choose for her major. I believe she, like us, is hoping we'll find Dan. She's selected basic courses plus one for fun—pottery, with a goal of making us all large hot-chocolate mugs. Classes are three days a week, so she will continue working at the Dairy Queen.

The day I come home and find Mitch in the studio is disconcerting. I'm sure he's contemplating using the space at last. Although he stands there quietly, barely moving, it feels like we'll be closing the door on Dan, even if it is his idea.

"You decided to take him up on it? To make it your space?" I ask, my voice barely a whisper.

"I guess. Yes? I don't know—Lil. I'm so torn." He doesn't look at me, and his shoulders droop. "I've been thinking. What if my working out here will encourage Dan to visit when I'm here? This would be the one place he'd show himself." I'm surprised we didn't think of this before. Mitch looks at me and asks, "Do you think I'm crazy? I've got to do something to move forward. This limbo is driving me mad." The anguish in his eyes matches my own. I hurry to his side and take his hands in mine.

"Mitch, honey. You're right. You're doing the right thing."

"You think so? Really? I'm so glad. I thought you might be upset—that would kill me." He pulls me close.

We hold each other for a moment before I step back and look around. "What are your thoughts? Are you going to keep the bed in here or—?"

"I thought I'd move my office out here and take the bed and dressers into the house to make a guest room. I want to keep it all—one because it's what Dan's used to, and the other reason, like that old car you love to drive, it belonged to your mom. It's all well-built furniture, not like the junk they sell now."

After thinking about it for a bit, I realize it's a great idea. We decide to go to the second hand shop on Saturday for a couch or loveseat.

"And maybe a comfy overstuffed chair and footstool to put where the bed is now," I add. "You never know. I might show up with my book once in a while. I'll read—you'll work. Sounds cozy. What do you think?"

"It sounds great. I'm getting kind of excited, yet guilty at the same time. But it's what he wanted, don't you think, when he put up that driftwood sign?"

"I believe it is. We both need to work on that guilt. We need to live! We aren't helping him by putting our lives on hold, waiting for him to come home. At this rate we'll be an emotional mess if he does return. And if, God forbid, he doesn't—" I can't go on. A sob escapes, and once more Mitch wraps me in his strong arms. It takes me a minute to pull myself together. I wipe my face. "We need to take care of ourselves if we're going to survive—meaning put one foot in front of the other, take care of business, and quit walking in the quicksand of what if's, shoulda, woulda, coulda all the time. I can only manage one minute at a time right now, but I'll work up to one day at a time."

"I know you're right, that's why I finally made a decision today to get off dead center and do something. And you know what? In spite of that niggle of guilt that rears its ugly head, it's exciting to make some plans again."

I hug him, knowing he's right. "I'll leave you to it. I need to change into something comfortable. Do you want my help or shall I fix dinner?"

"Dinner, I think. I'll be in after I strip the bed and break it down. I'll put the bedding in the washer. One step, two steps forward we will go."

As I return to the house, I'm humming. Was that movement I saw in the tree line by the garden? No, it's only a breeze blowing the branches. *How long will it take to quit seeing him in every shadow?*

Sarah isn't as receptive as we thought she'd be. She refuses to look at what Mitch is doing—or even talk to us about it. Her attitude hits me hard—she's always had such an easy-going personality. I'm not sure what to do with this semi-defiant young lady. She bites her lower lip as she watches Mitch carrying things in and out. When he asks for her help getting the guest room put together, she straight up refuses—probably for the first time in her life. I'm about to talk to her, but Mitch stops me, saying, "Let her be. She'll come around when she's ready."

Of course he's right. Barely two weeks later, we find her standing in the doorway of the studio when we come home from the store. She goes inside and looks around. A half hour or so later, she comes back in, walks up to her dad, and gives him a hug. "Good job, old man, good job." And the air is cleared.

Before long, Sarah and I are enjoying the cozy seating area while Mitch works at his drafting table. I find myself touching the tractor, like a talisman, before going in and then again when I leave. Both Sarah and Mitch do the same. A child's John Deere pedal tractor has become our touchstone.

• • •

Phone calls in the middle of the night never bode well. The ringing rips me from my sleep, and I answer before I'm completely awake. That's why I'm so confused when I hear Dan's voice. "You need to come right now, he got Sarah, he hurt Sarah, you need help Sarah now!" The agonized words sound like they're torn from his throat.

"Dan? Dan! Sarah's okay, she's asleep in her bed. She's okay, Son, she's okay." I nudge Mitch to wake him, put my hand over the phone. "Go check and make sure Sarah's home."

"W-what?"

"Go check Sarah." I whisper, then he hears Dan's voice boom from the phone. "She not okay, he hurt her, I go stop him, you get her. You come now! You bring Gamma car, she be safe."

"Dan, Son, it's okay, Dad checked, Sarah's in her bed asleep. It's okay, where are you? We'll come help you."

"No! I not need help. Saarraaahh I come help you. I kick his ass." The phone thunks like it's been dropped, and I hear the sound of feet running.

I hold the phone, willing Dan to return, but he doesn't. Finally, I hang up. Mitch is watching me. "What the hell? That was Dan? What was he saying about Sarah? She's sound asleep."

"I don't know. I don't know." My words slip out in a whisper. I take a sip of water. "He thinks she's in trouble, and we need to take the car—he called it Gamma's car, to find her." I want to cry, but the well is dry. Suddenly I realize I need to do something. I reach for the phone. Mitch isn't too happy when I tell him I'm calling the cops. But if they can find him, maybe he'll get the help he needs, and we need them to check on Ronnie Dean to make sure he doesn't try to hurt him.

It takes a few minutes to make the emergency operator understand what I need. She keeps asking if Dan's on drugs, but I'm finally able to explain that it's a mental health issue.

I sigh with relief when Officer Newsome calls to let me know that all seems well at Ronnie Dean's house. He tells me he knows Dan and understands that he has mental health issues, and assures me he'll keep an eye out for him. "We've been aware since you reported him missing, Mrs. Hawke. We've had a few reports that we've thought was him, but he's always gone when we get there. Once it was over on Buchannan— I think your old house, and the other was your husband's old construction yard. I didn't call because we never saw him. They say he moves like a ghost—there one minute and gone the next. I went to school with Dan, and I've regretted not doing more to stick up for him. You should know, Mrs. Hawke, I'll do everything in my power to bring him in safely, to get him the help he needs."

"We appreciate that, Officer Newsome. You don't know how much we appreciate that."

"If you hear from him again, don't hesitate to call us. I'll pay close attention to the pay phones when I'm on duty, and I'll share it with the station. Now, you folks try to get some rest."

Before I can respond, the call is disconnected. I tell Mitch, who's waiting impatiently to hear what I've been told. We sit close together, two shell-shocked parents. Our child is lost in his own mind, and our love can't fix him.

Chapter 58

"Thank you for seeing me on short notice, Mr. Bacon."

"That's okay, Lillian. I'm glad you called. I've not heard you sound as upset as you did when you called this morning. What's going on?"

I take a breath, a sip of water, adjust my blouse, and smooth my skirt. I know I'm avoiding answering the question. I'm attempting to wall in my feelings, pile a brick wall high enough that no pain can assail it. Finally, I begin. "Around two thirty this morning I was awakened by the phone ringing. When I answered, I recognized my son Daniel. He was upset, raving that someone was hurting his sister. He kept insisting we save her and wouldn't listen when I tried to convince him that she was safe in bed. He kept insisting we help her, but he wouldn't tell me where he was. Finally, he said he was going to 'kick his ass' and dropped the phone." I take another deep breath—I'd made it through.

He looks at me without blinking. I try to hold his gaze, but I feel like he can see through me. I drop my eyes and begin to fidget.

"Lillian," he leans towards me, hands together, resting on his knees. "You aren't in a staffing, giving a report on a patient. This is your life, your heart, your son. You need to rip the Band-Aid off the wound and let the blood spill. You need to feel the feelings—that's why we're here. Otherwise, you're wasting not only my time, but also yours. Now, once more, tell me why you're here."

Sometimes I hate this man, sitting there so smug, asking me to tell him how I feel. Nobody wants to hear how I feel right now—the poison might choke us all. I've worked damn hard to guard myself against the pain. *Now this ass wants me to lance the boil?* If I do, I'll dissolve into a puddle of goo and seep through the cracks to oblivion. *How do I purge it and survive?* I take a shaky breath. My hands are clammy. My face is flushed, and I feel sick to my stomach.

"How the hell do you think I feel? When I heard his voice I was so happy, so frightened. I wanted to slam down the phone and run screaming. I wanted to find him, to hold him, to save him. I wanted to rip that God damned sickness out of him. How do I feel?! I feel like a time bomb ready to explode. I feel impotent—a phony, a failure. I want to pound the shit out of something." I draw a shuddering breath. "But most of all? I feel like I want to quit—quit being patient, kind, understanding, strong." My voice is barely a whisper. "Most of all, I feel lost." By now I'm bent over double, my chest on my knees, my shaking hands clasped together, fingers intertwined hanging on for dear life. The only sound is the ticking of a clock and my sobs—my gut-wrenching, snot-flowing sobs. Finally, I take a stuttering breath, sit back, reach for a tissue, and blow my nose. As feeling returns to my numb extremities, I breathe deeply, begin to shiver, and rub my arms. Spent at last, I raise my eyes to his face.

He reaches out, touching my hand lightly. "Thank you, Lillian. Now, we can do some real work. You did beat the shit out of something—that wall you've been building, probably ever since you first realized Dan was different from other children. Look at you, Lil. You're still here, still standing."

"But I feel empty," I whisper.

"Good, we can begin to fill that void with tools to cope with what life throws at you. How many times have you sat in this chair and told your patients that? Don't you deserve the same?"

"I-I don't know. I guess that's why I'm here. Right?" I attempt a smile that probably looks more like a grimace.

"I'd say so. You filled a large trashcan full of crap today. Your job, when you leave this office, is to leave it here. You feel raw and vulnerable, and the temptation to pick that crap back up and slap it on to insulate you will be strong. You can resist it. You need to leave it here. We'll flush it as you walk out the door. This next week I want you to be aware of how you are feeling, honor those feelings, and journal about each and every one of them."

"B-b-but, what if I bleed all over my patients. How do I walk that tightrope?" I know it sounds sarcastic.

After a few minutes he replies. "What would you tell someone who asked you the same question?"

Wait a minute? Isn't that what I'm paying him for? Drawing another deep breath, I sigh and say, "Focus on the task at hand, take care of business, one step at a time."

"Does that sound like a game plan? Do you believe it can work?"

As I run what I've just said through my mind, I realize I believe it. "Yes, I do." We wrap up the session and make an appointment for next week.

"No cancelling. Your mental health is as important as anyone's. Make you your priority. An empty well helps no one."

• • •

Over the next months the phone calls continue off and on. Weeks pass with none, then for a spattering of days there will be multiple calls, always in the middle of the night. I continue seeing Mr. Bacon, and I'm feeling less remorse and guilt. I have a new mantra. *It isn't personal. It's the disease.*

Occasionally, the police call with news of a possible sighting. We're all getting better at taking it in stride. The winter months are the most difficult—we worry about him out in the snow and cold. Winters in Wyoming can be unforgiving. Mitch buys supplies and leaves them at Nana's bench in a large insulated container he's chained to one of the legs. We also leave winter clothes, boots, and a heavy coat there. When I shop, I look for foods that need little preparation, like instant soups and granola bars to nourish him. They're usually gone by the time we check, and we assure each other it's Dan. Between that and the phone calls, we know he's alive.

Mitch also continues in counseling, though he's found another therapist, one he relates to better. We don't talk about it much, but it seems to be helping.

The holidays go by in a blur and, before we know it, another summer is ending. Sarah decided she's going to the University of Wyoming this fall, so we're busy getting everything ready for her. Once more, we're grateful for Carl and the trust fund he left for her education. Dan's was used up for his treatment over the years, but hers has been untouched until now. She and Phil seem to be serious, and he's been good for her. Mitch and I are not quite ready for her to be all grown up. It means we have to let her go.

As she's sorting through her clothes, deciding which to take or leave or get rid of, talk turns to Phil—of course. He's rented an unfurnished apartment for the school year, so he'll be taking a load of furniture.

"Will he have any roommates?" I ask as casually as I can.

"No, Mom. He won't have any roommates. And no, Mom, I'm not planning on moving in with him. Remember, I've already rented a studio apartment in that old Victorian house you fell in love with."

I hold my hands up. "Hey, I didn't ask."

"You didn't have to. Your body language was shouting it."

"I'm a mom. What can I say? You're growing up. You're also human, and I don't want anything to derail your future."

"Like hearing I think I'm pregnant?"

"WHAT?!" Mitch roars into the room. He walked in on her last sentence, and he looks at us. It doesn't help that she begins to laugh. "I see nothing funny, young lady." He sounds horrified, and that makes it worse. I fight back giggles. His expression is priceless.

I reach out to him. "No, Mitch. You didn't hear what you thought you heard. Sarah is not pregnant. We're talking about her focusing on school not Phil. I said I didn't want anything to interfere with her future plans, and she said—and I quote, 'Like hearing I think I'm pregnant.' You only heard part of the conversation." Finally, he calms down and laughs at our joke, though he threatens not to give Sarah her surprise that's in the driveway.

But he does. It's an old 1955 23-window VW Samba bus he bought and refurbished. He had a mechanic look it over and complete any work it needed or might need in the near future. The interior has been gutted and rebuilt, including the seats. He left the last row of seats out and installed a bar across for hanging her clothes. The exterior was the final touch. It's a hippy van—bright flowers over a brown lower half and yellow top half, the colors of U of W.

"You got this for me?" Her voice choked.

"I did, pumpkin. You need more room than your little VW bug has. I know you've wanted a hippy van for a long time. When I saw this, it was in sad shape, but the timing was perfect. It's all safe and sound, with new, all-weather tires on it and some chains, just in case. I put a small toolbox in for you with some basic tools you might need, plus a fire extinguisher and some flares. You're all set for travel. We'll keep the bug here. Heck, maybe we can pry Mom out of Gamma's car for better fuel mileage." After hugs and a few tears, we get it packed and wave her on her way.

That night, as I'm falling asleep, the phone rings. I hear a guttural voice on the line. "I hate you!" The line goes dead, and once more I feel gutted. The calls continue through the night, but they lose their impact. By morning, I realize he was probably close by as Sarah packed her van and left. His sister's gone.

How can he protect her now?

∞

Chapter 59

Adjusting to our empty nest is a gradual process for Mitch and me. We miss our girl like crazy. The highlight of any day is a letter from her, telling us about her exploits. She's studying nursing with a mental health certification, though she has no plan to work in a psychiatric hospital. She and Phil limit their dates to the weekends so they can keep up their coursework and grades. They'll be home for Thanksgiving, but Phil will have dinner with his family and join us for breakfast on Friday morning.

Mitch does occasional work for a butcher, so he's bringing home a fresh bird at a discount. We're planning a simple meal this year—pies and rolls from a local bakery, canned cranberries, no sweet potato goo that no one eats but me, same for the green bean casserole and mince pie. This year I refuse to run myself ragged, and then be too tired to enjoy it all, especially my time with Sarah.

Thoughts of Dan always linger close, yet they no longer have the power to control my mind, moods, and actions. My daily prayer is for acceptance. Like the Serenity Prayer says, 'accept the things we cannot change.' I'm finally realizing the only power I have is the power to change me—and how I react to life as it happens. I might influence some situations, but I can't heal Dan by sheer will. I can rage against God for the unfairness of it all, but in the end I'm exhausted, and things are the same. Mr. Bacon reminded me when I said I wished Dan could be normal, that Dan is living his normal. That realization has helped me so much. The voices in his head are his normal self. When we medicate him, we ask him to function to our normal, like pounding a square peg into a round hole. Will he be safer that way? Of course, but right now he's doing what he can to keep from losing the voices. I'm learning to accept my feet of clay. I am human. I will mess up. I won't always know the answer or get everything right. I've given up my super glue and my superwoman cape. It isn't my job to fix everybody.

If I'm putting more effort into someone's healing than they are, I'm not helping either one of us. So this weekend I'm going to focus on what I have, rather than what I don't have. I'm sad Dan won't be with us and that we don't know how he's getting by. I pray daily he is safe and warm. But that black cloud I tethered myself to? I took a sword and cut that line. I close my eyes and see it floating toward the heavens. But being human, every once in a while when I'm hungry, angry, lonely, or tired, I make a loop in my rope and try to lasso it again.

I'm off on Wednesday, and the anticipation of Sarah's arrival has me pacing the floor.

"She won't get here any faster by checking every two minutes. Why don't I go pick up the pies and rolls from the bakery—they're closing early. Maybe you could chop the celery and onion for the stuffing."

"You're right. I need to be doing something, so chop veggies I'll do while you're at the bakery. You're a smart man, Mitchell Hawke. I don't care what anybody says."

Before I'm finished, a horn honks in the driveway. I dry my hands on my apron as I hurry out to the hippy van and jerk the driver's door open to hug my girl. But it's not Sarah. It's Reggie.

"Surprise!" Reggie, Tim, and Sarah yell.

"Aunt Reggie and Tim drove from Cheyenne to Laramie yesterday so we could surprise you. Dad, were you trying to sneak off? Was Mom trying to put you to work?" She throws herself into her dad's arms. And Tim is right behind her waiting for his turn.

Once in the house we're all talking at once. Tim's all smiles, a completely different boy than the pouty one that arrived last time. After we settle down with snacks and drinks, Mitch and I both notice him look toward the studio with a frown, looking a little sad. Mitch walks over to him.

"What's the matter, buddy?"

"I'm happy to be here, Uncle Mitch, but I was thinking about Dan. Mom said he left home because of his sickness. I was hoping he'd come home for Thanksgiving. Do you think if I went outside and called him, he might come home?"

"I wish—you don't know how much I wish." His eyes get misty. "I'm afraid it's more complicated than that." He tries explaining to Tim something we have difficulty explaining to ourselves. We know the words, but it's hard to absorb all the nuances of Dan's illness. They go to the studio so Mitch can give a pamphlet to Tim that explains schizophrenia better than he feels he can. Then they leave for the bakery before it closes.

The house rings with laughter and voices as Sarah and Reggie bring in the luggage, wrapping me in the warmth of family. Reggie gives Sarah a bad time about Phil when she admits to me she "kinda likes him a little bit."

"A little bit, my big toe. She made me drive so they could sleep together."

"Aunt Reggie!" She flushes bright red. "We were sitting up in the back seat. We did not sleep together." I've never seen her so flustered. I bite my lip to keep from laughing out loud.

"Wait a minute, missy. You were together? You fell asleep? Hence you two were sleeping together."

"Oh, you, Aunt Reggie. I'm going to make you rue the day you said that." When she dumps half a glass of ice water on Reggie's head, I lose it.

"Oh, stop!" I finally gasp as Reggie chases her around the table trying to get her back. Peals of laughter fill the house. My ribs hurt, my eyes are leaking—and the most hated sign that I'm getting older—I may have peed myself a bit.

This is the tone of Thanksgiving: love, laughter, and a few tears. It doesn't matter that the lace tablecloth isn't on the table, and nobody mentions the missing 'traditional' dishes. For once I know it's not the food that matters—only family matters. We rehash our last Thanksgiving together, laugh at the bumps, and talk of Dan without feeling like our

insides are being ripped from us—choosing to think of the good, not
the pain. Tim tells us how special the little red pickup is to him. He
won't let anyone touch it. And so the day goes, reminiscing, enjoying
one another—even an unplanned afternoon nap in front of the television. It's such a good day—my heart is full.

The next morning Sarah leaves to get Phil, since he left his pickup
in Laramie. She seems nervous—which surprises me. I wonder if she
chose breakfast today to guarantee no repeat of the boyfriend debacle.
Although we've met him before, he hasn't spent much time at our home.
She requested waffles with fruit and whipped cream, so Reggie and I
get started while she's gone. Sausage and scrambled eggs are added to
the menu, since not everyone can eat that much sweetness. Our timing
is perfect—we finish as Sarah and Phil arrive. But too late, I realize I
should have given him a chance to relax before serving breakfast.

"Glad you could join us, Phil." Mitch extends his hand. "How was
your Thanksgiving?"

"It was good, sir, really good. Thanks for inviting me. I'm looking
forward to getting to know Sarah's family better." He reaches for her
hand, but I see her glance out the door before taking it.

I welcome him and encourage everyone to take a seat before the
waffles get cold—or the whipped cream too warm. Phil's manners are
impeccable—they come naturally to him. Mitch and I look at each
other and smile when he holds Sarah's chair for her. Conversation flows
easily during breakfast, and after we've all eaten our fill, I suggest everyone move out to the deck while Reggie and I clear the table.

Sarah hesitates. I can tell she's concerned Dan might cause a problem. "It's going to be okay. It's not going to be a repeat of 'that' episode.
I promise you," her dad says to her.

"Are you sure? I feel he's close by. I've felt it ever since we got here,
but I haven't seen anything."

"He might well be, but he won't come up to the house. Okay?"

"It's okay, Sarah, I'm not going to do anything to make him think
you're in danger. He won't have to save you if I'm around." Phil says
quietly.

Mitch starts a fire outside as Phil, Sarah, and Tim watch. Reggie and I bring coffee and hot chocolate and join them on the deck. Once we sit down Mitch takes the bull by the horn. "So, Sarah's told you about her brother?"

"Yes, as a matter of fact I've known about Dan since the first day we met. I may even have him to thank for meeting her."

"How's that?" I ask.

"She never told you the story? It was a beautiful fall day. In fact it was the day after Thanksgiving three years ago. I stopped by the Dairy Queen for a Dilly bar, and as I was walking away, I noticed this lovely lady in the little park next to it. She was sitting on the ground with her back up against that big fir tree. I could tell she was crying. I started to leave—I didn't want to embarrass or startle her. Instead, I walked over and asked if I could help and gave her my hankie."

They exchange a glance that softens their features as Sarah resumes the story of her knight in not-so-shiny armor—ending with them exchanging phone numbers. "And the rest, as they say, is history!"

"You mean the nutty family didn't scare you off?"

"Aunt Reggie!"

Phil laughs, "No, I have my own nutty family, so I understood what Sarah was dealing with. My big sis' son, my nephew, is Down syndrome. That's not the same as your Dan, but we've probably experienced similar frustrations. Syd is basically non-verbal, he has little impulse control, and he's quick to anger. His anger usually flares when he can't make someone understand what he's trying to tell them. He's had years of speech therapy and behavioral modification, and he is much better. He doesn't do well in large groups of people, especially if he doesn't know many of them, and if he gets excited or tired. But when he's good—he's very, very good. I love him to pieces. Like Dan, Syd has a special talent. He excels in music, particularly the piano, which he began playing at about five."

"At five?" I ask.

"Yes, our grandma's a pianist, and one day she picked him up and put him on her lap, expecting him to pound on the keys like most little ones will. But after a few minutes of playing around on the keys he played the lullaby she sings to him. He's in his heaven when he's playing. He sits straighter, smiles, and makes the music of Angels. He only has to hear a song once, and he can play it. Like your Dan, he's one special guy. And like all of you, we wish we could fix him."

His story touches me deeply. I like this young man. I can tell Mitch does, too. I like the way he cherishes our daughter, and the respectful way he treats her as she shows him the studio, the new workshop her dad made, and around the yard. I do notice that she doesn't offer to take him to the creek or walk too close to the tree line.

Before we know it, the weekend's over. It's just the two of us in our quiet house, again—filled with good memories and hope for our daughter's future.

∞

Chapter 60

Winter hits with a vengeance. Mitch still leaves more food and supplies, hoping Dan, or someone else in need at least, can use it. He adds gloves, hats, heavy socks, and mufflers—usually all gone the next time he checks. Mitch winterized the Caddy, including new snow tires and a set of chains for good measure. Because we live five miles from town, he'd rather be safe than sorry.

He clears my windshield and pours my coffee by the time I'm ready to leave for work. The weather forecast predicts blizzard conditions by the end of day. Although it's sub-zero when I leave for work, the skies are blue, and the sun is shining. It will have to warm up if we're going to get snow.

Barely two hours after I get to work the skies open, the winds pick up, and we're in a whiteout. These winter squalls are nothing new, so I figure it'll let up before long—but it doesn't. Mitch calls at noon suggesting I try getting off early. The road forecast is already dire, and slide-offs are being reported all over. I arrange to leave after I finish my staff notes following a scheduled one o'clock group. I look for Marvin, our maintenance man, and bribe him with the promise of homemade chocolate chip cookies to put those damn chains on.

By the time I leave, the streets are treacherous. Luckily, some of the main intersections are sanded, and I only have to cross two. Unluckily, the road to our house is the worst. Wind gusts blowing into the side of my car threaten to push me in the ditch. One mile at a time I creep my way home. I can barely see past the front bumper, and I pray not to come upon another car—I'm not sure I'd see it in time to stop. I'm driving only ten miles an hour, concentrating on each mile marker post I pass.

Finally, I reach our driveway. Bless my sweet Mitch—he's shoveled it out, but it's already drifting over. I pull up the hood of my coat, wrap my scarf around my neck, and lift it to cover my mouth and nose. Taking a deep breath, I make a mad dash to the door, praying I don't slip and fall.

As soon as I'm in the house, I call for him so he knows I'm safe. Thankfully I didn't submit to his pressure to get rid of that old car. I'm sentimental about it because it belonged to Mom, and it's been my faithful ride for many years. I don't want one of those lightweight cars in a storm like this. I check all throughout the house. No Mitch, but I'm not worried—he's probably in the studio. I know he's here. His pickup is in the drive.

I change into jeans and a sweater and pull on my fur-lined boots after starting a pot of coffee. I fill a thermos with coffee, grab a bag of peanut butter cookies, and put on my winter parka before braving the storm.

Leaning into the wind as I step out of the protection of the house, I'm pummeled by the wind and snow, making it difficult to stay on my feet. I slip, almost falling. With the snow pounding down on me, I can barely see. *It can't be much farther.* Another gust hits me. I stumble over something, dropping the thermos as my feet slip out from under me. Thinking I must have strayed off the path, I feel around in the snow for the thermos. Now I'm frightened and disoriented. My hand brushes something solid, and I wrap my fingers around it. No, it's not the thermos, so I wipe the snow from my eyes. When I look down, I can't believe what I see. I see—*God! Nooo!*

A wailing voice rips through the wind—I realize it's me. Frantically, I try beating the snow off of him. I'm shaking him, but he's asleep. I try waking him—I shake him again—hard. I know CPR, but for the life of me I don't know how to do it now.

What do I do? He's so cold. Oh, God, so cold. I almost lay down beside him to warm him. *No, that's not right! I've got to call for help—get some blankets.*

I scurry up and run, slipping and sliding. I can't count the number of times I fall before I finally reach the house. Tearing the phone off the hook, I dial 911 and scream into the phone, "He's so cold, he's covered with snow." She asks for my name and address.

Dear God, I can't remember. Still shaking from the cold and the shock I tell myself to think. *Lillian, think, you have to do this or he'll freeze to death.* Finally, after a deep breath to calm myself, I give her the information. She tells me to stay on the line until help gets there, but I can't. *I have to go to him.*

"We're between the house and the studio out back," I yell and drop the phone. After ripping blankets off the bed, I fight my way back— back to where the love of my life is lying in the snow. Covering him with the blankets, I snuggle under them against him, rubbing his arms, trying to warm him. I lose track of time as we lay there in the snow with the wind howling and the snow drifting over us. *It's so-o cold!*

As though through a fog I hear, "Mrs. Hawke! Mrs. Hawke! You're safe now. We've got you. We'll get you to the hospital. You're going to be okay."

"No, not me, my husband. You've got to help my husband." Then everything goes dark.

• • •

Somebody stop that beeper. For God's sake make it stop! But it's still there—beep, beep, beep, beep. Such a muddle, all sounds are muted. Where's it coming from? I hear muffled voices that I can't understand. I'm trapped in a nightmare, and I can't wake up. I have to wake up. There's something I have to do. *But what?* I know it's important, but what is it? Through the fog I hear a muffled, "Mom, Mom. You have to wake up, Mom. I need you."

Sarah? No it can't be Sarah. She's in Laramie. But it sounds like her, and she needs me. I have to fight. I have to fight for Sarah. "Sarah?" my voice sounds like it's miles away. Somebody squeezes my hand.

"Mom, oh, Mom." A tear drops on my hand—I try to open my eyes. Slowly, I open them. Sarah is leaning over a rail, one hand brushing strands of her beautiful hair away from her face.

When I reach for her with my free hand, something stops me. "Where am I? Sarah, where am I?"

"You're in the hospital, Mom. Don't you remember?" Her voice is a hoarse whisper, sounding like it does when she's been crying.

"Was it an accident? The roads were horrible—lots of wind and snow." Beside Sarah another figure appears, wrapping an arm around her. "Reggie? What are you doing here?" Her face is wet with tears. I must be really beat up. But I don't feel any pain. "Reggie, you're scaring me. Where's Mitch? I want to see Mitch! Sarah, go get your dad." My voice is rising. I fight to get out of the bed. I need to find Mitch. *Why isn't he here?*

"Lil, please, you have to lie still—there's an IV in your arm. The nurse will be here in a minute. Hang on, honey—just hang on."

But I can't. *There's something I need to do.* It's important! Why can't I remember what it is? It's about Mitch—but what? As awareness blossoms, I'm still, feeling the snow on my face. And the wind—the wind so bad, so cold. I stumbled. I fell. He was cold, so cold.

"No! No! No! No! No!" I scream. I scream the scream of the damned. I hear Sarah and Reggie trying to calm me, but I can't stop.

A hand touches my wrist; a voice breaks through the pain. "Mrs. Hawke, I'm going to give you a sedative. You're going to be okay."

No, she's wrong, I'll never be okay, never—but I have to, Sarah needs me. I have to fight for her sake. Fight, I have to fight— Then oblivion washes over me.

They're talking. I should open my eyes—face the day and all it brings. I don't want to! I don't want to hear the words. I don't want it to be true. *Just let me stay in my cocoon for a few more minutes—please!* When I feel a soft hand on my arm, I still don't want to open my eyes, but I'd know my baby girl's hand anywhere. That's why I have to wake up.

"Mom? Mom? Mama, please," she begs. "I need you. I need you to wake up. The doctor says you're not hurt, so why won't you wake up?" The voice of a lost little girl cuts through my cocoon, ripping it apart.

I can't hide anymore. I force my hand to wrap around her fingers and squeeze. The bed shakes with her sobs. How can I leave her to face all this on her own. *I can do this, I can face this, I must, or I'll be lost forever.* I can't do that to her when she's just lost her dad. *Oh, my God.* I've thought the words. I can't breathe, but I must. Inhale, exhale and again. Baby steps—open my eyes. That's all I have to do—open my eyes. "Sarah, baby. It's okay, Mama's here. Shhh, sweet girl, shhh." Somehow, I manage to wrap my arms around her and hold her. Our tears blend together, but they can't wash away our pain. Another arm slips around me. For a moment, a split second, I think—but no, it's not. It's my sister shoring me up.

Rubber soles squeak on linoleum tile as footsteps approach. "I'm sorry, but I have to check your vitals."

I don't want to let go of them, but they step back to give the nurse room to do her job. Sarah asks her to bring me some broth or something to eat.

"How long will I have to stay?"

She pats my hand without answering my question. "The doctor will be here shortly. I'll get you something to eat."

I almost refuse the food, but when I look at Sarah and Reggie, I know I have to eat for them. So I say nothing. I want to ask about Mitch, but I don't want to hear the words. I'm not ready for that yet.

Doctor Parkin comes in as I'm drinking the broth the nurse brought. I'm glad to see his friendly face—he's been our family doctor for years. He hugs Sarah and asks how she's doing. She lies and says "fine." Reggie stands close to her, an arm around her waist—protecting her from what's to come.

Dr. Parkin takes my hand, and it begins—the questions about what happened. I hate reliving it in front of Sarah and Reggie, but with his encouragement I make it through. The words are spoken: Mitch is dead, a heart attack. There's nothing I could have done even if I'd been standing right beside him. It was instantaneous. That's supposed to make me feel better, but it doesn't. Although I've suffered some frostbite, there are no serious medical problems. He tells me I've been here three days, and I can be released. Once I learn Mitch is in the morgue here in the hospital, I ask if I can see him before I leave.

"You're going to be fine, Lillian. You're a strong woman. It's going to be hard, but that young lady needs you now—so you have to do this."

I'm tired of being strong. I'm so flippin' tired. I need to go home—as soon as I see my husband.

"I'll get an aide to take you to the morgue, then I'll fill out the paperwork for your release. Rest when you get home. Take care of yourself—eat, rest, and hold your family close."

Reggie and Sarah made that visit already, but insist they want to come with me. Yet I feel I must do it on my own. "Reggie, I need you to stay here with Sarah. This is something I have to do by myself. You take care of our girl."

Thomas is the aide who wheels me to the morgue. I struggle out of the wheelchair. I have to walk in there under my own power. *And I have to go alone.* I have to say goodbye to my soul mate, but I'm not sure I can do that. Thomas offers to help me—but I refuse.

It's been said that in death a person looks like he's sleeping. That's a lie. I've watched this man sleep many times. In sleep, life still emanated from him. There's none of that here. He looks like a wax image of my guy. There's so much I want to say, so many things. I thought we'd have more years. When I touch his cold hand, I'm suddenly enraged. How many times did I ask him to get a physical? How many times? Then I hear the voice of a shrew, saying horrible things to a dead man. "You selfish son of a bitch! How dare you do this? How dare you leave me alone, alone to deal with Dan—to spend the rest of my life without you? You promised me forever! It's not goddamn 'forever' yet. It isn't even close. I hate you, Mitchell Hawke. I hate—hate—hate that you won't be beside me when I wake up in the mornings. You won't be there to hold me when I fall apart. You won't be there to fill the supplies for our Dan—and how the hell do I let him know? How do I survive without you?" I'm pounding on his chest, tears coursing down my face. I'm angry at him, at God, but most of all at me. If I'd have left work when he'd called—if only I had come home earlier. And I fold.

Thomas picks me up and places me gently into the wheelchair. The rest of the time is a blur. People reassure me as we leave the hospital, but I can't answer. We're three robots going through the motions, wanting only to escape to home—yet hating the idea of a home where Mitch will no longer tell his silly jokes, won't be sitting at his drafting table while I curl up in the chair and read. Home—where I once felt whole and safe.

Chapter 61

Reggie and Sarah are treating me like a fragile piece of expensive crystal. Reggie drives too slow—as though a bump will shatter me, but the roads are smooth and clear now. As we get closer my muscles seem to tighten, and the hint of a headache slowly blooms. We pull in beside my car, behind Mitch's truck—my heart clutches. Before getting out of the van, I hesitate then walk slowly to the house. A faint musty, smoky smell lingers in the house as I come in. I wander through the rooms. Sarah and Reggie watch me—like they're waiting for me to fall apart. Needing to do something, I head to the kitchen to make a pot of coffee, but someone beat me to it. There's a full pot, still dripping, so I know it's fresh. "Who made the coffee?"

"What? We haven't had time, but I'll make some," Reggie tells me as she and Sarah follow me into the kitchen.

"No, it's already made. So, who made it?" Sarah walks slowly toward the table, reaches down, and picks up something lying there. She turns to me, eyes filling with tears. Her mouth moves but no sound comes out.

"What is it?" She's scaring me. She holds out a picture, painted only as our Dan can paint. Clouds are spewing snow over a background of grays, hints of purple, and hues of blues and greens, with a shadow of the studio—and a stairway reaching to the heavens. A man dressed in work clothes ascends, wings sprouting, toward an elderly woman—my mama, a middle-aged bald man—Carl, and a little wiry dog, Leo. All of them with sheer angel wings are reaching out to welcome him. Across the bottom, a blizzard rages—I almost feel the snow and wind buffeting me again. Our Mitch is on his way to heaven—to be reunited with loved ones.

Brushing my fingers over it, I stroke the figure of the man I love as he transcends to his heavenly home. It's Dan who made the coffee. He must have slipped out the back as we came in the front. Sarah and Reggie rush out on the deck, hoping to get a glimpse of him. They won't see him—he moves like a phantom on a whisper, barely moving the air around him. Once more I wonder how often he's within arm's length of us. I close my eyes, not wanting to look out there—to see the spot where Mitch left us. When I snap open my eyes, I only see the open path to the studio—the path my two guys followed to their dreams, not a snow bank covering Mitch—my love, my life. I open the door, still holding the painting, and walk to the studio.

A gentle hand touches my shoulder. "Mom? Do you think this is a good idea?" I pat her hand in reassurance. Sarah's grieving, too, not only the loss of her dad but also for her brother. We'll never see her dad again, and we can only pray for Dan. When I reach the studio, I place my hand on the tractor, the talisman that connects me now to both Dan and Mitch. I hesitate for a heartbeat before I enter the studio, holding the picture to my chest. Sarah and Reggie follow me.

As I move about the room, I touch treasured items, a sofa pillow I hold to my face, hoping a trace of Mitch's aftershave still lingers. I'm drawn to Mitch's drafting table where his design for the next project is still spread out. I'm surprised—Dan's easel, at the ready for his return, doesn't hold the family picture with the yellow monster in the background. It had been there since the day we found it. Despite the horrible shrouded figure, it brought us comfort. But it's gone. In its place is a rough pencil drawing of a wild-eyed man in a tattered long coat with long matted, unruly hair and a scraggly chest-length beard. On his feet is a shiny pair of new Red wing boots, the boot box in one arm and a large, lumpy bag thrown over his shoulder. Three small angels hover protectively over him along with his angel dog Leo. Printed down one side of the self-portrait, one word—SAFE. A shiver runs through me.

Reggie breaks the spell. "Come on, Lil. Your hands are freezing. Let's get you back to the house where it's warmer. I slide the etching over and place the stairway picture beside it, father and son together.

Touching my fingers to my lips, I transfer the kiss to both, then let her guide me to the house. Sarah leads the way, wiping tears as she walks. I have no tears—I am empty.

Untethered, I wander the house picking up items and setting them down. I hold my daughter as she cries and try answering her questions. Reggie heats chicken soup that's been left by friends—our fridge is filling fast. The doorbell has been ringing constantly since I came home. Reggie takes care of it while Sarah and I, paralyzed in our grief, ignore everything. I have no appetite, but I force myself to eat. I have to be strong for Sarah.

"Lil?" Reggie asks hesitantly. "I hate to bring it up, but we need to go to Wright's in the morning to make arrangements."

"Wright's? Who are they?"

Her hand covers mine. "The mortuary. Remember the paper you signed before leaving the hospital saying you want no embalming or autopsy? Since he's not being embalmed, I'm sorry, time is of the essence."

"Mama, don't put him in a box in the ground in a cemetery," she pleads. "He'd hate that, Mom. He'd really hate that."

I clasp her hand in mine. "I know, baby, I know. We talked about what to do in case something happened." *But it wasn't supposed to happen.* "He will be cremated—no fancy damn padded coffin. He always said he wanted to go out the same way he came into this world—'Starkers!' No clothing, just wearing his wedding ring. If they insist he has to be in something, his first choice was cardboard. If that won't work, then a simple pine box. In the spring we'll plant a Blue Spruce, we'll hold a memorial, and scatter his ashes at the base of it. It will be only family and a few close friends attending—he didn't want all that pomp and show, just a simple memorial." I look at Sarah, "Is that okay with you?"

Reggie fights back tears. Sarah wipes hers away. They nod in agreement. Lost in our own world, we sit quietly until the ringing phone breaks the mood.

"I'll get it. It might be Phil." Sarah reaches it mid-ring. It's a friend of Mitch who asks about holding a little 'celebration of his life.' He wants to know if we'd mind.

After talking to him, I realize how important it is to Mitch's friends. Who am I to take that away from them? He'll call me when the arrangements are made. The memorial that counts for us will be held in our backyard come the spring.

The next few days go by in a haze. I go where I'm directed, and I try being present for Sarah. At the turnout for the Celebration of Mitch's life, which is much larger than I expect, many fun-filled stories are told. Sarah holds my hand. I almost hear the words of praise for him, but they're drowned out by the words buzzing in my head—the words I never got to say to him.

Too soon it's time for Sarah, Phil, and Reggie to leave. I'm glad Sarah has Phil to lean on. He's so good to her. I know they're worried about me—but it's time. It's time for me to sink or swim, and frankly, I can't wait to go back to work where there are no ghosts to haunt me. Tomorrow is the day I'll get up, take a deep breath, and venture back into my life.

Chapter 62

"How are you today, Lillian?"

I stare at him while I search for words.

"You hate that question, don't you? How do you suggest I begin our session?"

"I don't know. How about, 'you heard any good jokes lately?'" My voice is the monotone I seem to talk in lately. Sarcasm slips out too easily.

He suppresses a smile. "Well, have you? Have you heard any good jokes?"

"Yeah, sure. Have you heard the one about the woman whose biggest dream was to grow up, marry a good man, have a houseful of children, and spend her time loving and nurturing them? No job other than being a wife and a mother. Then God said, 'No, that's not your path. I'll give you a troubled child to force you out of your comfort zone. You'll search for answers to help him, leading to a career that keeps you away from home for long hours while you frantically seek the magic to fix your broken boy.' Yet she failed at that. And just about the time she found solid ground and peace of mind, He looked down, wagged His Godly finger, turning the solid to liquid. I'm drowning. And now I've lost my rudder, my guiding light, my soul, and anchor. How's that for a joke, Mr. Bacon?"

Quietly he watches me, his eyes never leaving my face. I hold his stare, and he's the first to look away this time. He shifts in his chair and lays his pen on the table. His expression softens. "That's a shitty joke, Lillian. It's a shitty joke to pull on anyone. If it were me, I'd be pissed. So, what does a person do when something like that happens?"

"Maybe they just quit?"

"Do you think that's an option?"

"Sometimes I wish it were—to lay down and not wake up until the world makes sense again. Do you know something else I think? Sometimes I wish the EMTs had been slower, leaving us there together. No more pain, no more heartache."

"What keeps you going?"

"Autopilot, Mr. Bacon, autopilot. I wake up, force myself to eat, search for the mask I'll wear that day. Will I mingle and make small talk, isolate myself, paste on a smile or the expression that scares the bejesus out of anyone who comes too close? One step, then it's one step more. If I trip, I try not to slide all the way to the bottom, get up, brush myself off—and do it all again."

"How's that working for you?"

"Evidently not too damn good. I'm here, aren't I? Now where's your magic wand?"

He smiles wistfully. He knows I know the answer. "A wise woman once told me there is no magic, that we therapists have feet of clay, and our attempts to glue people back together will fail. She told me all we can do is be there to listen and help develop a roadmap for avoiding the pitfalls of self-destruction and self-pity—a shoulder to lean on and a supply of garbage bags for the crap. In the end, our patients have to do the hard work and empty the trash themselves."

"She sounds like a fool. You give her too much credit. Besides, she got most of that from you. Just give me the magic so I can pole vault over this crap—I don't have the energy to climb over it."

"What are you doing when you're not hiding at work?"

"That's when the fun begins. I managed to climb back into the bed we shared—that was a feat in itself. I sleep like a baby. You know how that is, don't you?"

"You mean sleeping a few hours at a time and waking up crying?"

"Have you ever tried going to work after a long night of thoroughly cleaning the pantry because you couldn't sleep?"

"Did it help?"

"You know, I think it did. I yelled at God, at Mitch, and at life, but in the end it was like coming to see you. It made me sweat, raised my anxiety level, and in the end, I accomplished something and felt good about it."

"Do you feel you're making progress?"

I take some time before I answer. "Yes, I do. At least now I'm aware I'm wearing a mask—not so much to hide, though, as to survive, to act 'as if.' I'm not denying my feelings. There are times I have to function—for that I dress up and show up, take care of what's in front of me, go home—then get up and do it all over again. I'm not hanging out at work so much anymore." I pause again, realizing that is progress.

"Do you know what my epiphany was in the wee hours of the morning I was tearing the pantry apart? That I'm saturated with mental illness and addiction—it seeps from my pores. If you cut me, I won't bleed. I'll ooze the pain of mental illness. When Dan first showed signs, I was determined to find the answers, but the more I learned—the more impotent I felt. What scares me—what really scares me, is that I'm doing my job by rote. That's unfair to my patients, but also to me. I'm better than what I've been giving. I ask myself if I'm doing it because I still love the job or if it's just for the paycheck? Either way, the idea of not having the job to go to right now scares the hell out of me."

It's his turn to take a deep breath. "I agree. You are making progress, and I respect your insight. Before leaping to the big job question, I encourage you to take some time. The best thing for you now is to acknowledge that pile on the table. Think of it as a block of cheese. You can't eat it all at once, so nibble around the edge, where the smaller problems are. You need to build your strength back before making the bigger decisions. Let your smaller accomplishments fill you first. Over time, some of what looks insurmountable today will take care of itself."

He looks at me, and I know he really sees me. "This week, look at that woman in the mirror—really look. Pull off the mask you wear to hide from yourself. To regain your confidence, say these words morning and night as you look yourself in the eye: 'I am special, I am valuable, and I am worth being well for.' Get back on a schedule. If it will help you sleep, wear one of Mitch's shirts—with a dab of his aftershave on it. Write him a letter, or many letters. Say anything, your hurt, anger, and your fears. Write it down, don't throw it away—and don't bring it to me. And remember, baby steps, one step at a time."

"I will do that. Thank you, Mr. Bacon. Next week? Same time?"

• • •

And so I do it. I wake up, get up, show up. With time, I start believing. The heavy weight that's kept me down so long finally begins to lift. I no longer feel like I'm swimming in cow manure. On the days I find myself backsliding into the darkness again, I ask myself what Mitch would want me to do. I can hear him say, 'Live, Lil! That's what I want you to do. Pull the life out of each and every day—anything else is a slap in my face.' I talk to myself or to him a lot lately. More and more I notice the little joys in life; a robin perched on the deck chair, the sun shining, a gentle breeze, the first flowers of spring. The biggest joy is the call from Sarah saying she and Phil are engaged. "Mitch, you'd be so proud of our girl, and I know you approve of Phil. She calls me three or four times a week to make sure I'm okay. She's in counseling in Laramie, and I can't wait for her summer break. We're going to have a wedding."

Then finally, there's the day I wake up with hope again and find myself singing as I fix my breakfast. It's a Saturday, and I make a decision. I'm getting a dog today at the dog shelter. With a dog I can talk all I want—people will think I'm talking to the dog. Of course, that means fencing part of the yard and putting in a pet door. I'll have to call Mitch's old hands who've offered to help.

I fall in love with a big black dog with a black tongue, a Shar Pei/Chow cross, six months old. Her name is Charlie. She doesn't have the wrinkles of the Shar Pei, only the loose skin, eyes, and ears of the breed. From the Chow, she has the thick cowl and thick curled tail. She's my constant companion when I'm home. Our favorite place to hang out is the studio. I didn't know if I could feel comfortable in there again, but once I slipped in with my book I felt my guys close by.

Since we lost Mitch there's been no signs of Dan, other than that day I came home from the hospital. The containers remain filled, though I rotate the contents once a week. I have no way to let him know we're planning the memorial for spring break. I've ordered an 8-foot Blue Spruce to plant between the workshop and the studio, praying the ground will be hard enough to get equipment back there.

When she calls to share the details about Phil proposing, we make plans. Listening to her, bursting with excitement, brings me out of the doldrums. The plan is still to keep the memorial simple. Reggie and Tim will be here, along with Sarah and Phil. We're inviting his family to join us, too, if not at the memorial, then to the meal we're planning after. We're making it a celebration of his life with a few of his favorite things.

It feels good to walk into work with a smile on my face. My co-workers notice right away, because this one makes it all the way to my eyes. Most smile back, but a few reach out and touch me as if to say, 'good job.' Sandra, our hugger, gave me a big one, and I didn't pull away. I didn't even have the urge to deck her. That's progress. The rollercoaster ride of my life hasn't stopped completely—but at least it's slowed down.

Chapter 63

The next few weeks fly by. I finally find the energy to purge the house of all the dead flowers and restock my groceries. I complete all the thank you cards and put them in the mail. Some things I haven't had the heart to do. There's no deadline on grief or instructions on how to handle it, so I'm gentle with myself—but not so gentle that I don't accomplish anything because it hurts. Facing Mitch's closet, dresser, and personal items will be the hardest. Sarah wants to be here to help. We've decided to donate most of his clothes to either the Serenity House or the Salvation Army. I'm keeping some of his shirts to use as nightshirts. I find comfort in wearing them—and I am sleeping better. Sarah wants his old work boots and a pair of his coveralls. If only Dan was here, we could give them all to him, but since he's not, maybe one day he'll stop in at the Salvation Army store and find some of them.

I spend more time in the kitchen, trying new recipes. Cooking for just one is hard, but I bought more freezer containers for the meals I prepare on weekends. I can just heat and enjoy a home-cooked meal when I'm tired. There will be enough for Sarah's homecoming, too. The house smells delicious—cookies, bread, and a hint of fresh paint—from the kitchen and bathroom facelift.

Charlie lies contentedly as I putter and follows me from room to room. If I'm having a bad day—or even a bad hour, she snuggles up to me. Before I know it, I'm feeling better. She sleeps on Mitch's side of the bed at night. I laugh, knowing Mitch might object to a dog in the house, especially on the bed and the couches. Maybe that's why we didn't get another dog after we lost Leo. Wherever I am, there she is. Oh, she can be a pain at times—like when she dug a hole in the yard when I first got her. But she was easy to train. With the pet door, housebreaking her was a snap—no accidents in the house so far. I love that she's a gentle lamb, but also protective. I'm keeping her in the house while the Blue Spruce is planted, just to be safe.

Coming home for the first time since Mitch died is tough for Sarah. We cry, we laugh when Charlie tries to make it better, and we stay up late talking. "Mom, I've been so worried about you, but it looks like you're doing okay. I was shocked when you got a dog—I thought you might be losing it."

"For a while, I thought I was. Seeing Mr. Bacon helps. Then one day, I thought 'what would Mitch think?' I knew he wouldn't be happy with me sitting on the pity pot all the time. Not moving forward is an insult to him. So move forward I do—not always smoothly, but this silly dog helps. She depends on me, she listens without judgment, plus she makes me laugh." Charlie knows we're talking about her—she rolls over for a belly scratch.

Blue skies and sunshine welcome us the morning of the memorial. The Blue Spruce, planted just days before, is a stunning backdrop for our ceremony. A cement-contractor friend of Mitch's built a hollowed-out pedestal with a brass door—a vault for our memory box. Above the door is a plaque inscribed with his name, the dates of his birth and death, plus "Husband of Lillian, father of Dan and Sarah. Gone too soon and missed forever. A tree planted to shelter us from the storms as he did."

Sarah and I write letters to put in the box. Reggie asks if she and Tim can, too. Of course, we agree. Besides the four letters, we include a small painting of our family done by Dan for Father's Day long ago. Dan was about five, Sarah, one, and Blue Bunny and Leo appear in it, too. It sat on Mitch's dresser where he saw it every morning.

After sprinkling Mitch's ashes around the tree, we work them into the soil as we share stories, shed a few tears, and laugh when we remember some of his shenanigans over the years. Each of us turns toward the tree line when we speak, hoping for Dan to be close by. We also speak of our love for him, how much we miss him and wish he were here with us. All the time Sarah is home, I look expectantly for some sign, a painting or something. He's done one for all our momentous occasions. I wonder where he is and how he's doing.

Sarah's July wedding is held in front of the Blue Spruce. She looks so beautiful. Her smile is dazzling. As a bride, in her simple sheath dress and ballerina slippers, with a new pixie-cut hairdo, she radiates happiness. Poor Reggie was nearly apoplectic when Sarah chose slippers over heels. "Can you imagine me walking in heels on the grass?" she asked. Finally, Reggie conceded she's probably right. "I'm a simple girl, with simple tastes, Auntie. I'll leave the flash to you."

When the pastor asks who's walking her down the aisle, she looks so lost. The confusion, sadness, and even fear, show on her face—it's the one thing we didn't consider. The plan was for the wedding to be in front of the Blue Spruce so she'll feel her dad is part of her wedding. How could we forget the walk down the aisle?

Gathering her in my arms, I hold her as she sobs. "Oh, Mom! Sometimes, for a few moments I forget—I forget he's not here and won't be ever again. Just when I think I can do it without him, something happens, and I don't think I can. How can I walk down that aisle without my dad?"

"Are you saying you don't want to do this? The wedding? Marry Phil? Or is it only the walk-down-the-aisle part?"

She pulls away, horrified. "The aisle, Mom, the aisle! I can't imagine not marrying Phil. I can't imagine my life without him. But I want to walk to him, to watch his face when he first sees me. I want that, Mom! What am I going to do?"

"What do you think Dad would say?"

She pauses for a minute, glances toward the studio, then to the Blue Spruce and back to me. As she wipes her eyes, a small smile plays on her lips. She says softly, "He will be walking me down the aisle. That's what he'd say. He's with me every step of the way. So, I need to take my mom's arm—and maybe her silly dog, too. 'We can do this' is what Dad would say, don't you think? Will you do it? Will you walk me down the aisle and give me away?"

And then I'm wiping my tears. I hug her again. "I'd be honored. And my silly dog, too."

• • •

"Who gives this woman?"

"Her dad—in spirit, Charlie girl, and I." I bite my lip to keep from crying as I place her hand in Phil's. Charlie gently nudges her toward Phil as I turn to take my seat, and then comes to sit quietly by my chair. Sometimes she's too smart. The mood lightens as everyone laughs at her antics.

Everyone has a good time. Laughter and music fill the air. Although there's dancing and a catered dinner, it's an informal affair. And there's love, so much love. Both Sarah and I occasionally scan the tree line, hoping for a glimpse of Dan—but once more, there is no sign of him.

Everyone throws rose petals at the happy couple as they make their way to the hippy van to leave for their honeymoon. They'll be gone a week, then come back to spend the rest of the summer with me. We've hired someone to do the clean up so Reggie and I can relax. But it's bittersweet when I have to wave goodbye to her and Timothy, too.

Sarah and Phil are still glowing when they return from their honeymoon. Charlie and I take the studio where I make up the hideaway bed so they can have the house to themselves. I was a newlywed once—I know they need their privacy. Besides, I like the studio.

It's then I decide to remodel it, to put in a small kitchen, and double it in size. I'm going to deed the house and property to Sarah and Phil for a wedding present. When they move back next year, it will work for us all.

Maybe one day they'll have grandbabies for me to spoil.

Chapter 64

Charlie's a great companion. She's always at the door to greet me when I come home. When I'm having a bad day, she stays near me, almost to the point of tripping me as I walk. When I start having nightmares, she pushes against me with her nose, then snuggles close to me as I go back to sleep. Some days I swear she can talk, as she always gets what she wants. The workmen remodeling the studio are under her spell. They bring her treats, stop what they're doing to play with her, and share their lunches with her when she begs—despite being asked not to. After work we walk to the creek, weather permitting, to see if anyone's picked up the supplies I've left in the storage container. Another winter's coming, barreling down on us like an avalanche, and I fear being buried under feelings of despair, so I continue to see Mr. Bacon.

• • •

"What do you hear from Sarah?"

"They're doing well—busy. She's taking a couple of extra classes so she can graduate with Phil in the spring. They plan to move back here since they've already received job offers. And—I'm giving them my house."

"You're what? Where will you live? And what prompted this?"

"I decided right after the wedding, while I was camping out in the studio to give them some privacy when they returned from their honeymoon. I felt more comfortable there, so I'm having it remodeled by enlarging the living area and adding a kitchen and laundry room. I sold some property adjacent to our old construction site, and I may sell the pickup, too."

"What did Sarah say when you told her?"

"She was shocked at first, then excited, especially when she realized I'd still be there, just not underfoot. It takes some pressure off them, too. We're both concerned about Dan's reaction should we find him or he comes home. Weren't you the one who told me not to put my life on hold and not worry about how Dan might react?"

"You've put a lot of thought into it. Are you still feeling trapped in your job? That seems to be an ongoing concern for you. If you weren't a counselor and could do anything you wanted, what would it be?"

"A gardener." *Where the hell did that come from?*

"A gardener?"

He's shocked—surprised at least. I didn't think I could do that.

"Why a gardener?"

I ponder this for a bit before I answer. "Because I'd be working outside, doing physical work—working up a sweat. In the spring you till the ground, plant the seeds, and nurture them. The sun warms the soil, and the seeds germinate before poking their shoots through. If you care for it, it produces food for you to feed your stomach while you nourish your soul."

"Is that anything like what you do now?"

"First of all, I'm not outside now. I'm cooped up in a stale building eight to ten hours a day, five days a week."

"All right, let's put the outside on the shelf. How about the rest of it, with the exception of eating your work?"

Ahhh! He knows me too well. He knew I'd jump on that right away. "Sorry, I'm not seeing it?"

"Lean back and close your eyes. Think about what you told me and layer it over what you do now."

I close my eyes, trying to still my mind. I do want this to work—I'm not trying to be difficult. "I see patients come into our facility who resist our help much of the time. To develop a rapport—breaking the sod—takes patience. Then we educate and nurture them to identify triggers, self-defeating behaviors, lead them to rise to the light of acceptance and willingness to change—like a blossom opening." *How many times have I said those same words to patients as they begin to grow and bloom?* My eyes open wide, and I sit up. "You know, sometimes I hate you."

"Yes, I know. So if a crop fails in your garden, do you quit—or do you simply try another crop? I'm not suggesting you stay in a job that's no longer fulfilling. All I'm saying is—don't throw it all away because a new master gardener is chopping up your garden. Now, the same question: if you could do anything, what would you do?"

No hesitation this time. "I'd set up a long term treatment program, where we would detox, stabilize, and provide group therapies, but also teach living skills. Patients would participate in caring for the facility, raising gardens, chickens, and other animals. They'd be assigned work tasks. A counselor would be involved in all stages. The Patient Council would attempt to solve any problems—with the counselor's assistance. Before discharge they will earn a GED if they hadn't graduated high school, learn to create a resume and how to dress appropriately for job interviews, open a checking account and balance their checkbooks. We would educate them to do more than parrot phrases and teachings back to us. If I ever win the lottery, that's what I'll do." All that must have been percolating in my head for some time.

"Have you ever talked to anyone about your ideal facility? Maybe you need to give it more thought, make a plan, and at least begin to flesh it out. You may never get it all, but who knows? You might find some like-minded people who would offer you a piece of it. If you don't speak up, none of it will happen. Don't slam the door on what you have until you've identified other options."

The seed is planted—back to those damn baby steps. One thing is certain—I love the work, but I hate the politics of the job. Executives who've never spent a day in the trenches make decisions based on the bottom dollar, without considering the population we serve.

• • •

As fall moves into winter I put out feelers in the community, talking to local judges as to what services are needed in the community. As the days get shorter and darkness comes too early, I dread each day that might bring chilling temperatures and snow. As the days hurtle toward the first anniversary—the day I fear reliving—an overwhelming sadness envelops me, and I feel as though I'm sinking into a dark bog, chilled to the marrow of my bones. Even Charlie's efforts to cheer me sometimes fail.

Making it even worse, the weather is so severe Sarah and Phil can't come home for the holidays. Then it's here—the anniversary of the worst day of my life. I drag myself out of bed, thankful it isn't snowing—but I'm running late, and traffic is a nightmare. As soon as I get to work we have a code green. There he is, a snarling, spitting, growling wild man, unrecognizable—until I see him strapped to the bed and look into those blue eyes of my Dan staring back at me. The shock of seeing him on the anniversary of the day we lost his dad almost takes my breath away. *Focus, I have to focus, I have to do my job.*

A gentle hand touches my shoulder. "Go home, Lil."

As if in a fog, I leave. I don't remember driving to the street where our lives started, where Dan was born. I have no idea how long I've sat here lost in thought. But, I don't belong here. I need to go home— home where it happened—but also where I belong now. I drive carefully, knowing I'm not really fit to be driving. Home—where Charlie's waiting.

I've found our boy, Mitch. He's alive—he's really sick, but he's alive. Something had to keep him going. I'm going to believe it's God and you, and that's what brought him to safety today. I haven't lost you both. Please keep us safe.

All the way home, I talk to him, my Mitch—my heart, who never lived to see his son again. I want to believe he's been watching over Dan—bringing him to safety because he couldn't do it himself.

Charlie's waiting, twisting and turning, crying out to me as I come in the door as if she senses something's off. "Well, Charlie. It's turned out to be one hell of a day." She pushes her nose under my hand, expecting to be scratched, and I comply. "You're a treasure, my friend. Our Dan's been found. I wish he'd known you. You always seem to know what I need." We sit that way with me scratching her ears as she thumps her tail contentedly, while I think about the maze of my life. How much longer can I go on like this? But first, I need to call Sarah.

"Hi, Mom? What's up? You don't usually call in the middle of the day. Are you okay?"

"Yes. I am," and when I say it, I realize I really am. "The day started out rocky. That's why I'm calling now."

"I knew it was going to be a rough one for you. It is for me, too."

"What I have to tell you should help. Dan's been found."

"What? What?! When? How? Did he come home? How is he?"

"He was brought in on a police hold shortly after I got to work. He's in bad shape—he's filthy. His hair and beard are matted, and his clothes are nothing but rags. His beard hid his face so that I didn't even recognize him—until I looked into those beautiful eyes."

"Did he know you, Mom? What did he say when he saw you?"

Gently, I tell her. "Oh, Sarah, baby. He didn't know me, honey. He was fighting any attempt to help him. The nurse was finally able to give him a shot, and it calmed him enough to get him in the observation room used for police holds. He was restrained when I left. The staff has their hands full—and I can't be a part of that. He's family."

"Why not? Mom, he needs you—you need to be with him. Damn. I need to get home to help you."

"Sarah, stop and think. First of all, you don't need to be on the roads right now—the weather is too unpredictable. As much as I'd love to see you, please don't try it. And you wouldn't be able to see him."

"But you shouldn't have to do it alone. I need to be there for you."

"Honey, I'll admit, when it first happened, I went a bit bonkers. I ended up on Buchanan across from our old house with memories flooding over me. I probably looked like a crazy woman," I say with a chuckle.

"It isn't funny, Mom."

"I know, honey. But sometimes when you're faced with overwhelming problems, it helps to find a spot to rest where you can laugh a little to give you strength to go on. It won't help Dan for us to go down the rabbit hole with him."

We talk until we both agree we're going to make it—on our own and with the support of others. I'm so glad she has Phil to hold her, wipe her tears, and give her strength. We'll talk every day for a while, until we can answer the question: "What's going to happen to Dan?"

Chapter 65

Over the next few weeks I'm able to get up, show up, and be present. The prognosis for Dan is not hopeful. It's highly unlikely that he'll ever be released from the state hospital. I'm able to see him, but he doesn't seem to know me. Although I spent the afternoon before he was transferred at his bedside talking and reading to him, it didn't rip me apart this time. I'm so thankful he's safe. It isn't about me and my feelings after all. He's never intentionally done anything to deliberately hurt me or Mitch or Sarah. It's his illness—its effects hit us like shrapnel, wounding us. It's our responsibility to take care of our injuries. Our love can't make him well—God knows we've tried.

"Before you ask, Mr. Bacon, I am doing all right. Not great, but in light of it all, I am at peace for the first time in forever."

"You were working when Dan was brought in?"

I sense his skepticism that I'm okay. I retell the story of Dan's reappearance as he watches, analyzing every movement I make and studying every nuance in my voice.

"And after all that, you say you're doing all right? How did you get there?"

As I say the words, "I let go, Mr. Bacon. I let go," I'm relaxed, my hands lie loosely in my lap, and I feel no anxiety—only peace. I'm not here for his approval. He's my co-pilot as I navigate this life. "I sat at my son's bedside. He had no idea who I was, where he was, or even what he was. Yet, there he was—inhaling and exhaling, on autopilot. For most of his life, I believed it was my job as his mom to keep him safe. It was then I realized I can't always do that. No matter how much I love him, I can't change his life for him. I felt myself being drawn toward the edge, tethered to him by a rope of my own making. As I was about to drop into nothingness, I cut the cord and stood on firm ground. Yet he did not fall or change. I can only change me."

"Does that mean you no longer care?"

"Oh, hell no. It means I care enough to take care of me—so if the day ever comes when he is well enough to reach for me, he'll find more than an empty shell. You're the one who's encouraged me to visualize what I want, and that's what I did. I closed my eyes and relaxed. A beautiful, white cloud appeared. Strong hands, cupped to hold something, stretched through the clouds toward me. Hugging my broken boy close to my chest, I reassured him I will always love him—but I was giving his care to God. Then I placed him in God's hands where he was gently cradled. When I opened my eyes, I was at peace. I know I'll forget at times and try to take him back, but for now, right this moment—I am at peace."

"You've done some good work, Lil."

"That's not all, Mr. Bacon. You know that job issue I've been agonizing over?"

"You've made a decision?"

"Yes, I let go of that, too. I tendered my resignation last week. It was time to take my own advice and do something. So I got off dead center and made a decision, even if it turns out to be wrong. Letting frustration and resentment build wasn't fair to my co-workers, my patients, and most of all, to me. This career found me—and it's served me well. I'll be forever grateful for having had it. I've helped people along the way, and I'm proud of the job I've done. But I'm tired. I'm getting old before my time, and I no longer have the patience for it. So, with some angst, much prayer, talking it over with Charlie—"

"Charlie? You're in a new relationship?"

I can't help laughing. He looks so confused. "No. Charlie, my dog." I stress the last word. "Remember, I've mentioned her—surely? Well, she's a great listener. And trust me, when she doesn't like what I'm saying, she walks out of the room—kinda like Mitch used to do." And I laugh again.

That brings a genuine smile to Mr. Bacon's usually serious face. "Ah! Yes, the dog. Sorry I interrupted you. Please continue—you were telling me how you came to quit your job."

"Anyway, short story, long. After going over my finances, I find I'm not rich—but I'm not dirt poor either. The house and property are paid for—the kids and I'll split the taxes. I live simply. I've paid into a 401K for years, so when I reach retirement age, I'll have that and my Social Security. The college approached me about teaching a couple of classes. That will provide some income and keep my brain working, plus it will get me out of the house. I've also been talking to a man who lost his son to addiction. He owns a horse ranch, and he's looking into developing a therapeutic community for people with mental health issues and addiction. There, they can work with the animals, learn to ride, as well as do other chores. He plans to build four cabins with two people per cabin, a cook shack, a meeting hall, and a large garden the residents will help care for. He asked me to be on the board of directors. He's already received one grant and is working on more. Plus, I haven't given up on my garden. I'm going to enlarge it and start a compost pit."

"You've been busy. Well done, Lillian. Well done."

"You planted the seed, Mr. Bacon, when you asked me what I'd do if I could do anything I wanted. You encouraged me explore my options, and I did. I'll admit, I got off course the closer we got to the anniversary of Mitch's death. We hadn't heard anything about or from Dan since the day Mitch died. Who would've thought the anniversary of one of the most horrific experiences of my life would be the impetus I needed to move on to the next chapter of my life?"

"Lillian, I have to admit, when you first came in I thought you might be in denial, that with Dan back—in the condition he's in, you could be in that dark cloud again. It's quite apparent that you're not. Obviously you have thought carefully about your decisions—beginning with letting go. Is there anything else? You've told me about your work prospects and your garden. What will you do with your free time?"

"Yes, indeed. I'm learning how to process food from my garden and share my abundance with the needy. I'm even learning how to quilt. And who knows, maybe I'll write a book."

∞

Chapter 66

I moved into my darling studio when Sarah and Phil returned. Phil found work with the Forest Service, and Sarah worked as an RN at the hospital for 3 years before returning to college to become a Nurse Practitioner. They blessed me with identical twin granddaughters, Mitchelina and Daniella, who bring so much joy to our lives.

When my garden took on a life of its own, I hired part-time help from Serenity House. Sharing the bounties with the halfway house and the new homeless shelter still brings me joy—and peace. Many summer weekends Sarah and I canned the fruits of our labors—she and Phil are as involved as I am. As the twins grew, we put them to work—and they've thrived.

The pedal tractor, standing sentinel at my door, remains the talisman on entry and exit. Quilting's become my new passion. Phil built me an antique-style quilting frame with pulleys that hangs in the main room of the studio, where I can pull it easily to the ceiling, out of the way, or drop it down to work on a quilt. The girls are now quite skilled at helping Nana sew those little stitches.

My Charlie girl lived and comforted me for many years—she passed quietly in her sleep. She rests under the blue spruce near Mitch, and I can sense her presence still. Phil also built a bench under the tree for me to rest, read, and tell Mitch about my days. He loves making furniture like Mitch did and spends hours in the workshop.

Dan remained in the state hospital. Eventually he did recognize us, but rarely acknowledged us on our monthly visits. He started painting again, and it's through his prolific paintings we know of his love for us. Many are of our family in a variety of situations, mostly around the dinner table or relaxing on the deck of either home. He seldom included himself with us—usually there's a shadowy figure watching from a distance. Reggie continues to sell them in her extraordinarily successful gallery. There are Dan Hawke paintings in all corners of the world now. Occasionally he shyly gave me one for my own. When I took him a picture of Charlie, he painted the most beautiful picture of my sweet girl. And the day he greeted Sarah with "Hi Sissy," our hearts almost burst with joy. His gift to her? A painting of the twins from a photograph she'd shown him of their first birthday. In their highchairs, with fists full of chocolate cake—smeared on their little faces and in their curly strawberry blond hair—their bright blue eyes, so much like Dan's, sparkle with mischief.

Dan died in his sleep on his 45th birthday. Although we're sad, he is finally at peace and with his three favorite people once again. His last painting is of him, lying peacefully in his bed. Flowing from the man in bed is a white, shadowy figure ascending toward the outstretched arms of his dad, Gamma, and Carl—with Leo, bright-eyed, waiting. Beside the bed is an old-lady version of me in a rocker, holding a book, looking upward, with Charlie by my side. We take that to believe I will live into old age; Dan somehow seemed to know these things.

We brought Dan's ashes home to rest beneath the blue spruce next to his dad. We plan a small memorial service with family and a few friends. Since he was born on the fourth of July, we'll light sparklers for his send-off. He never liked fireworks, but was fascinated by sparklers.

• • •

It's a beautiful summer day when Reggie and Timothy arrive. They're bickering as only they can. Timothy doesn't think his mother should be driving, but she's not ready to give it up. He's grown up to be the nicest young man. He's the first one out of the car.

"Aunt Lil!" He wraps me in a warm hug. "You look amazing. Have you been spending a lot of time in the sun? How's that garden grow-ing?" Then he lowers his voice. "You need to talk to your sister—she's no longer the driver she used to be. She scared the hell out of me. Maybe she'll listen to you."

"Like she's ever listened to me," I whisper. "Reggie, come on, get your fanny out of the car and give me a hug."

"Where's Sarah and the girls?" she asks as she hugs me.

Sarah is already running out of the house. "Aunt Reggie, I didn't hear you drive up. Mom, why didn't you yell? Girls, Aunt Reggie and Tim are here." The twins stand shyly in the doorway, arms entwined— miniature versions of their mother at 12. Dressed in shorts and tank tops, their hair in ponytails, tanned faces sporting a smattering of freckles, the only difference is the color of their barrettes. They love confusing people who can't tell them apart—the twinkle in their eyes tell me they might be up to no good before the day is done. Their shyness disappears when Reggie envelops them both in a bear hug and gently brings them with her to join the rest of us.

The day is spent visiting, looking through pictures, and reminiscing. Tim takes his fishing pole to the creek to see if he can catch a fish. I doubt he'll have much luck with two pre-teen, chatty girls following him.

In the early evening Sheila and Lester, Phil's parents, join us. Xandra and Doug from Serenity House arrive at the same time. They will soon be opening Dan's Place, a new facility, with money left to their organization from Dan's trust fund.

We take Dan's ashes to his final resting place. His last painting rests on his easel, and the one he painted for Sarah when she was little hangs nearby, along with a collage of their childhood Sarah put together as a tribute to him.

A gentle breeze kisses my cheek as each person shares a personal story about Dan. Most are about his talent. It's through his art we've learned the story of the man. I mostly listen, soaking in the love being shared. I wrote a letter to put in the vault, thanking him for all the opportunities he's given me to grow in my life because he was such a special boy—and especially for the lessons I've learned because of him through the years.

Timothy shares his memories of the first Thanksgiving he and Reggie spent with us. In his hands, he holds a little red pickup. "When we got here, I was afraid of Dan. He was so big, and he didn't say much—but I could feel him staring at me. I was in awe of his collection of toy pickups and other vehicles, and I couldn't resist this one. After scaring the dickens out of me, he brought it to me as an apology. Dan, I hope you know how much this pickup and your friendship meant to a little boy. Because I was blessed to know you, I'm going to be a psychiatrist to help people with mental illness. Thank you, big guy." With that, he gently places the treasured toy in the vault.

Reggie's contribution to the vault is the letter Dan wrote to her about selling his art. "It's the only letter I ever received from him, and I've always treasured it. If it weren't for Dan, my little gallery might never have made it. He's my highest-selling artist—everything I have I owe to Dan."

Sarah is the last to speak. "What I remember most about my big brother is how safe he made me feel when I was little. Many mornings when I woke up, he'd be sitting by my bed watching over me. The many good memories of him are the ones I hold on to. Although I've been so angry at times, it was never directed at him. It took a few counseling sessions for me to figure that out. It wasn't his fault. He was made that way; he didn't choose it. I have something for the vault, too." She takes a deep breath, reaches into a bag, and pulls out a blue bunny rabbit—reminiscent of the one from their childhood. After telling the story of how he'd given it to Gamma first, and then to her when she was born, to watch over them, she kisses it and holds it upward. "He's here to watch over us now that you're gone. Love you, big brother."

I could not have asked for a better farewell for my boy. Finally, I really let go, and now it's up to God to keep him safe. "Soar with the angels, my son. You're free, at last, to fly."

The End

Acknowledgments

First, I want to thank my husband Jim for his patience, support, and encouragement in my career as an addictions counselor, for believing I hung the moon, and for always being there for me—and especially for his patience in the last months of my quest to finish this, my first novel. You are my rock. You've always supported all my other writing projects, hobbies, and tangents I've been known to pursue over the years.

To JoAnn Miller, my biggest cheerleader, for encouraging me to stretch myself. We first met online in *Coffeehause for Writers* where we responded with a free write to a daily prompt. I wrote the first chapter of this story there, and you suggested I do more with it, reading it when I added to it, and encouraging me as it grew. When I hit the wall with writer's block, you gently encouraged me to 'keep writing.' Thanks also, Jo, for being one of my Beta readers, taking the time to not only read but review the Beta version.

Thank you, Theresa Flaherty, publisher, editor, and new friend, for taking a risk on this novice author and for your encouragement and patience through this process.

Vicki Flaherty, your input and suggestions were greatly appreciated as was your enthusiasm for this project.

Thanks to Tom Gothard, Glenda Miller, Joy Kicer, Bill and Marcie Southwick, Anna Beth Hubbard, Pam Burkett, and Lisa Flaherty for being Beta readers, for your time, enthusiasm, and response in doing what was asked of you. Words cannot convey my appreciation for the task you took on so willingly.

For all my friends on Facebook who encouraged me daily to write a bit more when I began a session. Many short stories have come from those encouragements. You all make my day brighter when you respond.

Doctors Eric Heidenreich and Richard Worst, psychiatrists, thank you for taking the time from your busy schedules to answer my questions regarding medications and symptoms. You are genuinely appreciated, as is the work you do.

To my children, having all of you has made me push myself to grow and become a better person. Our blended family has grown together through good times and some bad. I believe we are all stronger for it. Love is too small a word for how I feel about you. Also, to my grand-children, great-grands, and great-great-grands, I am so very blessed. I pray that all of you reach for the brass ring and follow your passions. It is never too late to follow your dreams. I am proof of that.

About the Author

Gayle Parish is a retired certified addictions counselor with over 25 years in the field, including work experience in a psychiatric/addiction hospital, half-way house setting, and private practice. Family  therapy, with the whole family unit involved, is most dear to her. Gayle is married, with a blended family of one daughter and six sons, many grandchildren, great and great-great grandchildren, who are her joy. Her husband of almost fifty years is her greatest supporter and cheerleader and a shoulder to lean on when life's journey seems too difficult.

https://gayleparish.wordpress.com

CPSIA information can be obtained
at www.ICGtesting.com
Printed in the USA
LVHW012354180921
698153LV00001B/2